Jack the Ripper

Jack the Ripper

The Murders
and the Movies

Denis Meikle

additional research by
Wes Walker

Reynolds & Hearn Ltd
London

This book is lovingly dedicated to my children, Sarah
and James, who still have a great deal to learn about
the world in general, but who already know more than
most of their peers about Jack the Ripper!

Frontispiece
Dr Jekyll & Sister Hyde (1971)
Opposite
Jack the Ripper (1959)

First published in 2002 by
Reynolds & Hearn Ltd
61a Priory Road
Kew Gardens
Richmond
Surrey TW9 3DH

A CIP catalogue record for this book is available from the British Library.

ISBN 1 903111 32 3

Designed by Peri Godbold.

Printed and bound in Biddles Ltd, Guildford, Surrey.

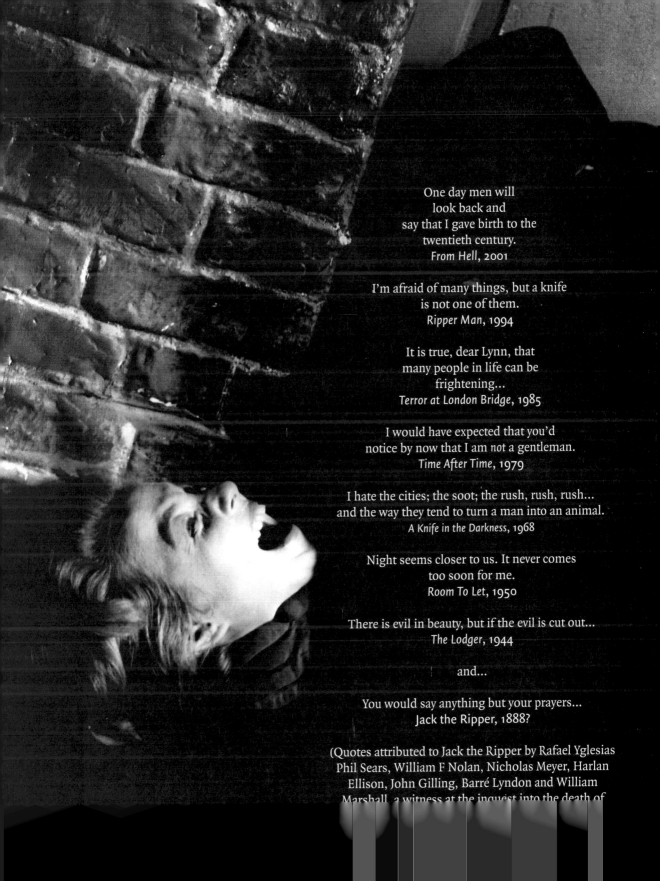

One day men will
look back and
say that I gave birth to the
twentieth century.
From Hell, 2001

I'm afraid of many things, but a knife
is not one of them.
Ripper Man, 1994

It is true, dear Lynn, that
many people in life can be
frightening...
Terror at London Bridge, 1985

I would have expected that you'd
notice by now that I am *not* a gentleman.
Time After Time, 1979

I hate the cities; the soot; the rush, rush, rush...
and the way they tend to turn a man into an animal.
A Knife in the Darkness, 1968

Night seems closer to us. It never comes
too soon for me.
Room To Let, 1950

There is evil in beauty, but if the evil is cut out...
The Lodger, 1944

and...

You would say anything but your prayers...
Jack the Ripper, 1888?

(Quotes attributed to Jack the Ripper by Rafael Yglesias
Phil Sears, William F Nolan, Nicholas Meyer, Harlan
Ellison, John Gilling, Barré Lyndon and William
Marshall, a witness at the inquest into the death of

Acknowledgements

This book came about through an article that I wrote for the American fantasy magazine, *Fangoria*. That article, entitled 'Featuring Jack the Ripper', was a retrospective on how the world's most notorious serial killer had been portrayed on screen, from his first (silent) appearance in Paul Leni's *Waxworks* to the present day, and it was commissioned to coincide with the October 2001 release of the film *From Hell*. To Tony Timpone, editor of *Fangoria*, who commissioned the piece and unconsciously set a larger wheel in motion – and to Marcus Hearn, of Reynolds & Hearn, who saw the virtue of expanding the theme to book length – I am profoundly indebted.

No project like this can be undertaken without extensive research and the help and goodwill of any number of sympathetic individuals. My thanks are therefore due to the following: Coral Kelly and Andy Aliffe of the Cloak and Dagger Club, and Dave Froggatt, for the loan of rare items from their personal collections and to Andy in particular, for his generous and unquestioning support throughout; Tony Timpone, Doug Murray, John Parnum, Adrian Rigelsford and Gary and Sue Svehla for the loan of stills; Amy Kastigar of the Ohio County Public Library, for background detail; Ian Crane, for the index.

Special thanks for the acquisition of much of the required material must go, as ever, to Chris Koetting, who is never less than willing to help out above and beyond the call of duty, and whose loyalty and friendship are a boon in any endeavour. And to Dick Klemensen, for invaluable assistance and the time that he spent in mustering the troops on my behalf.

Finally to my wife, Jane, without whose patient indulgence and practical assistance at every turn, the task of buckling Jack would have been made much more arduous.

Inset right: Part of the teaser ad campaign for *Jack the Ripper* (1959)

Contents

It **always happened to a lady of the night!**

sometimes it happened in an alley— sometimes in a dark hallway and sometimes in the middle of a scream!

TURN THE PAGE

Introduction

"In 1888, a series of brutal murders took place which heralded the age of the serial killer. They were committed in the East End of London, in England, by a man popularly known as Jack the Ripper."
Marshall Kane (Bruce Payne) in *Ripper: Letter from Hell* (2001)

J ack the Ripper: The Murders and the Movies is a study of the more than 50 films and television series episodes that have been inspired by events surrounding the infamous Whitechapel Murders, which took place in London's East End in the year 1888, and which history and legend have laid at the door of the pseudonymous 'Jack the Ripper'.

The screen image of Jack the Ripper has undergone no great revision in the 75 years between Hitchcock's *The Lodger* and the Hughes Brothers' *From Hell*, while, contrary to his relatively static representation on film, the alleged identity of the killer has continually been reappraised and revisited in an ever-increasing number of books, all of whose authors think that they finally have him unmasked.

Since the time of the original crimes, writers and researchers have tried to put a name, and a face, to Jack the Ripper. All have failed. Of the many who have sifted the evidence, such as it is, most have succeeded only in becoming party to the literary equivalent of a miscarriage of justice. As a result, interest in the Ripper murders among the priests of popular culture and the mass media continues unabated. The reason is simple: the notorious nickname by which the killer came to be known went unclaimed, just as he (or she?) went uncaught.

Every member of the historical cast seems to have been proposed as the murderer by a succession of ever more desperate authors, all too eager to prove their crime-busting credentials. If anyone has been missed, they will doubtless turn up as Jack the Ripper in some 'final solution' of the future. The names that are offered up for consideration as suspects might be fanciful, but our fascination with the question of who the killer actually was is still very real. Fiction writers and filmmakers, in turn, have cast both shards of light and mists of obscurity over what continues to be one of the greatest unsolved mysteries in the annals of crime. In their case, however, interest lies less in the solution and more in the dramatic possibilities inherent in both the period and the circumstances in which this particular monster is to be found.

The name alone, Jack the Ripper, is enough to conjure visions of dark streets swathed in fog and barely illumined by the citrus glow of sputtering gas-lamps, where rats scurry and gin-sodden whores make their teetering way home after a night 'on the town', only to find themselves confronted by the shadowy figure of a man in top hat and cape, clutching a Gladstone bag in one hand...

...a knife in the other.

It is one of the enduring images of late-Victorian London, powerful in itself because it freezes in time and place a period in British history which might otherwise have faded from memory, but emblematic as well, in that it shows up in sharp relief the gulf between rich and poor, between public displays of prosperity, and the nihilism and despair that infected much of the populace behind the scenes, where amoral emissaries of a capitalist oligarchy could prey on the most defenceless in society.

And get away with it.

A Punch cartoon
from 1888

THE NEMESIS OF NEGLECT.

"THERE FLOATS A PHANTOM ON THE SLUM'S FOUL AIR,
    SHAPING, TO EYES WHICH HAVE THE GIFT OF SEEING,
INTO THE SPECTRE OF THAT LOATHLY LAIR.
    FACE IT—FOR VAIN IS FLEEING!
RED-HANDED, RUTHLESS, FURTIVE, UNERECT,
'TIS MURDEROUS CRIME—THE NEMESIS OF NEGLECT!"

The
Murders

Chapter One
The Devil's Wind

What sad, black isle is that? It's Cythera, so they say, a land celebrated in song, the banal Eldorado of all the old fools. Look, after all, it's a land of poverty.

Charles Baudelaire, *Les Fleurs du Mal* (1857)

In 1888, Britain was the industrial, commercial and cultural nucleus of the civilised world. Her Empire stretched from Hudson Bay in the north east of Canada, to Guiana and British Honduras in South America, through South Africa's Cape Colony to Western Australia and the Solomon Islands, and on up to India, 'the Jewel in the Crown'. Those countries which remained independent of direct colonial influence nevertheless shared trading pacts or political alliances with Britain, to the extent that by the end of the 19th century, British interests were to be found in every continent on earth.

In a little less than 200 years, the British way of doing things had been extended, whether by coercion, education, good housekeeping practice or simple missionary zeal, to embrace one-fifth of the land mass of the globe. British sovereignty extended to 11 million square miles of territory and to more than 400 million people. Great Britain was the Nation of Nations, progenitor of the mightiest Empire in history, indisputable ruler of all she surveyed.

Presiding reclusively over this geographical colossus was Her Imperial Majesty, Alexandrina Victoria of the House of Saxe-Coburg, Queen of the United Kingdom of Great Britain, Ireland and the Dominions beyond the Seas, Defender of the Faith, and Empress of India, who had occupied the throne for 51 years, the last 26 of them as a widow.

The dawn of the steam age had led to the laying down of an arterial rail network in 1843 and, within a decade, Britain had become the 'workshop of the world', with its factories belching black smoke for 14 hours a day. Development blighted the rural landscape, and the consequent economic migration forced more people into towns and cities. The result was chronic overcrowding and poor sanitation, which brought about increases in crime, poverty, and disease: life expectancy among the working class was as low as 17 years, while infant mortality was as high as 50 per cent.

The 1875 Public Health Act went some way to improve things, but slum dwellings were by then widespread in every major city in the country.

The proud, robust, but palpably diseased heart of this great estate was London, a sprawling, multicultural "metropolis of the Empire," as William Cobbett christened her, whose roots had been laid by the invading legions of Imperial Rome in AD 50, and whose towering edifices and technological marvels, teeming ghettos and terrifying poverty had the ability to astonish and appal in equal measure.

Russian novelist Fydor Dostoevsky, author of *Crime and Punishment* (1866) and a survivor of four years' hard labour in a Siberian prison camp, wrote of London's Haymarket in 1863: "I remember seeing among the crowd of people in the street a little girl who could not have been more than six years old. Her clothes were in tatters. She was dirty, barefoot and beaten black and blue. Her body, which could be seen through the holes in her clothes, was all bruised. She was walking about aimlessly, hardly knowing where she was..."

Previous page: Jack the Ripper (1959)

Right: Cartoon commentary, circa 1888

By the 1880s, the whole of Europe nonetheless was casting envious eyes at the efficient way in which the Empire was managed (la belle France even had Anglophile clubs), and Bostonian Henry James, who had settled to the writer's life in London in 1876, was moved to observe that "nowhere else is there such a play of light and shade, such a struggle of sun and smoke."

The capital was the destination of choice for 'Dick Whittingtons' from all parts of the country and all across Europe, who sought health, happiness and the elusive crock of gold that waited for the lucky few at the end of the rainbow. They came annually in their tens of thousands: businessmen and buskers, artists and artisans, the newly empowered and the recently impoverished, the well-to-do and the wanton.

London, "the great cesspool into which all the loungers and idlers of the Empire are irresistibly drained," as Dr Watson remarked in A Study in Scarlet, could be reached by coach and steam-train from all corners of the British Isles. Befitting its status as the heart of the commonwealth, the life blood of commerce flowed to and fro by road, rail, river and canal, all of it channelled though finance houses in the single square mile that was the City of London.

Euston Station had opened in 1837 (with its Great Hall added in 1849), King's Cross in 1852, and the cathedral towers of St Pancras dominated the London skyline by the end of the 1860s. In 1863, the new Metropolitan underground railway was running trains through roofed-in trenches (so as not to disrupt the street-life of the metropolis) and came to be the subject of an etching by that dark poet of pen-and-ink, French illustrator Gustave Doré. Novelist William Makepeace Thackeray saw in the coming of steam the passing of old-fashioned horse power, referring to each as "old world, new world". Some, though, were determined not to go down without a fight: in July 1888, a stagecoach appositely named 'Old Times' broke the record of eight hours for the round trip between London and Brighton, against a wager of £1000.

In what Liberal Prime Minister William Ewart Gladstone had termed the 'West End' of the city – in the tree-lined terraces of Mayfair, Pimlico and Belgravia – were to be found the outward signs of certitude and security. But to the East lay the parishes of Spitalfields, Stepney, Shadwell and St Georges, with their thieves' highways, their workhouses, their gin palaces, their opium parlours and their grinding poverty. The West End of London was the playground for a people of plenty, while the East End represented penury for many of those whom George Orwell would immortalise as "the people of the abyss".

London was a city of four million souls at this juncture. Of the 900,000 domiciled in the East End, one-fifth were considered to be anything from unutterably poor to utterly penniless. In the years leading up to 1888, the East End of London had inexorably become home to the biggest motley of malcontents, militants, miscreants, misfits and madmen in the world: 18,000 inhabitants of Spitalfields alone were of foreign birth. Anyone in this multi-ethnic, multicultural mix had the potential to be a killer; many of them had been, were, or would be. One or more of them was to become the most notorious murderer in British criminal history.

With industrialisation in mid-century had come a factory mentality in all things: the leisured *bagnio* of Regency England had been replaced by the purely functional brothel. As early as 1857, the *Lancet* had estimated that one house in every 60 in London was a brothel and one woman in every 16 had taken to whoring as a means of eking out the most meagre of livings. In 1881, C E Howard Vincent, Director of Criminal Investigations at Scotland Yard, described the situation in central London to a House of Commons Select Committee: "From three or four

Marianne Stone in
Jack the Ripper (1959)

o'clock in the afternoon, Villiers Street, and Charing Cross station, and the Strand, are crowded with prostitutes, who are openly soliciting prostitution in broad daylight."

By 1888, the Metropolitan Police were documenting 1200 prostitutes of 'low class' in a specific area of the East End. Henry Mayhew and Samuel Bracebridge Hemyng, the two pre-eminent chroniclers of Victorian life, both disputed these 'official' figures and felt from their own experiences that the true picture required them to be incremented by a factor of ten. If Mayhew and Hemyng were correct, then nearer to 12 *thousand* casual whores were operating at a place and time which put them directly in harm's way.

Runaway population growth, decaying infrastructure, unrestricted influx of immigrants, failure to address social issues, inadequate legislation and inefficient as well as insufficient policing – all of these were setting the capital on a collision course with history. The sepoys who had engaged in rebellion against the East India Company during the Indian Mutiny of 1857 considered the bloody rampage which culminated in the Cawnpore massacres as having been spawned by a collective 'fever' which they called 'The Devil's Wind'. Something of the same now hung in the smog-choked air of London.

For it was into this iron-and-granite paean to Imperial power, this teeming termites' nest, this melting-pot, this gas-lit Garden of Earthly Delights, this divinely dangerous modern Babylon straddling rapaciously over the mighty River Thames, that Jack the Ripper – "master murderer of the age" – came to shock and scare and scandalise, and then to vanish without trace.

> London lies today under the spell of a great terror. A nameless reprobate – half beast, half man – is at large, who is daily gratifying his murderous instincts on the most miserable and defenceless of the community.
>
> The Star, 8 September 1888

The East End was effectively a city within a city; a poisoned sore which festered less than a mile from the towering splendour of Wren's St Paul's. In the heart of the East End lay Whitechapel, a seething, sodden, sudden-death slum, bounded by the smaller parishes of Spitalfields, Mile End and Shadwell. To the north of these was Bethnal Green; to the west, Shoreditch and the City; to the south, London Docks and the river; to the east, Stepney and St George's. The vagaries of the census-takers classed Spitalfields and part of Stepney in the Whitechapel registration area; thus, what became referred to as 'Whitechapel' actually took in several smaller parishes as well. (Only *one* of Jack's consensual victims was murdered in Whitechapel proper.)

The so-called Whitechapel district covered no more than a square mile, and it had developed over two centuries from its origins as a base for the silk-weaving expertise of thousands of Huguenot immigrants who had fled persecution in France at the end of the 17th century. Migrations from Eastern Europe had since added to the ethnic mix, and a lack of the most basic amenities exacerbated the conditions under which those already occupying the lowest rung of the social ladder were required to live. Heat and light were among the scarce commodities, their absence aggravated by the prevailing climate: the River Thames had frozen over in 1880, while the winter of 1885-6 had been the coldest for 30 years. The approach of autumn, with its chill, dark nights, signalled the onset of what was mordantly known as the 'starving season'. Street-crime was common, wretchedness was a universal currency, prostitution, destitution (with their attendant horrors of drink and drugs), premature or violent death – all were par-for-the-course in this part of London.

Many parts of Whitechapel were no-go areas for the Metropolitan Police, an uncharted territory held in check by citizen's committees, razor-gangs, slum landlords, or Jewish and Irish godfathers. Patrolling policemen went about in pairs, if they went about at all. In 1883, the Commissioner issued instructions that constables could carry side-arms if they wished, after two of their number were shot while on duty.

To be born into the back-streets of Whitechapel was to be sentenced to a short, sad life of squalor and misery. To live in Whitechapel was to know the depths of degradation to which human beings could sink. Whitechapel was hell on earth; it was the inexplicable dark side of Victorian capitalism, to which middle-class Londoners made token obeisance with their pennies in the poor-box at Sunday service. It was an omnipresent reminder of the evil in their midst, and it served as the conscience of the city. Whitechapel stood as testament to the phenomenon of economic depression, a tinderbox of ethnic tensions, political radicalism and social unrest. If there had been no Whitechapel, religionists and reformers would have found it necessary to invent one. If Jack the Ripper had not existed on his own account, then prevailing circumstances would have conspired to create him.

> "In all, Jack the Ripper is alleged to have committed 14 murders. The key word there is 'alleged'. Although as many as 14 killings were at times attributed to Jack, if we may become that familiar, it's commonly agreed upon that only five were actually his work; the others may have been 'copycat' killings. There are many theories as to who Jack was and why he committed the murders. Hollywood has been great at supplying us with those through the years and we'll look at some of them later on... But for now, these are the facts..."
>
> Professor Harswell (Tom Schreier) in The Ripper (1986)

Between 26 December 1887 and 13 February 1891, the East End was struck by a series of street-slayings, centring on the Whitechapel area. All of the victims were women of the 'unfortunate class', and it was not long before a number of these murders were denominated to a single assailant. The final tally remains open to debate, but contenders for inclusion in the killer's roster total 18 or more and range from an unknown woman, possibly two, in 1887 (commonly referred to as 'Fairy Fay'), to a young prostitute named Frances Coles in 1891. As to the detail of these murders, current opinion decrees the following:

According to an article in Reynolds News, an unknown woman (possibly two), whom author Terence Robertson christened 'Fairy Fay', was killed near Commercial Road on 26 December 1887. Two months later, Annie Millwood was repeatedly stabbed near George Yard, off Whitechapel High Street. She collapsed and died soon after, though not as a result of the injuries that she had received. On Whitechapel Road, on 3 April, Emma Smith was set upon, robbed and raped by three men. She died from a wound she sustained after a blunt instrument was thrust into her vagina.

Martha Tabram was killed on the morning of 7 August 1888, in the same George Yard. She was strangled, then stabbed 39 times with a short knife. There was no mutilation of the body, as such.

On 31 August, Mary Ann 'Polly' Nichols was killed in Buck's Row, near the Whitechapel Road. She, too, may have been strangled. Her throat was cut so completely as to almost sever

T G Abberline

A contemporary sketch of Detective Inspector F G Abberline

the head and her abdomen was sliced open. Nichols was the first victim to be 'ripped'.

Annie Chapman was strangled to death, or at least into unconsciousness, on Saturday 8 September. As she lay on the ground in Hanbury Street, near the Whitechapel Road, an attempt was made to decapitate her. Her killer then opened her up and removed her uterus with an efficiency that induced divisional police surgeon Dr George Bagster Phillips to report that "the work was that of an expert" and that removal of the womb had been the object of the exercise. From this surmise, the newspapers concluded that the 'ripper' was a doctor.

Elizabeth Stride was attacked and killed in Berner Street, off Commercial Street, on 30 September. Her throat was cut, but there was no evidence of other injury to the body. Popular opinion has it that her killer was interrupted. Less than an hour later, in Mitre Square inside the City of London, Catherine Eddowes was also partially strangled before her throat was cut and she was disembowelled. Her killer removed and carried away both her uterus and left kidney. Her face was mutilated: her nose was sliced off, and her cheeks and eyelids were slashed in a 'pattern' of sorts. On examining the body, the City Police Surgeon, Dr Frederick Brown, echoed Dr Phillips' comments about the nature of the beast who had committed the atrocity: "It required a great deal of knowledge to have removed the kidney." (Two weeks later, part of a kidney was sent to George Lusk, the new chairman of the Mile End Vigilance Committee; it was accompanied by a letter declaring it to be "From hell...") The murders of Stride and Eddowes, ostensibly by the same hand but certainly on the same night, are what became known as the 'double event'.

On 3 October, the headless torso of another unknown woman was found on a construction site in Whitehall, where work had begun on the building of New Scotland Yard. The arms were later recovered from the Thames.

On the morning of 9 November, Mary Jane Kelly was killed as she lay on the bed of her room in Miller's Court, Dorset Street. The extent of her injuries was such that it was impossible for the doctors to state accurately the cause of death. Her throat was cut and an attempt was made to remove her head. She was partially skinned and completely eviscerated; body parts were strewn around the corpse and piled onto a table next to the bed. Her features were comprehensively mutilated and her heart was missing, probably carried off by her killer.

On 20 December, Rose Mylett was strangled to death in Poplar, but she was not attacked with a knife and there was some disagreement as to whether this was a case of murder or one of accidental death (she had choked while under the influence of drink). Between 31 May and 25 June 1889, dismembered body parts of Elizabeth Jackson were fished from the Thames; an American press report referred to her as the Ripper's "tenth victim." On 17 July of that year, Alice McKenzie died in Castle Alley, Whitechapel, from knife wounds to the throat. She also suffered mutilations to the abdomen. Dr Thomas Bond, who had examined the body of Kelly, gave it as his opinion that "the murder was performed by the same person who committed the former series of Whitechapel murders." A second headless torso was discovered in Pinchin Street, St Georges-in-the-East, on 10 September, thought to be the remains of

Lydia Hart, though she was subsequently traced. There were mutilations to the abdomen.

On 13 February 1891, Frances Coles was attacked in Swallow Gardens, Whitechapel; her throat was cut and she died on her way to hospital. Finally, on 24 April 1891, Carrie Brown was strangled and stabbed (an attempt was made to disembowel her) in an East River Hotel room in New York – a long way from Whitechapel, to be sure, but close enough for the New York Times to headline: "Whitechapel Horrors repeated in an East Side lodging house."

There were numerous other assaults, such as that on Ada Wilson, who on 28 March 1888, opened her door to a man who stabbed her in the throat. Wilson survived. On 20 November, Annie Farmer stabbed herself and tried to blame it on the Ripper. And on 3 December, at King's Cross, Harriet North was also stabbed; she, too, lived to tell the tale.

These, or any number of them, have collectively become known as the 'Whitechapel Murders', although they should perhaps more accurately have been designated the East End Murders. According to the Metropolitan Police Force, under whose jurisdiction the majority of the murders were committed, the number of Whitechapel Murders was in fact 11, only a proportion of which (admittedly, a large one) was laid at the door of the pseudonymous Jack the Ripper.

As to *what* proportion exactly, opinions differed. Inspector Edmund Reid of Whitechapel's 'H' Division, who investigated the death of Martha Tabram and others, thought the number was nine; Superintendant Thomas Arnold plumped for a more conservative four; Detective Inspector Frederick George Abberline, seconded from Scotland Yard to head up the detective force in Whitechapel during the Ripper inquiry, also opted for four; while Detective Constable Walter Dew, who was first on the scene of the Kelly murder, gave the total as six, or possibly seven. Dr Percy Clark, who assisted Dr George Bagster Phillips on the autopsies of many of the victims, thought that it was more probably three. Other police surgeons, coroners, senior officers, and newspaper editors were equally at variance. An article in the London Times as recently as December 2000, relating to the film From Hell, still credited Jack with seven, despite much evidence to the contrary in the interim.

Even the designation 'Whitechapel Murders' is something of a misnomer. In the words of Detective Inspector Reid, who inherited the district from Inspector Abberline when he departed for the Yard in 1887, the Whitechapel Murders "were not peculiar to that division, for one was in the City of London, one in Bethnal Green, four in Spitalfields, two in St George's, and only one in Whitechapel." This tally equates with Reid's assertion that there were *nine* murders in the series, but it makes the point, all the same: 'Whitechapel' murders they were, so Whitechapel Murders they shall be.

It has generally been accepted for the last three decades (though not necessarily for the next three) that the number of the Ripper's victims was five: Nichols, Chapman, Stride, Eddowes and Kelly. These are now commonly referred to as the 'canonical' victims. In recent years, expert opinion has swung towards removing Stride from the so-called canonical list, which would bring Jack's tally down to four.

Whatever the true figure, it was soon acknowledged that some, at least, of the Whitechapel Murders were the work of a single individual, first by the newspapers (who postulated a link between the murders of Smith, Tabram and Nichols, following the murder of Chapman), then, more reluctantly, by the investigating officers themselves.

By the second week of September 1888, it was increasingly clear to all that a Monster was loose on the streets of Whitechapel. At the end of that month, the Monster had a name.

Comes the Ripper

Prior to this, the killer who stalked a single square mile of the East End of London in the autumn of 1888 had been referred to only in a glossary of outrage. A "perfect savage," roared one newspaper; "the most dangerous kind of lunatic," cried another; a "murderous maniac," exclaimed a third, while his victims were considered to have been treated with "inhuman and ghoul-like brutality."

When a sense of identity did begin to filter into the consciousness of the public and the opinion-makers alike, he was first nicknamed 'Leather Apron', after a number of women attested to having been verbally or physically abused by an itinerant who was given to wearing one. Author Leonard Matters wrote of 'Leather Apron': "Everybody was terrified of him, and the tough proprietor of one of the dens in Thrawl Street declared to a newspaper reporter that Leather Apron was so terrible a being that even he (the proprietor) would never think of being out after midnight without a loaded revolver."

Concerns about this particular individual appeared to be substantiated when a piece of such a garment was found at the scene of Annie Chapman's murder on 8 September, and 'Leather Apron' the killer remained until 10 September, when the *real* Leather Apron – a Polish Jew named John Pizer – was arrested on suspicion of the Nichols murder, only to be released some days later for lack of evidence. As the month drew to a close, the Whitechapel murderer was returned to anonymity and the 'penny dreadful' generalities of a press that was desperately in need of a replacement for 'Leather Apron' in its banner headlines.

In the meantime, it was the killer's profession which exercised the mind of the community at large. Slaughterman was the occupation of choice, though barber-surgeon ran it a close second. At the Chapman inquest, it was stated that a degree of medical skill had been present in the nature of the wounds inflicted on the body, and from that one off-the-cuff remark came the idea that a doctor was responsible for these most heinous of crimes. Not a demon barber, a demon doctor... No one knew for sure.

As an anonymous street-poet was later to pen in the assassin's name:

"I'm not a butcher,
I'm not a Yid,
Nor yet a foreign skipper,
But I'm your own light-hearted friend,
Yours truly –"

The rhyme was allocated its exit line by the signature on a letter (and follow-up postcard) which was delivered to Central News on 27 September, and which intimated knowledge of the crimes. The missive was written in red ink and read as follows:

"Dear Boss – I keep on hearing the police have caught me, but they won't fix me just yet. I have laughed when they look so clever and talk about being on the <u>right</u> track. That joke about 'Leather Apron' gave me real fits. I am down on whores and I shan't quit ripping them till I do get buckled. Grand work the last job was. I gave the lady no time to squeal. How can they catch me now. I love my work and want to start again. You will soon hear of me with my funny little games. I saved some of the proper <u>red</u> stuff in a

The original 'Dear Boss' letter

ginger beer bottle over the last job to write with but it went thick like glue and I can't use it. [Empty ginger beer bottles were among the few items found in Mary Kelly's room after her murder.] Red ink is fit enough I hope ha ha. The next job I do I will clip the lady's ears off and send to the police officers just for jolly wouldn't you. Keep this letter back till I do a bit more work then give that out straight. My knife's so nice and sharp I want to get to work right away if I get a chance. Good luck. Yours truly – Jack the Ripper."

The sender had added a postscript:

"They say I'm a doctor now ha ha."

The puzzle appeared to be coming together, at least in the eyes of the image-makers: the back-alley murderer who struck between the hours of midnight and dawn now had a profession, a pseudonym, and a psychology of sorts. He was a doctor (despite his denial), he called himself Jack, and he ripped the girls "just for jolly".

"Send both of these items to the press agencies right away. The whole world must know what kind of a monster this is and the kind of sinister jokes he's attempting to play, and that way, we'll manage to track him down. Any reader who knows any handwriting that is similar to the murderer's is to notify us immediately."

Inspector Dorne (Hans Nielsen) in *The Monster of London City* (1964)

When the Ripper finally revealed himself in the last week of September, his nominal appearance was greeted with initial amusement. Central News confessed to having viewed the letter as "a practical joke" (which it quite possibly was). Other commentators gave it short shrift or dismissed it out of hand as a hoax. By 6 October, facsimiles of both letter and card were posted on walls all over London in an attempt by the police to secure the public's help in identifying the handwriting. Hoax it may have been, but the killer's 'signature' was widely accepted as genuine. On the same day, the *East London Advertiser* headlined "'The Ripper' seen…" a shout which was echoed by its readers on numerous occasions in the weeks that followed, whenever anyone suspicious caught their eye. Before the month was out, "Jack the Ripper!" had become the cry of the streets.

A *Punch* cartoon of 13 October, entitled *The Pandemonium of Posters*, commented on the profusion of lurid images which were now such an insidious part of the London scene. The accompanying rhyme contained a sentiment which was still being echoed a century later, in respect of a glut of equally lurid horror videotapes.

"How strange that a civilised city ho! ho!
Tis their fatuous dream to consider it so!
Which is nothing too lovely at best, should bestow
Such a liberal licence on spoilers!
These mural monstrosities, reeking of crime,
Flaring horridly forth amidst squalor and grime,
Must have an effect which will tell in good time,
Upon legions of dull-witted toilers."

The autumn of 1888 was not the first time that Londoners had found themselves in the grip of a 'Monster' terror, or been shocked by the barbarities of human villains. According to author Peter Haining, a 'Human Ghoul' with a propensity for throat-slashing and dashing his victim's brains out stalked the vicinity of Fleet Street in 1785, though this may be a conflation of the legend of Sweeney Todd and the better-documented case of the London 'Monster', a virulent street-pest who took great delight, and undoubted sexual pleasure, from stabbing passing females with a variety of sharp implements, including swords, between 1788 and 1790. The Monster's outrages caused panic on the scale of the Ripper scare a century later, with notices posted to the effect that the attacks were carried out "by a MONSTER" who sometimes "dressed in black." A hapless Welshman named Rhynwick Williams was eventually tried and convicted of these crimes, though given the numbers of young toffs and rake-hells who were parading around London at the time with a similar psychological bent, it is more than possible that the Bow Street Runners plumped for the wrong man.

A more viable precedent for Jack the Ripper was the hysteria induced by the urban legend of 'Spring-Heeled Jack' in 1837-8, much exaggerated since in books by Haining, Charles Berlitz and others. Jack, an English forename with a long history stretching back to the dark ages, was common parlance for everyman, or 'fellowman', in the 18th and 19th centuries; Jack Tar (a sailor), Jack Pudding (a buffoon), Jack-of-all-trades, Jack-in-the-box, and the American Jack o'Lantern, the Halloween pumpkin, were some among many. It was also used as a generic in all manner of colloquialisms, such as 'yellow jack' (for yellow fever). Nursery tales told of Jack the Giant Killer and Jack and the Beanstalk; nursery rhymes, of Jack and Jill and Little Jack

Horner. Ballads and chapbooks retailed the adventures of real-life rogues like Jack Ketch and Jack Sheppard. And jolly Jack Tars went equipped with jack-knives. In Shakespeare's day, 'playing the jack' meant to deceive and lead astray, and that is precisely what the joker referred to as a 'spring-heeled' jack, rather than by the sobriquet of Spring-Heeled Jack, set out to do.

When a series of assaults against defenceless women in outlying districts of London were reported as having been carried out by a strange figure who subsequently 'leapt' away, the perpetrator was accorded the name of 'Spring-Heeled' Jack and he soon became a creature of the night who vomited blue and white flame, and whose eyes were 'balls of white fire'. He also sported the conical hat of a wizard, the mane of a lion, horns, clawed hands, a fish-scale suit and rocket-propelled boots. The gullibility of the Lord Mayor of London in publicising a letter from one of Jack's alleged victims spread panic like wildfire among the populace and created numerous other sightings which persisted right up to the 1850s. Modern sources credit Henry Beresford, Marquis of Waterford, as the original prankster. (A variant of this legend can be found in tales of the 'Mothman', as recounted in a number of UFO-related books by author John A Keel.)

Towards the end of the 1850s, a spate of "phantom garottings" plagued the capital – where victims were subdued by a choke-hold from behind – while the phenomenon of the random knife assault against an innocent passer-by, in the manner of the attacks perpetrated by the London Monster, continued into the 20th century. It is worth noting that arbitrary acts of violence against individuals, mostly females, and often committed by organised gangs of ruffians, were not confined to London, or even England, in the 19th century; their like, and worse, can be found in all the major towns and cities of Europe, as well as in the Americas.

Gothic villainy also trod the boards of travelling theatre troupes throughout the 19th century, and three-act plays like *Spring-Heeled Jack; or, the Terror of London* were a staple of Victorian melodrama long before the terror of 1888. By the 1880s, 'penny dreadfuls', 'shilling shockers' and popular playhouses were still "packing 'em in" with vigorous accounts of murderous scoundrels whose activities had bordered on the monstrous, like Sweeney Todd, the 'demon barber' of 1790s Fleet Street, or 'Squire' William Corder, murderer of Maria Marten at the Old Red Barn in Polstead, Suffolk in 1827.

The corollary of Victorian propriety was prurience and a quest for sensationalism, both of which went hand-in-hand with the materialistic sensibility that had been brought about by Imperial power. But if sensation was to be found in the arts, whether highbrow or low, then none was more sensational than Thomas Russell Sullivan's theatrical adaptation of Robert Louis Stevenson's *Strange Case of Dr Jekyll and Mr Hyde*, which premiered at the Lyceum Theatre in the Strand on 4 August 1888, and proceeded to run concurrently with the Whitechapel Murders.

Punch magazine's theatre critic spoke for all who saw American actor Richard Mansfield in the dual role when he wrote, "I must defer my criticism of *The Strange Story* until I have quite recovered from the awful jumpy, creepy, crawly effect produced on me by Mr Mansfield's extraordinary performance last Saturday night. It is a ghastly extravaganza, with a marvellous 'transformation scene'." The twin horrors of *Jekyll* and Jack became inseparable in the collective imagination, and they have remained so ever since. On 8 September, after the murder of Polly Nichols but on the very same day that the body of Annie Chapman was found in Hanbury Street, the *East London Advertiser* commented that the murderer "issues forth at night like another *Hyde* to prey on the defenceless unfortunate class."

The barbarous nature of the crimes was worrying enough: "Nothing so appalling, so devilish, so inhuman – or, rather non-human – as the three Whitechapel crimes has ever

HORRIBLE LONDON; OR, THE PANDEMONIUM OF POSTERS.

happened outside the pages of Poe or De Quincey. The unravelled mystery of 'The Whitechapel Murders' would make a page of detective romance as ghastly as 'The Murders in the Rue Morgue'," opined the *Star* in September. But beyond the singular degree of brutality employed to dispatch the victims, there were other commonalities to the murders which helped to plant the idea of a 'Monster' killer in the public mind: he went about his gruesome business unheard and comparatively unseen, like a thief in the night; he left no clues; he taunted the police on their ineffectiveness; above all, he exhibited no obvious motive for his choice of victim, or for the random slaughter in which he engaged.

> *"We've had eight weeks of statements; eight weeks of questions. We've looked at every butcher, doctor, cook, knife-grinder within ten miles of here. We've questioned almost every resident of Whitechapel. We've had interpreters for Jews, Poles, Germans, French. We've got police on almost every corner... But he's still out there... Someone, somewhere, knows something."*
>
> Inspector Abberline (Michael Caine) in *Jack the Ripper* (1988)

Following the murders of Stride and Eddowes – which brought the number of victims accredited to Jack to five or even six, depending on the source of the report – the clamour for the apprehension of the killer rose to fever-pitch. With little forensic science to aid them in their investigations, the police were powerless in the face of a new and unknown enemy. This was a crime spree with no parallel in peacetime history, one the like of which no civilised society had encountered before. It was what the world of the 20th century would come to recognise as *serial* murder.

The shock-wave from the 'double event' was felt throughout the East End, and it reverberated in the columns of every newspaper.

The *East End News* for 5 October reported on a speech to the Whitechapel Board of Works, given by the Reverend Dan Greatorex the day after the murders: "Whitechapel has become notorious all over the world as a place to be shunned and feared, and if the supposition once gains a hold that it is unsafe for a woman to be in Whitechapel streets after nightfall, the result must be utter ruin of all trade." His sentiment was echoed by the *East London Advertiser* for 6 October: "The worst feature of the murders is the manner in which the panic seems to be growing." In one of several heartfelt pleas along similar lines to the *Times*, Lord Sydney Godolphin Osborne begged for more consideration to be given to an East End which "for many years has been known to have been in a social condition utterly devoid of the commonest attributes of civilisation, so saturated with all that can contribute to heathenise as to be a standing shame to the nation."

Whitechapel, at the time, was filled to bursting with a great many obvious suspects. Even then, Jack eluded his pursuers. One of the first journalists to research the subject in detail, Leonard Matters, made several salient points when it came to elucidating the nature of this conundrum:

The killer either lived within, or had intimate knowledge of, the area in which he operated; he was likely to have reconnoitred the scenes of his attacks, to ensure himself of an escape route in the event. He either lived alone, or was engaged in a profession which allowed him to come and go at all hours, without anyone suspecting him. He either used, or was used to dealing with, prostitutes. So far, so good. But more bewilderingly, there was something about him which put him above suspicion in their eyes: at a time when no lone woman was safe on

A Punch cartoon
from 1888

the streets – when the biggest manhunt for the most dangerous killer in criminal history was underway in Whitechapel – each of Jack's victims went to their deaths voluntarily. None struggled. None screamed. And none saw it coming. Right to the last, they remained untroubled by the man who cut their throats.

Many authors have inferred from this seeming anomaly that the Ripper must therefore have been above reproach in demeanour, what the women of Whitechapel might have thought of as a 'toff'. The ease with which Jack claimed his victims certainly opens the door to conspiracy theory, but it can equally well imply the opposite: that he was already known by sight to the women on whom he preyed, who were therefore as unsuspecting of him as they might have been of a husband or lover (who form the highest percentage of 'domestic' murderers, in any case).

Years of Hollywood moralising in the metaphorical milieu of the horror film have rammed home the message that ugliness is often only skin deep, and that the heart of an angel can reside within the breast of a beast. The corollary to this is that a propensity for atrocity can lurk beneath a skein of normality. Cultural liberalism invites the former, but social preconceptions have inhibited the latter. Yet most modern serial killers have turned out to be ordinary, unprepossessing everymen: the boy next door, the attentive husband, the quiet clerk, the local odd-job man, the community nurse or doctor. Despite the weight of evidence that exists to show where monsters actually come from, society continues to resist the unappetising truth and remains conditioned to expect the outward signs of sin. The figurative fiends of film have always been taken too literally.

The Whitechapel Murders consensually ended, as far as anyone can tell, in a literal blaze of gory. The mutilated remains of Mary Kelly were discovered in her tiny lodging at number 13 Miller's Court, Dorset Street, six weeks after the double event, by Thomas Bowyer, rent collector and jack-of-all-trades for John McCarthy, who owned the property. In the heart of the metropolis, a young woman had been done to death, dissected, and disassembled of her flesh in the dead of night, with her body-parts dispersed around the room.

None who witnessed this last-known example of the Ripper's handiwork was able to erase the sight from memory. McCarthy described the scene to a reporter from the *Times* on the following day: "It looked more like the work of a devil than a man. The poor woman's body was lying on the bed, undressed. She had been completely disembowelled, and her entrails had been taken out and placed on the table. It was those that I had seen when I looked through the window and took to be lumps of flesh. The woman's nose had been cut off, and her face gashed and mutilated so that she was quite beyond recognition. Both her breasts too had been cut clean away and placed by the side of her liver and other entrails on the table. I had heard a great deal about the Whitechapel murders, but I declare to God I had never expected to see such a sight as this."

> *"You've never seen anything like it this side of Hell... What animal could have done this?"*
> Inspector Lestrade (Frank Finlay) in *A Study in Terror* (1966)

Exactly how 'Jack the Ripper' had gone about this atrocity has puzzled investigators for over a century. The door of the room was locked, the key allegedly missing, and the means of ingress known only to Kelly, her lover Joseph Barnett, and a few other intimates. A fire had been lit in the hearth in which items of women's clothing were burned. Kelly's movements prior to her murder have been the subject of endless speculation; her movements *after* death, even more so.

Most writers employ the phrase "mutilated beyond recognition" when they come to describe the condition of the corpse, which begs the question: how, then, was Kelly recognised? "By the ear and the eyes," was Joseph Barnett's response at the inquest by which he meant, presumably, the *hair* and the eyes, his enunciation creating an error in translation by the clerk of the court. Barnett and others who viewed the body were positive that it was Kelly, even though there was little left to go on. This made a mockery of Carolyn Maxwell's inquest testimony that *she* saw Kelly outside Miller's Court on the morning of 9 November, hours after she was supposed to have been murdered by Jack the Ripper, and again later, standing with a similar man to one she was seen with the previous evening.

Friday 9 November was the occasion of the inauguration of the new Lord Mayor of London, when the streets were humming with expectancy as thousands of people readied themselves to witness the spectacle; not a day that would

Artist's impression of Mary Kelly, from *The Illustrated Police News*

easily be confused with another. The hue and cry was up by 11.00 am, less than three hours after the time that Maxwell said she spoke with Kelly, yet experts insist that Maxwell must have been mistaken. In relation to the later identification of the body, it would seem that she was.

After the death of Mary Kelly, the notorious nickname by which the murderer would now go down in history took on a resonance of its own, its very utterance suffused with horror. But by then, by common consent, Jack's black crusade was already at an end. Taken in the round, this means that 'Jack the Ripper' haunted the back streets of Whitechapel for a mere seven weeks from the end of September to the second week of November 1888. From this small beginning – 40 days of terror, in effect – sprang a near-mythological monster whose power to enthral both serious researcher and casual observer alike has remained undiminished for more than a century.

> *"Thanks to Jack the Ripper… thanks to this brutal killer – yes, thanks to him – the world is watching Whitechapel. And I'll tell you this, it's not the killings by a demented hand that the world finds horrible. No. It's the murder by poverty; the murder by misery; the murder by hunger. In Whitechapel… Whitechapel! The cry of the starving, the moan of the sick… For years, we've tried to get one paragraph into the newspapers to expose what's happening here. I've been myself to the editors, hat in hand. 'It's not news', they said… Well, now it is news. One man has made us news…"*
> Dr Murray (Anthony Quayle) in *A Study in Terror* (1966)

In 1884, the Earl of Derby had reflected on the increasing numbers of women who were taking to drink, while in 1888, a retired judge named Henry Keene published a paper on "The Disorder of the Age" which fretted about a widespread "*mal du siècle*." A leader column in the *Spectator*, commenting on the murders in Whitechapel, regretted the shift of blame from individual malefactor onto society as a whole, giving as its reason that "At present, the Devil is disbelieved in." If the Devil is in the detail, then the detail of the Ripper murders engrossed the nation and many other nations besides. Around the world, the popular view of Jack the Ripper was maniac at large, while the more informed views of the police and enlightened social commentators had him as severely maladjusted (to put it mildly), quite probably mad, but almost certainly a by-product of the environment in which he operated. It was to be the popular view which prevailed.

Comparisons with similar crimes which have taken place since, as well as the application of modern detection techniques like 'psychological profiling', tend to suggest that the police had the right ideas from the very beginning: the killer was a local man with local knowledge, or else he was a seaman of some kind, temporarily disembarked at nearby London docks. But fact was married to fiction by the sensationalist practices of less scrupulous sections of the "yellow" press, man was turned into Monster, and the myth was born while Jack was still engaged in his nefarious pursuits. Rumours spread suspicion, which in turn prompted accusations and innumerable false arrests; vigilance committees were set up; hoaxers garbed in the appropriate costume arrived in the district in droves, to be confronted by policemen dressed as women! The entire investigation descended into a shambles, with policemen on the beat running after each other's tails like the Keystone Kops, and it ended in failure and ignominious resignation for General Sir Charles Warren, Chief Commissioner of the Metropolitan force.

The London police were not entirely to blame, though. Riven with internal squabbles, the various squads that were attached to the Whitechapel inquiry at different times and in different places were always hampered in following some good hunches to satisfactory conclusions. Even before the murder of Mary Kelly, Jack the Ripper had become a monster who could not be caught; had he been so, the killer – in whatever guise he may finally have appeared – is likely to have failed to satisfy the preconceptions of a populace in whom the idea of exotic conspiracy had already taken hold. It is a notion best exemplified by the behaviour of the Ripper 'industry' since, whose proponents have invariably preferred the more extravagant theories to those favoured by the police on the ground at the time.

Since no single one of the Whitechapel Murders was officially solved, it follows that the remaining non-canonical victims all met their deaths at the hands of other unknown assassins. If a proportion of that remainder were *also* to be considered as the work of a lone killer, then the *real* Monster of Whitechapel was never even christened, let alone caught. Yet history, or the perception of it, has forgotten the Whitechapel Murders as such and remembered Jack the Ripper – one man who is still held to be responsible for the most audacious killing-spree in the annals of British crime.

Sympathy for a Devil

On 15 April 1891, Thomas Alva Edison demonstrated his Kinetoscope in New York and the cinema was born, less than three years after the last Ripper murder. Louis Lumière, with his brother Auguste, gave a first public performance of his Cinématographe in December 1895,

A Study in Terror (1966)

and with *L'Arrivée d'un train à la Ciotat* in 1896, the 'movies' were big business right across the continent. Long before the creation of Hollywood in 1912, a European film culture was well established.

National film industries were soon developed, and with them came films which opened a window on the outlook and obsessions of the nations which sired them. While American studios sought to capitalise on the mass-market appeal of the new medium by offering knockabout comedies and one-dimensional melodramas, the filmmakers of Europe lost no time in putting their own cameras to more evocative use.

The early German cinema reflected the dark Teutonic psyche that had fathered all manner of myths and monsters from Siegfried to Faustus. It was expressionistic in tone and the 'horror' film, like Gothic literature, was consequently born in Germany of mood-pieces like *The Student of Prague* (1913; remade in 1926) and, most famously, Robert Wiene's *The Cabinet of Dr Caligari* (1919). And it was the shadow-scapes born of a cinematic sensibility centred on the mighty Ufa studios in Neubabelsberg, near Berlin, which proved the ideal environment for Jack the Ripper to make his first appearance on screen.

"*Spring-Heeled Jack – the notorious character – pounced suddenly and silently upon his victims...*"
Screen caption from *Waxworks* (1924)

A minor diversion en route to Jack's premier engagement was *Waxworks* (*Das Wachsfigurenkabinett*), filmed in 1924 by German expressionist director Paul Leni from a screen-play by *Nosferatu*'s Henrik Galeen.

Waxworks was a portmanteau or omnibus film, comprising two separate tales held together by a framing narrative. The format derived from literary anthologies of ghost or mystery fiction and was much favoured in the early days of silent cinema. Richard Oswald used it in *Tales of the Uncanny* (*Unheimliche Geschichten*; 1919), as did Fritz Lang in *Between Two Worlds* (*Der muede Tod*; 1921), but it was employed most successfully in Ealing's *Dead of Night* (1945), and most often in Amicus productions of the 1960s and 70s, from *Dr Terror's House of Horrors* (1964) to *From Beyond the Grave* (1973).

A young man (Wilhelm [later director William] Dieterle) is hired to write 'back' stories for the wax exhibits in a fairground attraction. The tales that he concocts around the semi-fabulous figures of Haroun al-Raschid, Ivan the Terrible and Jack the Ripper are subsequently dramatised to form the individual episodes. In the case of the latter, the inter-titles in *Waxworks* make unequivocal mention of Spring-Heeled Jack, rather than the Ripper ("Spring-Heeled Jack – the most amazing character of all times"), although he is clearly based on the Whitechapel murderer: as depicted by Werner Krauss (who had played the monstrous Caligari in Wiene's film, and would go on to play the Devil himself in *The Student of Prague*; 1926), he sports a long overcoat and homburg hat, with a white silk scarf thrown over his left shoulder; in his hand, he holds a knife.

The characters of al-Raschid and Ivan were played by Emil Jannings and Conrad Veidt, Weimar Germany's equivalent to Lon Chaney and still best-known for his chilling portrayal of the deadly somnambulist Cesare in *The Cabinet of Dr Caligari*. With such an illustrious cast, *Waxworks* was almost a silent screen version of Roger Corman's *Tales of Terror* (1963), with Veidt (still in Cesare mode, all wide-eyed and predatory), Jannings and Krauss substituting for Vincent Price, Peter Lorre and Basil Rathbone.

Dr Jekyll & Sister Hyde
(1971)

The first tale is an Arabian Nights fantasy aping that in Lang's *Between Two Worlds*. Jannings hams it up unmercifully as the lecherous Caliph of Bagdad, but Leni seems uncertain whether to play the awkward narrative as comedy or drama, throwing in a smattering of Douglas Fairbanks-style acrobatics for good measure. The second episode is the more successful of the two. Scriptwriter Henrik Galeen reserves his most chilling prose for Ivan: "Ivan was a blood-crazed monster on a throne, who turned cities into cemeteries..." All-powerful but paranoid, he takes pleasure in watching poisoned victims breathe their last in time to the sand that drains from an oversized hourglass. Thinking himself to be poisoned at the climax, Ivan goes quietly insane trying to prevent his own demise by forever turning the hourglass around. These two tales form the bulk of *Waxworks*; aside from our introduction to him in the prologue, Spring-Heeled Jack's appearances are limited to a few scenes in the closing minutes:

Having completed his stories, the young man falls asleep in front of the figure of Spring-Heeled Jack. The figure comes to life and pursues both the narrator and the daughter of the exhibit owner around the fairground. There is an effective shot as Jack turns to camera in the background while the lovers embrace, but in an attempt to create an hallucinatory ambience, Leni constructs the sequence from double exposures of fairground scenes over close-ups of the fleeing duo. This might have been innovative in 1924, but it seems rudimentary now and betrays none of the mesmeric qualities to be found when similar tricks were deployed in the likes of *Metropolis*, made two years later. Given the nightmare potential of hero and heroine chased by a knife-wielding killer, and the fact that the film was scripted by Galeen, who wrote *Nosferatu: a Symphony of Horrors* for F W Murnau, the sequence is surprisingly static, and ends with the writer being stabbed by Spring-Heeled Jack then waking to find that he has instead

A contemporary woodcut of 'Spring-Heeled Jack'

jabbed himself with his own pen. "I dreamed that Spring-heeled Jack stole you from me," the hero explains to his new-found love in the romantic finale. Variants of the 'it was all a dream' denouement would crop up in genre films throughout the twenties, usually to no better effect than here.

The whole film is heavily influenced by *Caligari* (including its setting of a fairground) and is doggedly surrealist in tone, but it betrays little of its predecessor's hypnotic power to enthral. Leni left for Hollywood after this, where his mocking style found similar outlet in *The Cat and the Canary* (1927). Veidt followed soon afterwards, memorably to portray the grimacing Gwynplaine in Leni's version of Victor Hugo's *The Man Who Laughs* (1928).

The 'real' Spring-Heeled Jack made his only film appearance in a 1946 Bushey production entitled *The Curse of the Wraydons*, adapted from the Victorian melodrama *Spring-Heeled Jack; or, The Terror of London*, which had been 'doing the rounds' since the 1860s. The film was one of a series to feature Newcastle-born Norman Carter 'Tod'

Slaughter, the king of the barnstormers, whose lip-curling, moustache-tweaking, eyeball-rolling turns as a veritable one-man rogues' gallery of Victorian villains, from Sweeney Todd to the Chevalier del Gardo (*The Face at the Window*; 1939), were quite without peer, even if they smacked a little too much of 'The Perils of Pauline' by the 1940s.

Slaughter had a unique way with him, and his malevolent grin perfectly conveyed the sentient insanity that was invariably required to lurk beneath the dandified exterior. He was the living embodiment of the flesh-creeping laugh that emanates from Renfield in Tod Browning's *Dracula* (1931). He was not, however, Spring-Heeled Jack on this occasion but Philip Wraydon, the insane Chief of a cut-throat band of Bonapartist sympathisers and dispossessed heir to the Wraydon fortune. Jack was Jack *Wraydon*, a wronged Hussar played by Bruce Seton (later to find fame on TV as 'Fabian of the Yard'), who comes by the name through his evasion of the Bow Street Runners. "Already fate plays into our hands. Captain Jack Wraydon, our wonderful Spring-Heeled Jack, will be laid by those heels and either shot or hanged!" Slaughter hisses, as he plots his downfall. The rehabilitation of 'Jack' had taken place in the original, which miraculously transformed the character from bogeyman into heroic avenger.

Slaughter's character bows out of *The Curse of the Wraydons* in typical style: crushed to death between the hydraulic walls of an oubliette. But the actor lived to leer another day, unlike the mythical Spring-Heeled Jack, whose legend was finally consigned to history at the close of the film.

If *Waxworks* proved to be a model of reticence when it came to dealing with Jack in 'Spring-Heeled' guise, no such reservations were allowed to dilute the impact of his inaugural appearance as Ripper in *Pandora's Box*.

> "ATTENTION! WOMEN OF LONDON
> *For some time, a man has been attempting to lure young girls and women into dark areas to murder them. Unfortunately, in four cases he has succeeded..."*
>
> Poster on a Whitechapel wall in *Pandora's Box* (1928)

In 1893 – when to all intents and purposes, Jack the Ripper was still at large – a 29-year-old German playwright named Benjamin Franklin 'Frank' Wedekind, son of a German-American father and Swiss mother, wrote a play called *Erdgeist* ('Earth Spirit'), which was greeted with derision and not produced on stage until 1902. In 1894, Wedekind expanded the theme of this earlier work and penned *Die Büchse der Pandora*, which also met with hostility and was not staged until 1905. He subsequently combined the two under the title of *Lulu* but even that was not the end; Wedekind continued to tinker with his 'Lulu' plays for the remainder of his life and, to this day, they can be performed in a number of versions.

The two plays, taken as a whole, were an outspoken attack on German bourgeois mores and sexual hypocrisy. The conduit for Wedekind's assault on Berlin culture at the turn of the century was the central character of Lulu herself, a femme fatale in the classic mould. "The personification of primitive sexuality," Wedekind said, "who inspires evil unawares." To ensure that his point was taken, Lulu's last fling, "unawares," is conducted in a London garret with a lover whom Wedekind considered to be the ultimate embodiment of that evil: Jack the Ripper.

If the United States and Britain had now accepted the enfranchisement of women, patrician German society still exhibited a deep fear and mistrust of it. This was exemplified in post-war

German cinema by its various versions of *Alraune* (in which a prostitute is inseminated with the 'bad seed' of a hanged murderer and gives birth to a girl without a soul), Brigitte Helm's seductive robotrix in Fritz Lang's *Metropolis* (1926) and Marlene Dietrich's psychological destruction of poor, distracted Emil Jannings in *The Blue Angel* (1930). While America had come to accept the vamp, the 'It' girl, and a dozen other euphemistic variants of the sexually aware, rather than socially subordinate, 'tart with a heart', Germany still had the *valkyrie* to contend with in its national psyche – mythological warrior women who condemned men to death with a single stare, as immortalised by Wagner's *Der Ring des Nibelungen*.

Wedekind's Lulu was in that tradition: a sex-siren, luring men to their doom with a flutter of her eyelids; a victim, in truth, of the erotic impulse in a male-dominated world, but no less dangerous for that. Provided that she conformed to her predestined role as mistress, her predatory nature could be contained, but afford her position and power – emancipate her, in other words – and that way led to ruin and dusty death.

The supremacy of German cinema between the wars gave free rein to writers and filmmakers to embark on ever more daring explorations of the human condition. Among them was Georg Wilhelm Pabst, one of the great directors of the decade, who was influenced by Soviet cinema and Sergei Eisenstein. *Pandora's Box* had been filmed as *Lulu* in 1917, and again in 1923 with Swedish actress Asta Nielsen in the title role. Neither of these had featured Jack the Ripper and both had moderated the play's polemic. Pabst went back to Wedekind, but he went much further afield in terms of his casting. While many European actors and directors were now following a career path across the Atlantic to the US and Hollywood, Pabst sought to reverse the trend by hiring American starlet Louise Brooks to play the role of the intrinsically German Lulu.

The decision created an atmosphere of enmity on set (Brooks' co-star, Fritz Kortner, barely spoke to her throughout the shooting), but Pabst stuck to his guns. He already risked critical wrath by exposing the hedonism and decadence of German culture, and that is precisely what he received; not even Lulu's authentic demise under the knife of the Ripper was enough to assuage the doubters. Nevertheless, *Pandora's Box* is one of the last great masterpieces of the silent screen, and the film exerts the same fascination on the viewer as Lulu does on her lovers. As a critique of male-dominated Weimar Germany – an anything-goes, patrician free-for-all – *Pandora's Box* is devastating; in consequence, the film did little business on release. This was not wholly to do with its subject-matter, as the advent of 'talkies' in 1929 rendered it something of an anachronism. (Europe had held back on moving over to sound due to the expense of retooling the studios.) But its reputation has grown steadily ever since, not least for a climax in which Jack the Ripper, albeit briefly, is allowed to exhibit more humanity than the rest of the supporting cast put together.

According to Wedekind, who opened his first Act by having a ringmaster invite the audience to enter his menagerie and witness the behaviour of "the beasts within," Lulu was "not a real character" but a figurative one, and she represented unbridled sexual impulse. She is Lust, one of the seven deadly sins, and around her, Wedekind mounted an uncompromising display of all of the others. Wrath was uniquely reserved for the Ripper.

Nowadays, Jack the Ripper is seen as a 'mutilation murderer', rather than a sex-killer, where rape is the primary motivator. There was no rape; in fact, there was no evidence of sexual activity of any kind at the scenes of his crimes. *Lustmord*, in Jack's case, is a misreading. He is as likely to have been the abused as much as he was the abuser: a sexual inadequate, who found expression for his rage among those who flung that inadequacy in his face – a long way from the power-figure of myth, and of later film treatments. In this important respect, Frank Wedekind got it wrong and G W Pabst got it absolutely right.

> " – *you are under the mistletoe – now you must let yourself be kissed.*"
> Jack the Ripper (Gustav Diesel) in *Pandora's Box* (1928)

Pabst's Lulu is the archetypal good-time girl, to whom sexual adventure is but another expression of love. In the original (toned down for the screen), she has been pimped by Schigolch, her adoptive 'father', since childhood, and being free with her favours is second nature to her by the time the film opens at Act Three of Wedekind's play, with Lulu about to marry her magnate lover Ludwig Schoen (Kortner). After much intrigue, she finds herself on trial for his murder. Her entourage of 'dependants' contrive her escape and she flees to London via a tramp steamer. A second murder implicates Countess Geschwitz, a lesbian admirer of Lulu's and the only one to offer her unconditional love. On the run and down on her luck, Lulu takes refuge in a Whitechapel lodging-house but she is forced onto the streets to fund her existence. Enter Jack the Ripper, and exit Lulu.

The fascination with Lulu stems from of the fact that she is not so much a character in her own right as a symbolic representation of woman the world over: used, abused, misunderstood, maliciously accused, almost sold into white slavery, prostituted on the streets of London, and murdered by Jack the Ripper. Asta Nielsen had played her as a wanton seductress, inverting Wedekind's thesis in the process, but Louise Brooks invested the role with a beguiling insouciance, making it much clearer that she was the victim of the piece and not the villain.

The newly discovered propriety of the late 19th century had cloaked the bawdy tart of recent vintage in the language of euphemism: in London, she was a streetwalker or a 'lady of the night'; in Paris, a *boulevardière* or *demi-mondaine*. At the lower end of the economic scale, she

Gustav Diesel as Jack the Ripper in *Pandora's Box* (1928)

was a 'fallen woman' or an 'unfortunate'. She thought of herself as an actress or model (both of which guises Lulu adopts). French poet Charles Baudelaire wrote of her as "a sort of gypsy, wandering on the fringes of society: a perfect image of the savage that lurks in the midst of civilisation" (*Le Peintre de la vie moderne*; 1863), while pre-Raphaelites Dante Gabriel Rossetti and Holman Hunt painted her in Romantic hues. However she was perceived, she still helped to oil the wheels of the Industrial Age and fuel the engine of economic progress. Brooks' Lulu was in this mould.

When forced to defend her role in the film, Brooks compared it with her own experience on the stage: "I knew two millionaire publishers, much like Schoen in the film, who backed shows to keep themselves well supplied with Lulus," she wrote, only to become more forthright still when reflecting on the Berlin society that Pabst had targeted: "At the Eden Hotel where I lived the café bar was lined with the better priced trollops. The economy girls walked the streets outside. On the corner stood the girls in boots advertising

Jack the Ripper (1959) flagellation. Actors' agents pimped for the ladies in luxury apartments in the Bavarian quarter. Racetrack touts at the Hoppegarten arranged orgies for groups of sportsmen. The night club Eldorado displayed an enticing line of homosexuals dressed as women. At the Maly there was a choice of feminine or collar-and-tie lesbians."

Despite his plea of neutrality, Wedekind's view of Lulu was ambivalent: she was a sexual temptress enticing men to their deaths on the one hand, an innocent corrupted by male desire on the other. Pabst held to the latter view with regard to his doomed heroine, and directed Brooks to become a blank canvas through which the audience would take their own message from the film; Josef Von Sternberg used the same approach with Garbo at the fade-out of *Queen Christina*. This revision makes Lulu's climactic encounter with Jack the Ripper all the more poignant:

On Christmas Eve, two lost souls find each other on the foggy streets of London: Lulu, now reduced to whoring to keep her 'father' in food and drink, and Jack the Ripper, a psychological soul-mate, who is also driven by urges over which he has no control. Both are beyond society's power to redeem them, but not beyond redeeming each other.

Jack has no money to speak of, but Lulu takes pity on him and takes him back to her room. For a moment, his inner demon is stilled by Lulu's innocent charm and instinctive act of charity. For a moment, it appears as though love might finally conquer all, even lost love on a lost highway in London. But Jack cannot deny his compulsion to kill, any more than Lulu can defy what fate has in store for her. A bread-knife from a nearby table finds itself in the hand of the Ripper. Lulu closes her eyes and, by the light of a lone candle, resigns herself to a last embrace. Brooks' own reflections on the scene were uncompromising: "It is Christmas Eve and she is about to receive the gift which has been her dream since childhood. Death by a sexual maniac."

The climax of *Pandora's Box* is potent and moving, though it has to be said that, like much else in the film, Jack the Ripper (while sympathetically played by a forlorn Gustav Diesel) is merely another instrument of Pabst's allegory, the final abuser of women.

In a subsequent version of the play, variously subtitled a sex or 'monster' tragedy, Wedekind had the Ripper slaughter Lulu *and* the Countess Geschwitz, with the murder of Lulu taking place off-stage; Jack reappears carrying her womb wrapped in newspaper. A film adaptation in 1980 by Polish writer-director Walerian Borowczyk utilised this climax, and burnished the whole with a sensuous colour scheme and incidental music modelled on Saint-Saens' overture *Dance Macabre*. Anne Bennent's Lulu is merely pretty and promiscuous, though, and Udo Kier's dapper Jack the Ripper conducts himself like a hit-man for the mob. Mopping up after the murders, he gives voice to his thoughts in a dubbed line straight out of a Sergio Leone spaghetti western: "That was a hell of a lot of work... I'm just a goddamn lucky fella." This crude rendition was, however, closer in spirit than Pabst's film to an earlier draft of Wedekind's play, in which Jack pondered how much money he could obtain from the London Medical Club for his anatomical acquisition, the 'box' of the title being a vulgarisation for the item in question.

Many more Lulus have surfaced since *Pandora's Box*, both before and after Borowczyk's adaptation, such is her enduring cinematic appeal. (A Paul Aster project of 1998 – *Lulu on the Bridge* – was intended to feature Mira Sorvino as an actress playing the part of Lulu in *Pandora's Box*.) The majority of these films have added nothing to Wedekind's original and little to Pabst's vision of it, beyond increasingly explicit sex scenes, which were the reason why most of them were made in the first place. Deprived of a consummate artist like Pabst to give him a Romantic air and cast him as a victim of fate, like Lulu herself, Jack the Ripper was thematically relegated to the squalid reality of Whitechapel back-streets, where he was now destined to play out the preferred role that popular culture had already set aside for him, as murderous monster of the night.

German cinema, the home of expressionism, had drawn on Wedekind's plays from the 1890s for its version of Jack as social outcast, a notion that befitted the psychological themes to which its filmmakers were wed. But in the Ripper's own less polemical stamping-ground of English letters, it had been a different story.

As the 'naughty nineties' took on an air of cultural decadence in Britain and Europe and, after the turn of the century, blossomed more robustly into the Jazz Age in America, the first and by far the most famous fictional treatment of Jack the Ripper in English saw print in its original form in the January 1911 edition of McClure's Magazine, a monthly periodical based in New York. It was written by a 42-year-old French émigrée named Marie Adelaide Belloc Lowndes, and it was called *The Lodger*.

The Movies

Chapter Two
Tales of the London Fog

"Monster?" repeated Mrs Bunting absently. She was trying to hear the lodger's footsteps overhead; but her husband went on as if there had been no interruption: "It wouldn't be very pleasant to run up against such a party as that in the fog, eh?"

Marie Belloc Lowndes, *The Lodger* (Methuen; 1913)

Marie Belloc Lowndes penned two versions of *The Lodger*, an early short story of some 11,000 words and the later novel, which expanded the story to book length and almost 80,000 words. But *The Lodger* was not the first fiction to feature Jack the Ripper.

Margaret Harkness brought Whitechapel's most infamous export into *In Darkest London* in 1889, published under her pseudonym of John Law. Harkness shared the beliefs of Marx and Engels; her novels about life among East London's poor were socially aware and highly politicised, with indigent characters blaming their travails on the controversial influx of foreign nationals, particularly Jews.

Suspicion had fallen on the indigenous Jewish community from the very beginnings of the Ripper scare, partly because of a widespread belief that Yiddish custom condoned ritual sacrifice, but it reached its zenith after the double event, when the killer himself might consciously have attempted to stoke the fires of racial hatred by chalking an anti-Semitic accusation on a wall. In an effort to redress the balance, *In Darkest London* cast Jack as a slaughterman who takes refuge in the ghetto, but nevertheless confesses his sins as a Gentile: "People must eat and someone must kill beasts; but to kill makes a man like a cannibal, it gives him a thirst for blood, and I got to feel at last that nothing would quench my thirst but human blood, human flesh." The recipient of this confession is a Salvation Army officer, an idea which found an echo in Pabst's masterpiece, *Pandora's Box*.

Its worthiness not in doubt, what *In Darkest London* lacked – and *The Lodger* provided – was plot. A snatch of gossip overheard at dinner more than 20 years later by writer and socialite Marie Belloc Lowndes turned Jack the Ripper from fact into fiction.

Marie Belloc Lowndes was born Marie Adelaide Belloc in the small French village of La Celles St Cloud, near Paris, on 5 August 1868. Her father was barrister Louis Belloc, her mother was Elizabeth 'Bessie' Rayner Parkes, a suffragist and granddaughter of clergyman, chemist, and political radical Joseph Priestley (who had identified oxygen in 1774, but was later forced to emigrate to America when his views on the revolution in France made him unpopular in England), and her brother was Hilaire Belloc, who was also to make a name for himself, ironically, as a right-wing conservative, as well as writer, biographer, and poet.

A staunchly Catholic family, the Bellocs moved to England in 1872, and Marie Belloc, like her contemporary Margaret Campbell (better known by the pseudonym of Marjorie Bowen), had her first story published when she was a mere 16 years old, in 1884. She was soon writing articles for a number of magazines and periodicals but, in her own estimation, the "real beginning" of her career as a writer came in 1888, the year of the Ripper murders. By 1890, she had become a regular contributor to the *Review of Reviews*, a literary digest founded by

Previous page:
From Hell (2001)

William Thomas Stead, campaigning editor of the *Pall Mall Gazette* for much of the 1880s.

In these early years, Marie Belloc's speciality was French literature and literary affairs and, in 1895, she published an interview with Jules Verne in *Strand Magazine*. But she was rapidly becoming part of the literary scene in England, and already kept company with the likes of Henry James and Constance and Oscar Wilde. In 1896, she wed Frederic Sawrey Lowndes, a sub-editor on the *Times*, to become Marie Belloc Lowndes; in the years that followed, she and her brother Hilaire would count among their circle of friends such leading lights of English and American letters as H G Wells, G K Chesterton, Arnold Bennett, Cicely Hamilton, George Bernard Shaw, Ford Madox Ford and numerous other members of the literary *glitterati* of the turn of the century. A decade later and Marie was being invited to dine at Number 10 Downing Street with Liberal Prime Minister Herbert Asquith.

During this period, and as a consequence of her professional curiosity and bent for social discourse, Marie Belloc Lowndes also acquired a taste for crime, although she later denied that such was the case: "I am no more interested in crime than I am in any other human activity; indeed I may go further and say that I have always been far more interested in the ordinary – perhaps I ought to say the extraordinary – relations of men and women, than I am in murder." Nevertheless, she engaged in long debates with her peers about a number of high-profile cases, including those of Constance Kent, Charles Bravo and Dr George Lamson, who was hanged in 1882, and she attended at least one murder trial (that of the Seddons, in 1912).

Marie Belloc Lowndes

Mystery (and detective) fiction was on the upswing during the last years of the 19th century, largely due to the phenomenal success of a series of tales featuring Sherlock Holmes, a technological sleuth created by Arthur Conan Doyle. Not that these new fictional fields were confined to male practitioners: the coming century was bringing with it new freedoms for women as well, and as many female authors now sought to abandon their traditional preserve of romance (or romantic mysteries of the Radcliffe and Reeve schools, sustained by Marie Corelli at the turn of the century in *The Sorrows of Satan*; 1895) to pursue stories of detection instead, eventually surpassing their male counterparts. Foremost among them was Baroness (Emma) Orczy, best-remembered for *The Scarlet Pimpernel* (1905) but an avid writer of detective fiction also, whose *The Case of Miss Elliott* (1905), *The Old Man in the Corner* (1909) and *Lady Molly of Scotland Yard* (1910) all had an influence on Lowndes.

A suffragist and one of the founding members of the Women Writers Suffrage League, Mrs Lowndes had published the first of what were to be more than 40 novels in 1904: *The Heart of Penelope* was succeeded by *Barbara Rebell* (1905) and *The Pulse of Life* (1907), both character-driven studies charting the changing role of women in society. Several of these early works enjoyed a deal of critical success – *Barbara Rebell*, in particular, was held in fond regard by a devoted readership – but, with the growing popularity of mystery fiction, and her own ambivalent leanings in that direction, Marie Belloc Lowndes decided on a change of tack.

It was a decision which she would come to view with some regret in later years: "I have always believed that had I continued to write the kind of books that I began writing, and which I naturally preferred writing, I should probably have made, for me, a very much greater and better reputation than that which has fallen to my lot." Sir Arthur Conan Doyle, creator of Sherlock Holmes, expressed similar reservations over the shadow cast on him by his creation; for Mrs Lowndes, however, there were compensations: "On the other hand the fact, of which I was long ignorant, that I possess hidden away what is called a 'plot mind' became of very great importance to me as a writer..."

Marie Belloc Lowndes was the very epitome of 'ladies who lunch'. With her connections, her ear for gossip, her 'dowry' of £200 (a legacy that her husband had graciously donated towards her pursuit of a literary career) and her inveterate interest in crime and criminals, no one was better placed than she to pen a fiction about a glut of murders which had taken place in London almost a quarter of a century before. What Mrs Lowndes' 'plot mind' came up with in this regard was *The Lodger*, a tale of middle-aged couple Robert and Ellen Bunting, domiciled in a house off the Marylebone Road and down on their luck, who decide to let the upper floors of their home to a mysterious stranger who arrives on their doorstep one dark, dismal November afternoon.

The Lodger was published in the January 1911 issue of the American monthly *McClure's Magazine* (volume 36, number 3); the story ran across 16 pages and was accredited to Mrs Belloc Lowndes, "Author of 'The Decree Made Absolute'."

McClure's had been founded in 1893 by Irish-born publishing magnate Samuel Sidney McClure and by 1911 it featured an eclectic mix of fiction, features and 'muckraking', the disparaging term for the 'scandal-sheet' approach to journalism that McClure had instigated in 1903 in response to increasing competition in the marketplace. Retailing at 15 cents, *McClure's* had published Stevenson, Doyle and Rudyard Kipling, among other native authors, and it was proactive in bringing British writers to the attention of the American public. McClure's brother Robert headed up the magazine's London office, to which managing editor Willa Sibert Cather was seconded for 12 months, beginning in June 1910. Lowndes had offered her story to Cather, who purchased it for the January issue.

Marie Lowndes was to record in her diary how the original idea had come about: "*The Lodger* was written by me as a short story after I heard a man telling a woman at a dinner party that his mother had had a butler and a cook who married and kept lodgers. They were convinced that Jack the Ripper had spent a night under their roof."

The artist Walter Sickert, whose own impressionist paintings of London life were to render him a Ripper suspect in later years, told a similar story at table. According to Osbert Sitwell in *Noble Essences*, Sickert would tell of having taken rooms in Mornington Crescent, in the London Borough of Camden. During his stay, his landlady informed him that the previous occupant had been a consumptive veterinary student, whose curious behaviour and propensity for wandering the streets between midnight and 6.00 am had led her and her husband to believe that their tenant was none other than Jack the Ripper. The belief was compounded by the fact that on his return from these excursions, the young man would then pace the floor until the first edition of the morning newspaper went on sale and he could slip out to purchase a copy; on further investigation, the landlord discovered by the traces in the fireplace that his strange tenant had burnt the suit of clothes that he had been wearing the previous evening.

Sickert did not feature in Lowndes' circle of friends (although his biographer, Osbert Sitwell, did), but a casual acquaintanceship, such as her "man at a dinner party", is not beyond the bounds of possibility, wide and embracing as her social circle then was. Other elements of the Sickert tale certainly found their way into Lowndes' story, above and beyond its basic premise of two married ex-domestics who were convinced that the Ripper had "spent a night under their roof," as did similar hearsay passed off as fact by one Dr Lyttleton Stewart Forbes Winslow.

In his *Recollections of Forty Years*, Forbes Winslow also relates a tale purportedly told him by the landlord of premises in Finsbury Square who, in the summer of 1888, had let some rooms to a C Wentworth Bell Smith. According to the landlord's wife, Smith was given to "obsessive writing on religious matters," "late comings and goings," and would insist on washing his own shirts. Bloodstains were found in his room, and he was generally regarded by his landlady to be a lunatic, with delusions centring on "Women of the Streets." However she had come by it, it was a version of this apocryphal tale which sparked Marie Belloc Lowndes' imagination, but there was more to *The Lodger* than merely the fictional recreation of a classic murder mystery.

With *The Lodger*, Mrs Lowndes had penned a Tale of Terror as well as one of mystery and detection. She was an admirer of the work of Lafcadio Hearn (*In Ghostly Japan, Kwaidan*; 1899, 1904 respectively) and Henry James (*The Turn of the Screw*; 1898), and she both knew James personally and dined with him often. The decades preceding *The Lodger* had seen the flowering of the Victorian ghost story, a logical development of the fascination with Spiritualism and other esoteric religions which had filled the vacuum left by disillusionment with the established church during the last years of Victoria's reign.

In the same year that *The Lodger* was published – 1911 – Bram Stoker uncovered *The Lair of the White Worm*, M R James disinterred *More Ghost Stories of an Antiquary*, Algernon Blackwood rode *The Centaur*, Elliott O'Donnell revealed the secrets of *The Sorcery Club* and Gaston Leroux unmasked *The Phantom of the Opera*, itself a cross between the two genres of Terror and mystery which other writers were also attempting to bridge, through characters such as 'psychic detective' John Silence in Algernon Blackwood's case (*John Silence, Physician Extraordinary*; 1908) and 'Carnacki' the ghost-hunter in that of William Hope Hodgson.

Ghosts had as much to do with *The Lodger* as did Jack the Ripper, in fact. Story and subsequent novel were both written at 9 Barton Street, in the London borough of Westminster, the Queen Anne terrace that was home to Marie Belloc Lowndes and her family for more than 30 years, from 1909 to 1940. Not long after moving in, Mrs Lowndes became aware that the house was 'haunted'. She committed her impressions to her diary: "I constantly heard steps going across the hall and then the sound of the same steps going up the staircase."

Compare this to Mrs Bunting's behaviour in the story: "She opened the door leading into the bedroom behind, and there, closing the door quietly, stepped back into the darkness and stood motionless, listening. At first she heard nothing, but gradually there came the sound of someone moving about in the room just overhead..."

As far as Mrs Lowndes was concerned, from this point on, the house in Barton Street harboured a 'lodger' whom she never saw, only heard. With her husband spending long hours away in the evening at his post on the *Times*, she had settled down to the "life of a happy widow" by her own admission, and was writing full-time as a result (she had produced a book a year from *The Heart of Penelope* in 1904 onwards). With her heightened awareness of any unusual sound, any creak of the floorboards, the seeds of her most famous work were unconsciously being sown.

The activities of this "poltergeist," as Lowndes referred to her nocturnal companion, became increasingly pronounced: "The first time I supposed they were the steps of my husband coming back from the *Times* office late at night," she wrote, "and when they stopped on the little landing outside my door, I used, if awake, to call out to him. Now and again, if he was very tired, he would not open the door and would go straight on to his own room, but almost always, knowing I was awake, he would open my door, come straight into my room and we would have a talk. But again and again, after having heard heavy footsteps on our staircase, I would after a while hear sounds in the hall below and then steps on the stairs. The second time it was my husband."

Marie Lowndes had harboured thoughts of a 'haunted house' tale, but while her inveterate curiosity was aroused by Spiritualist theory (despite being a devout Catholic), and she was as willing as her peers to give credence to the latest anecdotal evidence concerning the afterlife, the traditional ghost story was a pasture not only well-trodden but fenced and ploughed for all it was worth by recognised masters in the field. In her heart was a Tale of Terror, but in her subconscious 'plot mind' was something more cerebral and altogether more realistic. Not a phantom, but a phantom *fiend*.

A snatch of conversation overheard at dinner, a half-forgotten memory revivified and placed *in situ* – namely, the house in Great College Street, Westminster, where the young Marie had spent most of her childhood, as well as the first 13 years of her marriage – and all the elements which had been formulating over the previous 18 months finally coalesced to form *The Lodger*.

Mrs Lowndes had created a ghost story, but *her* ghost was a man – an elusive, ethereal killer from a bygone age. A monster who was all too real and tangibly threatening. The plot of the story was as follows:

Settling into his rooms on the upper floors of the house, the Buntings' new lodger begins to exhibit certain peculiarities of behaviour which make Mrs Bunting suspicious of him, especially as the neighbourhood has recently been stricken by a spate of gruesome murders. Her husband is less prone than she to flights of fancy and offers a plausible explanation to account for the lodger's idiosyncratic manner, but even he is eventually forced to suspect that lodger and killer are one and the same, and his continuing presence in the house becomes a source of concern to both of them.

Events reach a climax when Bunting's daughter Daisy (from a previous marriage) comes to stay. The lodger senses a purity in Daisy which is in sharp contrast to his perception of the rest of her sex, and he invites her to show him around Madame Tussaud's waxworks exhibition. Fearing the worst, Mrs Bunting goes with them as chaperone. The three descend to the Chamber of Horrors where, at the same time, the Commissioner of Police and his French counterpart are engaged in a conducted tour. Mistakenly concluding that Mrs Bunting, for whom he has professed much admiration thoughout, has betrayed him, the lodger makes his escape by a side exit, though not before venting his ire on his innocent landlady. He never returns to his rooms, and some days later, a body identifiable as the Buntings' erstwhile lodger is fished from the Regent's Canal. (In the later novel, Lowndes dropped this scene – a gesture towards the fate of Ripper suspect Montague Druitt – and settled for the disappearance alone.)

The Lodger's name is Sleuth, a curious choice, at best, but one which Mrs Lowndes evidently found amusing; the lodger even spells it out for his new landlady: "S-l-e-u-t-h," he announces, adding, "Think of a hound, Mrs Bunting, and you'll never forget my name." Any initial jocularity in his manner is soon replaced by incidences of word and deed which become increasingly idiosyncratic:

> *The two men passed into the hall together. The house seemed blackly dark in comparison with the lighted-up road outside; and then, quite suddenly, there came over Bunting a feeling of mortal terror, an instinctive knowledge that some terrible and immediate danger was near him. A voice, the voice of his first wife, the long-dead girl to whom his mind so seldom reverted nowadays, uttered in his ear the words, 'Take care!'*
>
> *"I'm afraid, Mr Bunting, that you must have felt something dirty, foul, on my coat? It's too long a story to tell you now, but I brushed up against a dead animal, a dead rabbit lying across a bench on Primrose Hill."*
>
> *Mr Sleuth spoke in a very quiet voice, almost in a whisper.*
>
> *"No, sir; no, I didn't notice nothing. I scarcely touched you, sir." It seemed as if a power outside himself compelled Bunting to utter these lying words. "And now, sir, I'll be saying good night to you," he added. He waited until the lodger had gone upstairs, and then he turned into his own sitting room. There he sat down, for he felt very queer. He did not draw his left hand out of his pocket till he heard the other man moving about in the room above. Then he lit the gas and held up his left hand; he put it close to his face. It was flecked, streaked with blood.*
>
> Marie Belloc Lowndes, *The Lodger* (1911)

In the story, the first murder takes place in Whitechapel, with the next four unspecified as to location. The sixth occurs in the Marylebone Road. (A letter allegedly written by the Ripper, and found in a pillar box in Marylebone Road on the same day that Kelly's body was discovered in Miller's Court, read: "Dear Boss – I shall be busy tomorrow night in Marylebone. I have two booked for blood – Yours, Jack the Ripper.") The final murders in *The Lodger* take the form of a 'double event', though perpetrated in King's Cross, rather than in Whitechapel. These obvious parallels aside, the narrative is punctuated throughout by an additional weight of knowing detail about the Whitechapel Murders.

Mr Sleuth arrives carrying a leather bag. (The newspapers had reported that Mrs Fanny Mortimer, a witness to the murder of Stride, had seen a man with a "black shiny bag" at the crime scene; Leon Goldstein, the man in question, was later exonerated of any involvement, but the image of the bag-carrying killer became a fixture of the case thereafter.) He sports rubber-soled shoes. (After the 'double event', and at the insistence of Sir Charles Warren, beat constables had experimented with different types of rubber-soled boots to try to make themselves as silent as the man they sought.) He exhibits a distaste for open fires, consigning his suits to the flames at regular intervals. (By all accounts, the murder of Kelly had been enacted by the light of an open fire, in which items of clothing were burned.)

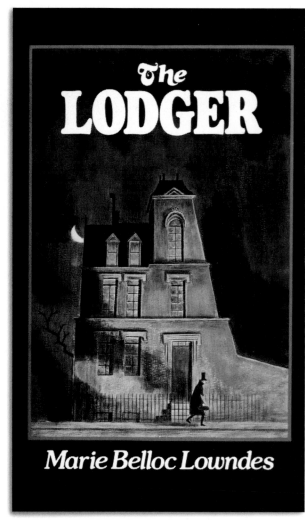

The LODGER

Marie Belloc Lowndes

Ripper centenary paperback edition of *The Lodger*.

This, then, was Marie Belloc Lowndes' *Lodger*, circa 1911. He gives his name as Sleuth, but he is the "Liverpool and Hamburg man," as her fictitious Commissioner of Police, Sir John Burney, proposes him to be (amended to the 'Leipzig and Liverpool man' in the novel). In short, and in the short story, he *is* Jack the Ripper.

1913, though, things had changed. In the novelised version of the tale, Jack the Ripper was noticeable by his *absence*.

Jack the Avenger

Publication on both sides of the Atlantic was commonplace by the early years of the 20th century, as was transatlantic travel by sea, at least until the *Titanic* went down on 15 April 1912. Marie Lowndes, a liberal conscience, thought the sinking of the *Titanic* was a folly of the idle rich; she attended the official inquiry in May, partly because her great friend and mentor, W T Stead, had perished in the disaster, and she was distressed to find that every ship's officer, in her view, was "trying to shield first the captain, second the company, and third himself," despite the loss of 1,513 lives in the tragedy, many of whom were women and children.

Some months after this event, William Leonard Courtney, literary editor of the *Daily Telegraph*, commissioned Marie Lowndes to write a novel for serialisation in the paper in the manner popularised by Charles Dickens and still à la mode at the time (though Lowndes' story was to be the first instance of its employment in the *Telegraph*). "I remembered *The Lodger*," Lowndes recalled. "I sent him the story and he agreed that it should be expanded. This was a piece of great good fortune for me..." And for the whole Ripper industry, as it was later to become. Success was immediate: "As soon as the serial began appearing... I began receiving letters from all parts of the world, from people who kept lodgings or had kept lodgings," its author reported with delight.

In accepting Courtenay's offer to turn her short story into a novel, Marie Lowndes opted to put aside more personal projects in favour of a purely commercial one. In so doing, she sought to enlarge on her original rather than rewrite from scratch, so all the main ingredients of the story were to remain essentially unchanged. This immediately presented a problem. The story had been wholly predicated on the notion embodied in the anecdote about the Mornington Crescent 'lodger', which in terms of Mr Sleuth came down to: was he or was he not Jack the Ripper? A question that was not definitively resolved, even at the climax. The short story had thus become a Tale of psychological Terror, told almost entirely from Mrs Bunting's point of view, and drawing on the house in Great College Street and the ghostly visitations in Lowndes' present abode for both its setting and its atmosphere.

In the short story, Lowndes was careful never to mention the Ripper by name, leaving it to her readers to make the connection. But she did offer up an unequivocal hint: "At last the unhappy woman fell into a deep, troubled sleep; and then she dreamed a most terrible and unnatural dream; hoarse voices seemed to be shouting in her ear, ''Orrible murder off the Edgware Road!' Then three words, indistinctly uttered, followed by '– at his work again! Awful details!'" The three words "indistinctly uttered" are 'Jack the Ripper', but in the same passage from the novel, the missing words no longer have any relevance.

A single hint in the short story had been enough to raise the possibility in the reader's mind as to the identity of the stranger to whom Mrs Bunting rents her rooms, but the novel was required to operate on a larger canvas and mere suspicion could not be maintained for some two dozen separate chapters. The probable truth of the lodger's identity had therefore to be established at an earlier stage in the proceedings and the dynamic of the piece altered to one of moral dilemma, where the Buntings had not only to decide what to do about their suspicions but when and how, especially in light of the possible threat posed to Bunting's daughter, Daisy.

Another factor bore equal consideration. The original had, of necessity, been set in period, but this had presented its author with few problems as the very presence of the Ripper decreed the (unspecified) date, and much of the narrative was concerned with Mrs Bunting's innermost thoughts and feelings, in any event, which obviated the need for further historical detail. To continue this in the novel would have required a degree of extra research. Marie Lowndes made a fateful decision: the novelised version of *The Lodger* would be set at the same time in which it was written, some 24 years *after* the Whitechapel Murders. Accordingly, it was no longer possible for Mr Sleuth to be Jack the Ripper and a new murderer – 'The Avenger' – was created in his stead: "At last the unhappy woman fell into a deep, troubled sleep; and then she dreamed a most terrible and unnatural dream. Hoarse voices seemed to be shouting in her ear: 'The Avenger close here! The Avenger close here!' ''Orrible murder off the Edgware Road!' 'The Avenger at his work again.'"

The idea of Ripper-style killings was too strong a concept to abandon in toto, however, and Lowndes conversely added *more* material relevant only to the Whitechapel Murders into her expanded version of the tale, in order that the 'allusion' be maintained.

The literal figure of Jack the Ripper correspondingly vanished from the pages of *The Lodger*, but Sleuth remained the Ripper in all but name. The decision to push forward the period of the story by a quarter-century created the paradox that, by common consent, *The Lodger* was about Jack the Ripper. And yet the events of the novel take place in 1912. The repercussions of this were to reverberate in every film version of the story, whose writers failed to take account of the anomaly and inadvertently introduced anachronisms into the tale as a result, but they would also afflict other aspects of Ripper cinema long after *The Lodger* had been filmed four times over.

Like Mary Wolstonecraft Shelley, whose original ghost-story version of *Frankenstein* became Chapter Three when she was persuaded by her husband to elaborate it to book length, so the opening of the first version of *The Lodger* – "'There he is at last, and I'm glad of it, Ellen. 'Tain't a night you would wish a dog to be out in'" – found its way to the top of Chapter 14 in the full text. This was a by-product of the linear structure which Lowndes applied to the novel, where Mrs Bunting's reflections on events which had taken place before the point at which the reader joined the short story version was enlarged upon to provide an extended prologue to the novel, as well as 13 preceding chapters!

The plot was further expanded to have Daisy installed in the household from the outset. This enabled the inclusion of a romantic subplot involving a police detective named Joe Chandler, which heightened the tension with regard to Daisy's welfare and also facilitated discussion of the murders on an ongoing basis between Chandler and Mr Bunting. The climactic trip to Tussaud's was complemented by an earlier excursion to Scotland Yard's famous Black Museum, courtesy of Chandler again, as well as attendance at the coroner's inquest on one of the victims by Mrs Bunting herself. In all other respects, both short story and novel remained essentially the same, and Mr Sleuth meets no more conclusive an end in the second draft than he did in the first. The Avenger, like the Whitechapel murderer, is thus never officially apprehended.

Marie Belloc Lowndes' serial thriller about a serial killer was published in novel form in 1913 by Methuen in Britain and Charles Scribner's Sons in the United States. Reaction to the book in literary circles was less than enthusiastic. "When it came to sending a quotation for an advertisement for the American edition, I was not able to find even one sentence of tepid approval," Lowndes noted; it had received not "a single favourable review." But its lukewarm reception by the critics was not reflected in its sales figures: "*The Lodger* sold something like half a million at sixpence in the Reader's Library," she informed her diary.

In the refined and genteel turn-of-the-century world of letters, there was no more refined or genteel a practitioner than Marie Belloc Lowndes. Yet this kind, diminutive, cultured and sensitive soul set in motion a fictional monster who, in multifarious guises, was to cast a shadow on celluloid for what is now close to a century. Lowndes may have harboured regrets that her claim to fame was ultimately to rest on *The Lodger* but, in the event, the story was an untypical gamble which paid off handsomely: "Had I not written *The Lodger*, I should never have been commissioned, as I was constantly commissioned, during the years that followed, to write what I now call thrillers."

The climax of *The Lodger* might have had some bearing on a silent screen novelty item of 1915, called *Farmer Spudd and His Missus Take a Trip to Town*. Made by the Gaumont company and partly filmed inside Madame Tussaud's itself, the short was directed by J V Leigh, who also played the farmer of the title. The Spudds visit Tussaud's, only to fall asleep in the Chamber of Horrors where they dream that the waxworks come to life. If this helped to inspire Paul Leni, it did little to encourage interest in *The Lodger*. Marie Lowndes had to wait a full 13 years before anyone in the film business saw real cinematic potential in her sixpenny best-seller.

> "Good morning, ladies and gentlemen. Today, as promised, we begin our study of crime in the cinema with a look at perhaps the most famous series of murders ever committed: the Whitechapel Murders, those committed by Jack the Ripper. I say they are perhaps the most famous because more than any other series of crimes in history that I know of, the Whitechapel Murders have been the subject of many, many films, especially in the British cinema. So, we'll start with the most popular..."
>
> Professor Harwell (Tom Schreier) in The Ripper (1986)

In 1926, a 26-year-old assistant director and sometime title designer, art director and general factotum with Gainsborough Pictures returned to England after a stint in Germany, where he

had been given the opportunity by studio head Michael Balcon to direct his first full-length feature film. His name was Alfred Hitchcock.

Title-card for Alfred Hitchcock's *The Lodger* (1927)

The son of a Leytonstone greengrocer, Hitchcock's elevation to the role of director with Gainsborough had initially been impeded by the hostility of a less-talented rival, but his prospects received a much-needed boost from working both at Ufa's studios in Berlin (as assistant director on *The Blackguard*; 1925) and Emelka's in Munich, where he had himself directed *The Pleasure Garden* (also 1925) as part of a co-production arrangement between Gainsborough and Münchener Lichtspielkunst. Hitchcock learned much in Germany, and most of it was to find its way into his next feature.

Some years before, the director had seen a theatrical adaptation of the Lowndes novel by Horace Annesley Vachell, a playwright whose own *Lord Camber's Ladies* was produced by Hitchcock for Gaumont-British in 1932. (The stage version was called *The Lodger: Who Is He?* The suave and sinister Lionel Atwill had made his Broadway debut in the title role when it played New York in 1917.) Thinking that it might serve as the vehicle in which to put some of his new-found ideas on film theory into practice, in the still largely experimental arena of silent cinema, Hitchcock settled for *The Lodger* as his next project. Perversely, he then cast former chorister and current romantic screen icon, David Ivor Davies – best known by his stage name of Ivor Novello – in the lead.

Cardiff-born Novello was a matinée idol and prolific composer of some of the best-loved musical numbers of his day; in 1914, he wrote 'Keep the Home Fires Burning'. His career as a romantic leading man dated back to 1919, and in 1923 D W Griffith had cast him opposite Mae Marsh in *The White Rose*. In 1925, he had starred in *The Rat* for Gainsborough (based on his own play), followed in 1926 by *The Triumph of the Rat*, both of which were directed by (Jack) Graham Cutts, who had just dispensed with the services of his assistant director, one Alfred Hitchcock.

Cutts, who was a *company* as well as film director with Gainsborough, protested against the choice of Novello for such an unsympathetic role and a compromise was reached. House scriptwriter Eliot Stannard overhauled the novel in Novello's favour, and production went ahead as planned. The antipathy expressed towards the film by Gainsborough distribution associate, C M Woolf, led to it being shelved immediately on completion, the third of Hitchcock's fledgling efforts to meet such a fate. *The Lodger* was eventually saved from oblivion by a timely makeover from editors Ivor Montagu and Adrian Brunel, at the instigation of Balcon, and its resultant success finally put Alfred Hitchcock on the cinematic map.

> *"The seventh golden-haired victim of the mysterious murderer known as The Avenger was discovered on the Embankment early this evening. A woman witness describes the murderer as wearing a scarf covering the lower half of his face."*
>
> Telegraph message in *The Lodger* (1927)

Hitchcock's version of *The Lodger* was appended with a subtitle, *A Story of the London Fog*, in order to play upon the mystery element (with the whole changed to *The Case of Jonathan Drew* for US release). Fog had been an intrinsic part of the London scene for half a century, and the capital remained subject to 'pea-soupers' – what in Victoria's heyday were often referred to as 'London particulars' – until the Clean Air Act of 1956, which was passed after more than 4,000 people had died of respiratory disease in the Great London Smog of 1952. The pseudonymous 'Walter', author of the notorious sexual biography *My Secret Life* (which was privately published the same year as the Ripper murders), had confided to his small and select band of readers the advantages to be had from fog: "Foggy weather is propitious to amorous caprices." The disadvantages had already been pointed up by Mrs Lowndes, and Hitchcock utilised them to the full in his desire to show that fog was just as propitious to murderous ones.

Unconsciously pointing up the temporal paradox embedded in the novel, Hitchcock took the Lowndes book at face value and gave it a contemporary setting of 1920s London (dispensing with its Jack the Ripper connection in the process). The original provides the plot for the first half of the film: a killer is preying on young women; a mysterious stranger arrives at the Buntings' lodging house; his curious behaviour arouses suspicion. From this point on, Hitchcock was on his own.

Because of Novello's involvement in the film, lodger and murderer could no longer be one and the same. A new subplot had therefore to be created to explain away his behaviour. For the story to remain essentially intact, the now-innocent lodger had to be given a motivation whereby his actions could parallel those of Mrs Lowndes' *guilty* lodger, yet be circumspect in the final analysis. As these actions involved skulking in his room and going out in the dead of night to wander the streets, as well as quirks of personality (such as asking for the removal of the pictures of young women which adorn the walls of his room), the only way that this could be achieved was to have him 'shadow' the real killer. To do such a thing required a raison d'être, and that left Eliot Stannard with only one scenario: the lodger has a vested interest in the case, arising from the fact that someone close to him was a victim of The Avenger. He is therefore trying to catch the killer for himself.

So far, so good. But the script fluffs the logical conclusion of such a plot, in which the protagonist would surely get his man. In the worst of all possible outcomes, the Avenger is nabbed off-screen and his identity, and inclusion in the film, is seen to be superfluous, a narrative contrivance that Hitchcock subsequently christened the 'MacGuffin'. Novello, to his credit, saw the error of Hitchcock's way and corrected it in his own remake of 1932.

In the revised plot, Daisy becomes attracted by the mysterious stranger (who reveals himself as Jonathan Drew), while her detective beau grows correspondingly hostile. A love triangle develops, in an allusion to the triangular calling-cards which the Avenger pins to his victims (one of many visual cues that Hitchcock deploys throughout the film). Inspired by jealousy, Chandler arrests Drew and slaps a pair of handcuffs on him, but he manages to escape. Finding refuge in a bar, he tells Daisy of his sister's murder at the hands of the Avenger. The 'cuffs' are spotted and a mob gives chase, but he is rescued in the nick of time by a contrite Chandler, now privy to the recent apprehension of the real killer.

The climax sees the lodger dangling by his handcuffs from iron railings, while the mob set about him in a straight lift from Chaney's *The Phantom of the Opera*. Rescue comes via the *deus ex machina* of a telephone call which relays the message that the real killer has been caught. The crucifixion motif is very clever in the silent screen's over-obvious way with symbolism but, by this point, the story has moved a very long way from Jack the Ripper.

> *"If your suspense revolves round the question: 'Is he or is he not Jack the Ripper?' and you reply, 'Yes, he is Jack the Ripper', you've merely confirmed a suspicion. To me, this is not dramatic. But here, we went in the other direction and showed that he wasn't Jack the Ripper at all."*
> Alfred Hitchcock talking about *The Lodger* in 1967

Novello enters the piece like Max Schreck in *Nosferatu*, with piercing eyes and the lower half of his face muffled by a scarf. Hitchcock had seen and admired F W Murnau's unlicensed 1922 adaptation of *Dracula* while in Germany, so the lodger's appearance, motionless at the door as it is opened to camera by Mrs Bunting, is conscious *hommage* to the scene where Graf Orlok enters Hutter's bedroom. As an example of stagecraft, this opening is impressive in a Gothic way, but so overstated is the lodger's introduction that he simply *has* to be innocent in this version, just as the opposite is true of Uncle Charlie for the same reason in Hitchcock's later *Shadow of a Doubt* (1943).

The Lodger (1927)

Conceptually, the film is a polemic about the persecution of innocence, a favourite theme of the director in subsequent years, obsessed as he was with Catholic notions of guilt and original sin. *The Lodger* was a Tale of Terror, however, not a peg on which to hang philosophical considerations.

As a piece of narrative construction, Hitchcock's *The Lodger* is deeply flawed. Some of its unsatisfactory plot development might have arisen through the requirement that Novello be innocent, thus turning the novel on its head, and some of it might have been exaggerated by the reconstruction work carried out, in part, by editor Ivor Montague, which finally enabled the film to go from shelf to screen and on to success some months after it was originally completed. Montague reduced the intertitles from 300 to 80 and

French poster for *The Lodger* (1927)

suggested the re-shooting of scenes to plug the gaps. Of the changes that Montagu proposed, Hitchcock advised Francois Truffaut in 1967 that he reluctantly "agreed to make about two," but the director's characteristic immodesty may have prevented him from confessing to more.

Hitchcock had wanted to retain a sense of ambiguity about the lodger's motives right to the end of the film, a sensible enough ploy with the lodger occupying pole position in the narrative. But with Ivor Novello on board, no such equivocation was possible. (When Hitchcock attempted to repeat this strategy in *Suspicion* [1941], the casting of Cary Grant had a similar effect.) The engendering of doubt as to the lodger's innocence or guilt was only practicable with an unknown in the role, and Novello was too well-known at the time for an audience to have suspected him of serial murder for long. With the stratagem thus undermined, and the focus switched from the aged Buntings to the lodger as star of the show, Hitchcock's *The Lodger*, almost out of necessity, instead transforms into a showcase for technical virtuosity.

Critics tend to view the film in relation to themes that 'Hitch' developed more fully in his later work, such as mistaken identity and the concept of the 'wronged' man. All well and good in context, but as an adaptation of *The Lodger*, the film is less noteworthy; it is Hitchcock's *The Lodger*, not Mrs Lowndes', just as it was Hitchcock's *The Birds*, not Daphne du Maurier's. The emphasis is on style over content, with the individual tricks in the magician's bag being viewed as more important than the act in the round. And tricks there are aplenty, as well as abundant allusions to the Christ-like sufferings of the Drew character, wistful and melancholic in his Romantic isolation.

The film's most celebrated shot is one in which the lodger is seen through a 'glass' ceiling, pacing the floor of the room above in obvious agitation. The 'ceiling' was conjured up by the props department to compensate for what might have proved a more effective use of sound. But the most memorable sequence in *The Lodger* is one of sound, albeit in visual representation only: Mrs Bunting lies awake in her bed, ears pricked by the indefinite movements of her mysterious lodger as he embarks on one of his nocturnal prowls. He creeps stealthily down the stairs to the door, as his landlady follows with her eyes what she *senses* to be his trajectory. Only here does Hitchcock put aside his obsession with montage and play the suspense theme straight, employing lessons clearly learned from his sojourn at Emelka.

This sequence comes closest to capturing not only the mood of Terror evoked by the novel, but that which was likely to have prevailed among the isolated denizens of the East End during the actual Ripper scare: after the murder of Mary Kelly, most of the witnesses to the event could only pronounce upon what they had *heard* during the fateful night.

If Stannard and Hitchcock had stuck to suspense instead of chicanery, the end product might have been much improved in relation to its source. As it is, *The Lodger* was nevertheless released to great acclaim after all the re-jigging. "Possibly the finest British production ever made," was one critical comment, although its eventual reception may have had as much to do with the presence of Ivor Novello as the proficiency of Hitchcock. Novello certainly thought so, for he cast himself in the same role again only six years later.

From *The Lodger*, Ivor Novello went on to *The Constant Nymph* (1928), which became the most popular British release of its year, but he returned to his old role in a sound remake after spending some time kicking his heels in Culver City in search of Hollywood stardom. With

Maurice Elvey at the helm on this occasion, Novello was able to exercise a degree of control over the new production. Elvey was a more conventional stylist than Hitchcock, but the film is none the worse for that.

Novello had sold the idea to Twickenham Films chairman Julius Hagen, and he complemented a pedigree script by Paul Rotha and actor-director Miles Mander by contributing his own dialogue. As the star of the show, he naturally wished to ensure himself some good lines. Novello was no mean author, and the lines that he wrote are also among the best in the film.

> *"Good evening. I saw your card… You have a room to let?"*
>
> Angeloff (Ivor Novello) in *The Lodger* (1932)

If the 1927 *The Lodger* had borrowed from *Nosferatu*, the 1932 film borrowed from Tod Browning's *Dracula* (1931), with Novello adopting an East European accent and attempting to sound like Lugosi's Count. (A camp pose that he subsequently adopted on stage in a series of

Cover art for
The Lodger

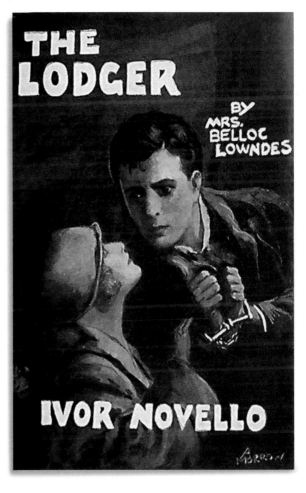

hugely popular 'Ruritanian' musical extravaganzas like *Glamorous Nights* and *The Dancing Years*.) Elvey also takes his cue from Browning, divesting the film of expressionistic nuance and deferring to the modernity of Hollywood-style horror. The lodger himself is a Byronic hero, burdened by guilt and tormented by a secret past. He wanders the streets at night, confiding to Daisy: "I like the fog." By way of compensation, he is cast as a composer, thus affording Novello the opportunity to tinkle out a few melodies on the piano.

In this version, the Avenger is the 'Bosnian Murderer' and the lodger a Bosnian émigré named Angeloff, but Elvey's film leaves even less room for doubt about its protagonist's eventual innocence than Hitchcock's did, despite his cryptic utterances and occasional attempts to justify the killings. "Beast, you call him," he reproaches his landlady. "But how do you know that he too is not innocent? – That all these crimes are just a madness; the beast that is in all of us coming to the surface. How do you know that he knows what he does?" "All the more reason that he should be shut up and put out of his misery," Mrs Bunting replies. "Put out of his misery… Yes… That is what *should* be done," Angeloff acknowledges, recalling Lugosi's elegiac line in Dracula: "To die, to be really dead, that must be *glorious*."

The plot travels much the same road as its predecessor, and only parts company with it in the last reel. Having escaped from his police

American lobby card for *The Phantom Fiend* (1932)

captors as before, the lodger arranges to meet Daisy in a park, but she is confronted by the killer instead. Angeloff turns up in the nick of time, and he throttles Daisy's assailant with the handcuffs. He then explains that the Avenger is his brother, an escaped lunatic, whom he has been hunting all along.

The film is remarkably forthright in its treatment of the murders. "Gash across throat, head almost severed," says a newsman, while reporter Jack Hawkins (in only his second screen appearance) notes of one victim that "Her throat was slit from ear to ear," at which point Elvey cuts to Angeloff sliding a bow across the strings of a violin, an effective juxtaposition that inspires a shiver of horror even today. Another sequence foreshadows the suggestive thrillers of RKO producer Val Lewton. A young woman enters a park alone. We follow her for a while, expecting the Avenger to strike, but nothing untoward happens and the scene ends. Moments later, a second woman enters the park; again, we expect the killer to strike. As we follow her also, she walks past the body of the first.

In sharp contrast to the Hitchcock film, the climax of this *Lodger* packs the expected punch. Daisy is searching for Angeloff in the park. She spies a handcuffed figure in the fog, and approaches it from behind with the entreaty "Michel...?" The figure turns around, and it is the Avenger. What was soon to become a cliché creates a genuine *frisson*, and although Novello plays both roles with the minimum of makeup to differentiate them, he manages so credible a transformation into the deranged Stefan that for an instant, it is difficult to believe that he and

Michel are one and the same. Stagey and melodramatic it may be to modern eyes, but the scene gives some idea of the hold that the Lyceum's Richard Mansfield was able to exert on the audiences of his day with little more than acting technique to aid him. The handcuffs turn out to be the killer's knife, held between both hands.

There is an allusion here to the case of Victorian journalist and author George R Sims, whom Marie Lowndes had complimented by referring to him obliquely in *The Lodger* and who was himself arrested on suspicion of the crimes because he matched a description of a man alleged to be Jack the Ripper: "It was quite a pardonable mistake. The redoubtable Ripper was not unlike me as I was at the time," Sims remarked subsequently.

Elvey's film has predictably been passed over in the retrospective rush to praise Hitchcock, but the 1932 version of *The Lodger* is much the more effective of the two productions. It was re-released in an abridged form in 1935, under a new title, *The Phantom Fiend*.

"I'll look forward to seeing you in Whitechapel…"
Slade/Jack the Ripper (Laird Cregar) in *The Lodger* (1944)

The $1 million profit which had been generated by Universal Studios – the 'home of the monsters' – at the end of 1939, rising to $3 million by the end of 1942, encouraged other majors to dip their toes into big-budget horror. Opting to leave the 'creature features' to Universal, rival studios sought a more psychological base for their own excursions into the genre, as well as a more literary pedigree. Twentieth Century-Fox added *The Lodger* along with *Hangover Square* to their roster in 1944 and 1945 respectively, both of them starring Laird Cregar and both directed by John Brahm, whose evocation of Gothic landscape in Fox's *The Undying Monster* (1942) had been second to none.

Fox producer Robert Bassler was the guiding hand behind *The Lodger*. Bassler was an admirer of the Lowndes novel and he hired playwright and screenwriter Barré Lyndon to provide the script. (Lyndon, real name Alfred Edgar, was the author of the original play on which Paramount's *The Man in Half Moon Street* was based.) The writers of the two previous versions had gone by the book; Barré Lyndon, mindful of the fact that the new film required a Gothic flavour, went back to *both* sources. But Lyndon did more than return *The Lodger* to what was presumed to be its correct period. He also rolled back the element of amateur detection that Stannard, Rotha *et al* had brought to the fore, refurbishing the story as the Tale of Terror it had been to begin with. The revision introduced the anachronisms which had waited to undermine any such 'authentic' adaptation, but it also meant that Lyndon felt no qualm about naming the *real* villain of the piece in the film's opening scene: Jack the Ripper.

The 1944 version of *The Lodger* was directed by German émigré John (Hans) Brahm, and the influences of expressionism and Black Forest myth were stronger on Brahm than they had been on Hitchcock, weaned, as he was, on *puppenspielen* and theatrical adaptations of Goethe's *Faust*. This time around, the tale was treated with due respect, rather than serving as a mere prop for technical trickery. The plot was as before, but set in period dress and reverted to the conclusion that the lodger is, in fact, guilty. The name 'Sleuth' is discarded in favour of a less idiosyncratic alternative – Slade –

Teaser poster for *The Lodger* (1944)

which the lodger borrows from the 'Slade Walk' through which he passes on his way to the 'Burtons' (itself amended from Bunting).

The decision to set this *Lodger* in 1888 uncovered the pitfalls which had lain in readiness for any such move. Tower Bridge, which was not built until 1894, can be glimpsed in the background of the film's closing shot, but that was down to production design. More integral was Lyndon's employment of fingerprinting to detect the killer; fingerprinting was a forensic science not in use at the time of the Whitechapel Murders. Had it been so, researchers might have been saved a century of further investigation.

The novel's reference to fingerprinting comes during the Buntings' visit to the Yard ("We've records here of over two hundred thousand men's and women's fingertips!" Chandler informs them), but Mrs Lowndes disavowed it as a means of advancing her plot, to ensure that the lodger's guilt remained equivocal. Lyndon fixes on it to confirm suspicions which are already in play at this juncture, thereby furnishing the film with its most glaring error of fact. "If my ideas are right, I'll make Jack the Ripper's own fingers tie the noose that'll hang him," Inspector Warwick (George Sanders) declares.

In a decision as open to Freudian interpretation as the notional motive of the murderer himself, Fox head Darryl F Zanuck vetoed the idea of the Ripper killing prostitutes and decreed that he should target actresses instead. In centuries past, the two were considered interchangeable, so no real harm was done. Zanuck's appendage to Mrs Lowndes' story did not improve it, but top-notch Fox production values and the performances of a cast reared in the old studio system are graces which outweigh minor quibbles such as who, precisely, is done to death.

The film is opulently mounted and populated by familiar faces from the British expat community, which was a fixture of Hollywood at a time when Brits could play something other than villains in American films. Consequently, *The Lodger* both looks and sounds right. This air of authenticity is more than skin deep: there is a real feel for period in this forties' West Coast slice of Victoriana. The flair for verisimilitude is, however, restricted to middle-class life. *The Lodger's* depiction of the working classes is stereotypically lax: all are jolly roustabouts, singing and dancing in the streets, with an unfeasibly high quota of Pearly Kings and Queens among their number.

Sir Cedric Hardwicke lends weight to the character of Burton, George Sanders is his effortlessly smooth self as the investigating officer (without any competition from the lodger for the hand of the lady, in this instance), and Merle Oberon is lustrously beautiful under the soft-focus lensing of her fiancé Lucien Ballard, the film's renowned cinematographer. But *The Lodger* truly belongs to its titular star: Philadelphia-born, Winchester-educated Laird Cregar, the Hollywood noir 'heavy' who carved a place in cinema history for himself through the brooding intensity of his work here.

> "You corrupt and destroy men, as my brother was destroyed. But when the evil is cut out of a beautiful thing, only the beauty remains..."
>
> Slade/Jack the Ripper (Laird Cregar) in *The Lodger* (1944)

Merle Oberon and George Sanders in a publicity pose from *The Lodger* (1944)

With the lodger recast as Jack the Ripper, he required kitting out with a suitable rationale. Lyndon kept the religious mania of the Lowndes novel but coupled it to a reverse reading of the plot from the 1932 version, in which the protagonist's brother was the murderer: Slade's brother is dead as the result of an ill-starred liaison with an 'actress' and his sibling is out to

Laird Cregar

gain revenge (a concept which cropped up again in *A Study in Terror* in 1966). The script's verbalisation of Slade's warped psychology is pure hogwash, but Cregar acts it out as though *he* believes it, which is all that matters in the final analysis.

Cregar's performance ranks as one of the screen's great essays in villainy. He manages to exude both charm and menace at one and the same time, and although relatively inanimate throughout most of the film, much is revealed of his inner torment by clever lighting and the merest trace of a tick on his tortured features. The cerebral air that Cregar instils into the character makes all the more shocking his sudden, violent outburst against Merle Oberon's Kitty at the climax. It is at this point that man and mania become one, as Cregar's face contorts to compensate for cautious staging that dictated an *off-screen* appearance of the Ripper's knife during the struggle. And Oberon seems to be genuinely frightened in the scene, as well she might have been in the clutches of a 20-stone Ripper.

A parting threat to Mrs Bunting is all that features in the novel, but film adaptation demands more. Having been foiled in his attempt to stab Kitty, Slade is pursued through the 'flies' of the theatre to a final confrontation played out against a backdrop of the Thames. Cornered and snarling, like a wild beast at bay – eyes bulging, teeth bared – he throws himself into the river, and into the annals of unsolved crime. These scenes are startling – as frightening as anything from Universal at the time – and along the way, Brahm serves up one of the most extraordinary shots in the history of the horror film: Slade lumbers across a catwalk towards camera, as the lights from the theatre below shine up through the slats to play stroboscopically over his maddened features. Slade has delivered his own eulogy earlier in the film – "Deep water is dark, and restful, and full of peace" – though how he actually manages to reach the Thames from a window in Whitechapel's 'Palace of Varieties' is another matter.

John Brahm had kept faith with the fact that *The Lodger* started out as a Tale of Terror, not one of crime, mystery and (failed) detection, and 75-year-old Marie Lowndes lived long enough to see her work on screen in a form that did justice to it at the third attempt. Perhaps the best critique of Brahm's version came from Mrs Lowndes herself. In the second volume of her autobiography, she recalled, "During the second world war, when mothers and children were being evacuated from London, a friend of mine heard a person in a crowded train turn to a woman, whose child was howling, and exclaim, 'Your baby must have seen *The Lodger!*'"

Within months of the film's release – but after shooting was complete on a follow-up, *Hangover Square* (from the novel by Patrick Hamilton) – Samuel Laird Cregar was dead, at 30 (not 28, as usually stated), from a heart attack brought on by the crash diet which had reduced his weight by a third for the reprise. An immense talent in more ways than one, Laird Cregar's gift to cinema was his performance in *The Lodger*, where he will forever be the personification of Marie Belloc Lowndes' most famous creation.

> *"Good evening… I see you have a room to let."*
>
> Dr Fell (Valentine Dyall) in *Room To Let* (1950)

If Barré Lyndon failed to wholly appreciate the difficulty of adapting *The Lodger* as a story of Jack the Ripper, mystery writer Margery Louise Allingham did not. Allingham, a contemporary of such as Agatha Christie, Dorothy L Sayers and Ngaio Marsh, and the creator of amateur sleuth Albert Campion, had penned a play in 1948 for broadcast on the BBC entitled 'A Room to Let', which borrowed both the period and the mysterious lodger of the Lowndes novel, but still managed to centre its action on Jack the Ripper.

A plotter of mysteries herself, Allingham proved to be more astute than Lyndon at discerning the disparities between the two versions; a play that appeared on the face of it to be straight plagiarism turned out, in fact, to be a quite different narrative.

What Allingham did was essentially very simple: she held to the central theme of the novel whereby a stranger takes rooms in a lodging house, and to the approximate period in which the action takes place (1904 in this instance; the year of the writer's own birth), but she removed the allusion to the *original* crimes and was thus able to incorporate the Ripper into her tale by have him become a tenant of the house 16 years *after* he has escaped from the asylum where he was incarcerated in 1888.

Allingham had found the perfect solution by which to square the circle of *The Lodger* and its connection to the Ripper, and her version was filmed in 1949 by Hammer/Exclusive.

Mrs Lowndes could have done much the same, and better retained the narrative dynamic of her original story. But she had gone a different route. This clever piece of lateral thinking ranks Margery Allingham on a par with her peers. Marie Belloc Lowndes died on 14 November 1947, and so was spared the knowledge that a more satisfactory answer to the problem she faced in 1912 had existed all along.

> Sergeant: *"Most like a 'hiss'. Queer, that."*
> PC Smith: *"Oh aye, what's queer about that?"*
> Sergeant: *"Bit of a trademark of his, it was. No mistaking it. November the 9th 1888 the last we ever saw of 'im or 'eard of 'im."*
> PC Smith: *"What are you talking about, Sarge?"*
> Sergeant: *"Nothing much. Just a fancy… Only it did bring to me mind someone called Jack the Ripper."*
>
> Reginald Dyson and Charles Mander in *Room To Let* (1950)

Room To Let was scripted by John Gilling, who was later to become a prolific journeyman on Hammer stages. The main narrative is formatted in flashback: three men meet for dinner to discuss the 'Willow Street Murder', one of whom, former reporter Curly Minter (Jimmy Hanley), was present at the scene of the crime. Minter relates how, as a young news-hound, he began to suspect that a Dr Fell, in lodgings at the home of a Mrs Musgrave and her daughter Molly, was really an escaped lunatic from The Towers, a local asylum stricken by a catastrophic fire. Fell is overbearing, and he holds the Musgraves virtual prisoners in their own home.

Constance Smith
and Jimmy Hanley in
Room To Let (1950)

Further digging by Minter connects Fell to the Whitechapel murders of 1888, but when he alerts the police, the doctor is discovered shot dead inside a locked room with the wheelchair-bound Mrs Musgrave lying prostrate at the bottom of the stairs.

The film concludes with Minter's dinner companion providing a solution to the mystery (again shown in flashback) in which Fell carries the crippled woman to his room to do away with her, only to have her shoot him before she tumbles back down the stairs. Minter, who is first on the scene, has himself arranged the mysterious locking of the door in order to protect his future mother-in-law.

Elaborating the theme of the insidious house-guest into a 'locked room' mystery (a staple of the crime genre) is merely illustrative of the vogue for puzzle-plots which was still current at the time of the film's production. The narrative dynamic of *Room To Let* turns on Minter's investigation into the 'missing' patient in the asylum fire, to whom no one in authority will attest. This is by far the most interesting aspect of the tale and one which has not gone entirely unnoticed by writers seeking the identity of Jack the Ripper. (*The Secret of Prisoner 1167, Was This Jack the Ripper?* by James Tully; Robinson, 1997.) The failings of a social order which institutionally turned its face against unpalatable truths are underscored by the paltry nature of the objections that are raised by Mrs Musgrave when thoroughly modern Molly (Constance

Smith) suggests a course of action which will evict the lodger from his rooms. Her misplaced sense of propriety exemplifies that which almost certainly would have inhibited the apprehension of the real Ripper, had he indeed proved to have come from a better class of society.

Allingham acknowledges the source of her inspiration with several nods in the direction of *The Lodger*: Fell says that he is from Leipzig, and later remarks, "Curious, isn't it, that I should be the lodger?" Knowing reference is also made to the anomalous employment of fingerprinting: "These were early days. The police weren't very scientific then," Minter says, in relation to the problem of the locked room.

Valentine Dyall's Dr Fell, with his trademark 'hiss' or sharp intake of breath, is genuinely creepy in the tradition of Tod Slaughter, and Slaughter's ghost, tricked out with Gainsborough period opulence, could still be seen twirling its whiskers on the periphery when small conceits like *Room To Let* gave way to the full-blooded melodramatics of Hammer Horror only a few years later. "I shall begin again, where I left off," he informs Mrs Musgrave, his eyes afire with missionary zeal. Nothing if not persistent, Jack the Ripper showed up in the script tray of writer Jimmy Sangster, this film's assistant director, after that transformation had come to pass.

The Allingham solution to the puzzle posed by *The Lodger* was unique. Future films would either deal with Jack the Ripper on his home ground or turn him into someone else, as Mrs Lowndes had chosen to do.

In cataloguing the curiously inaccurate addresses where he "made a cross" in 1888, *Room To Let*'s Dr Fell pays particular attention to Miller's Court, the scene of the Kelly murder and a real 'locked room' mystery in itself.

On the discovery of Kelly's body, the door of number 13 was found to be locked or bolted – a report in the *Times* of 10 November referring to a 'spring' or Yale lock, though there is no independent corroboration for this. The type of lock might logically obtain on who had been able to open or close the door and, like all 'locked room' mysteries, the answer to this one question is likely to be the key to the whole affair, yet no one appears to know for certain exactly what style of lock was fitted to the door. Kelly had claimed that the key to the room was lost, but that entry could be gained by reaching in through a side window and unlocking (or unbolting) the door from the inside. The broken window which enabled this procedure

Valentine Dyall and Constance Smith in *Room To Let* (1950)

appears to substantiate the loss of the key and is better explained in this context than as the alleged result of a fight with her lover, Barnett, given the location of the missing pane of glass. If that were so, only Kelly or those to whom she imparted the information could gain entry to the room, which effectively eliminates the idea that the Miller's Court murder was opportunist in nature.

Four years after being in peril of Jack the Ripper in a low-budget British film, the radiant Constance Smith found herself in the same situation in an equally low-budget American one. In 1953, Brahm's version of *The Lodger* was taken out of mothballs and dusted down to provide a programme-filler for Twentieth Century-Fox, through one of the many 'shadow' companies which had been set up for the purpose. Rising star Jack Palance was drafted in on the strength of his memorable turn as the cold-blooded killer in George Stevens' *Shane*, while Smith did duty as Lily, with the more outmoded 'Daisy' once again relegated to the name of the housemaid.

> *"Your police methods will never trap the one you call Jack the Ripper. You may be right about the periodicity, but I doubt if the beast you describe can be sated… He must do his work again!"*
>
> Slade/Jack the Ripper (Jack Palance) in *Man in the Attic* (1953)

Man in the Attic was a straight remake of the 1944 film, utilising Barré Lyndon's original script, but with some timely revisions by Robert Presnell Jr. Perfunctorily directed by Argentinian-born Hugo Fregonese, an action specialist perhaps best known for *Blowing Wild* (shot the year before with Gary Cooper, Barbara Stanwyck and Anthony Quinn) and *Harry Black and the Tiger* (1958; with Stewart Granger), it treads the cobbled ground with indecent second-feature haste. "Mr Slade is the Ripper!" landlady Mrs Harley tells her maid halfway through the proceedings, thus undermining the atmosphere of increasing apprehension on which the story had always depended, not to mention the sense of security felt by Slade and on which his stay at the house is predicated.

The Whitechapel street scenes carry a certain economic conviction, but the mighty Thames is reduced to a stream on the backlot and the Harleys' well-furnished home is a distinctly American one of post-colonial design. The film's uncertain sense of time and place is further hampered by a cast of supporting players who speak in Irish-American accents, with the single exception of Daisy (Tita Phillips), who effects a mock-cockney delivery of such ineptitude that it might have served as the model for Dick Van Dyke in *Mary Poppins*. Composer Hugo Friedhoffer concocted his own 'dainty ditties' for the music-hall scenes, although they are similarly out of sync with the period in mood, melody, and metre, and sound suspiciously like rejects from the same year's *Gentlemen Prefer Blondes* or *How to Marry a Millionaire* (both Fox productions).

Man in the Attic is also afflicted with cinematic conventions which had only recently come into being through the wave of science fiction films emanating from Hollywood. Key sequences are staged, scored and played as though the Harleys' attic is home to an extra-terrestrial alien in human form rather than Jack the Ripper, an impression compounded by the whitewashed sterility of the household as a whole, with its conceptual affinity to the featureless landscapes in the apocalyptic thrillers of director Jack Arnold.

In concert with the sense of dislocation created by the film's mise-en-scène, the usual errors of incidental detail were now beginning to crop up with tiresome regularity: a police inspector tells of a man hanged outside Newgate Prison "six months ago," when Newgate was demolished in 1880 to make way for a new Central Criminal Court building, while Lily dances the Can-can on stage, which was prohibited in England at the time of the Whitechapel Murders. The reliance on fingerprinting to establish the killer's identity is a hangover from the 1944 film, the blame for which must ultimately rest with Marie Belloc Lowndes, however, not Lyndon or Presnell.

Presnell's tinkering with Lyndon's script comes down to removing some of its archaic mannerisms and substituting lines of dialogue thought to be more idiomatic at the time. "He cuts their throats, then uses his knife like a doctor who's gone mad!" Harley says of the

Constance Smith and
Jack Palance in *Man
in the Attic* (1953)

Ripper in the slack syntax of the studio hack. "Jack the Ripper... What a revolting, stupid name!" Slade blurts out, like the high-school weed who has been made a laughing-stock by the classroom bully.

Palance invests the role of Slade with a measure of sympathy and that edge of tension which was soon to become his trademark. Laird Cregar had presented himself as strange and aloof, and fascinating because of it, but Palance is a basket-case of a different and more modern kind: vulnerable and psychotic by turns, though the extent of his psychosis is not revealed until the last reel of the film. The Ripper of this version is a matricide, who has already slain his much-hated mother and is now locked into repeating the deed at regular intervals, for no reason that the script feels obliged to enlarge upon. The only glimmer of insight is an inadvertent one: "Perhaps the police are searching for someone who doesn't exist," Slade suggests at one point, cancelling out over 60 years of diligent investigation at a stroke.

The majority of the last two reels is a shot-for-shot remake of Brahm's film, but his climactic chase backstage in the theatre is side-stepped in favour of a more vigorous outdoor pursuit between two Hansom cabs. At a time when the 'western' was the most popular form of screen entertainment, this was presumably the closest that the makers of *Man in the Attic* could come to a covered wagon outrunning a band of renegade Indians.

Like Connie Smith before him, Rhys Williams, who played Mr Harley in the film, also encountered Jack the Ripper again, although, in his case, it was in a quite different guise.

Hitchcock and Novello had each done their best to reduce the Ripper to the level of a subordinate player in an altogether different drama; in their versions of *The Lodger*, the killer might well have been any old maniac on the loose, so peripheral was he to the narrative perspectives of both films. Laird Cregar had gone some way towards redressing the balance in favour of Marie Lowndes, but subsequent versions from Hammer and Fox had played the theme out to the point of cliché. In the late 1950s, the British horror film underwent a boom which coincidentally was spearheaded by the company responsible for *Room To Let*. Hammer Film Productions did not itself attempt to revive the fortunes of Jack the Ripper – at least, not for over a decade – but the man who was charged with creating its pantheon of monsters did, albeit for another company in the field.

Jack's formative years and sometimes troublesome search for a sense of cinematic identity were almost over; the next time he appeared on the big screen, it was in a starring role and under his own name.

Jack on the Box

"Tonight, I'm going to tell you another strange and unusual story of the unexplainable which lies behind the veil..." So intoned Boris Karloff at the start of each episode of an unsold television series called *The Veil*, which the veteran actor hosted for Hal Roach Studios in 1958.

The Veil was one of a flurry of supernatural anthology series produced for television the same year, including John Newland's *One Step Beyond* and Rod Serling's *The Twilight Zone*. Where *The Twilight Zone* offered up fictional tales of fantasy, *One Step Beyond* and *The Veil* both purported to dramatise real tales of the occult or, in the case of *The Veil*, precognition. Unlike its competitors, however, *The Veil* was cheaply shot and too often populated by casts of unknowns. The exception was an episode entitled 'Jack the Ripper' which, like most of Karloff's introductions for the series, was filmed at Associated British Studios, Elstree. The film featured a more solid roster of British faces, including Niall MacGinnis (who, the previous year, had given the cinema its best-etched portrait of a 'black magician' in Jacques Tourneur's *Night of the Demon*) and Clifford Evans, later to star for Hammer in *The Curse of the Werewolf* and *The Kiss of the Vampire*.

Boris Karloff had encountered the Ripper once before in 1958, when he shot two films back-to-back for Producers Associates and director Robert Day. The first of these was *Grip of the Strangler* and the second was *The Doctor of Seven Dials* (released in 1963 as *Corridors of Blood*, and the better of the two). In *The Veil*, Karloff did little more than provide a running commentary on the proceedings in hand, but in *Grip of the Strangler*, he effectively played the notorious killer himself.

Boris Karloff and Tim Turner in *Grip of the Strangler* (1958)

James Rankin (Karloff) is a novelist and social reformer who sets out to prove that Edward Styles, the 'Haymarket Strangler', was innocent of the murders of five women for which he was hanged in 1860. Twenty years have passed, but in the course of his investigations Rankin unearths the surgeon's knife that Styles allegedly used to stab his victims after strangling them; clutching the knife has the effect of turning him into a mad killer and a new spate of murders ensues. It transpires that Rankin himself was the original Haymarket Strangler, his memory of the crimes erased by guilt – "I, myself, am the man that I've been hunting!" he tells his wife – and he pays for the discovery of his Jekyll-and-Hyde persona with his life.

Execution at Newgate in *Grip of the Strangler* (1958)

Originally shot as *Stranglehold*, *Grip of the Strangler* is closer in mood and feel to the Whitechapel Murders than many later productions whose only connection with the case is the use of the word 'Ripper' in their titles. The film is set in 1880, but the Ripper makes a nominal appearance: when Inspector Burke (Anthony Dawson) trawls the dusty archives of Scotland Yard for the files on the Haymarket Strangler, the camera pans across two boxes labelled 'Constance Kent' and 'Jack the Ripper'. Constance Emilie Kent was jailed for 20 years in 1865 for the razor-murder of her infant stepbrother, Francis, when she was just 16; she would still have been incarcerated at the time. The Ripper murders, on the other hand, did not occur till eight years afterwards. (By a curious coincidence, Kent has been nominated as 'Jill the Ripper' by some sources; the Whitechapel Murders took place three years after she was released.)

No explanation – other than the rejection of his advances – is offered for the type of victims chosen by the Strangler, but they are all showgirls, as per the 1944 *The Lodger* and the later *Man in the Attic*, and originally totalled five in number. But more to the point is the manner of their deaths. In order to avoid comparison with the crimes of Jack the Ripper, the killer in the film is called the Haymarket Strangler; he might just as easily have been called the Haymarket Ripper, because he only partially strangles his victims, before butchering them with a knife. In an overly complex plot – too clever by half for its own dramatic good – the knife is the catalyst to reviving memories of murder in Rankin which have laid dormant for 20 years.

> "Styles – the poor wretch – would have no use for a surgeon's knife. But Tennant would. He was a doctor..."
>
> James Rankin (Boris Karloff) in *Grip of the Strangler* (1958)

Karloff acquits himself better than might be expected of a 70-year-old in the grip of crippling arthritis, though his portrayal of a man in the grip of mania is strictly from the Universal school of horror. (He was to perform a similar feat in *Corridors of Blood*, but under the influence

of anaesthetic on that occasion.) In contrast to the tunes featured in *Man in the Attic*, Jean Kent's 'Cora' delivers an authentic Victorian music-hall ditty as a bonus.

The film's grasp on dates may have been shaky, but a real attempt was made both by *Grip of the Strangler* and its companion-piece to provide an authentic backdrop for the horrid happenings, rare in low-budget shockers of this sort. In *Corridors of Blood*, it was the 'rookeries' of Seven Dials and the depiction of surgical conditions in London's hospitals in an age before the discovery of anaesthesia; in *Grip of the Strangler*, it was the execution of Edward Styles in the pre-credits sequence. Styles is hanged in front of a baying mob, on a scaffold erected outside the gates of Newgate Jail. In 1864 alone, eight felons were executed at Newgate in similar conditions to Styles in the film, watched by crowds of onlookers, sometimes thousands strong, who filled the roads and houses next to the prison and who were catered for by all manner of hawkers and street-traders. After witnessing such a public hanging in 1849 (though not at Newgate), Charles Dickens wrote: "The conduct of the people was so indescribably frightful, that I felt for some time afterwards almost as if I were living in a city of devils."

The part-strangling, part-stabbing murders in *Grip of the Strangler* were an elaborate contrivance designed to facilitate a plot that depended on the original killer hiding a murder weapon which his amnesiac other self could accidentally rediscover, long after the event: "Half-strangled, then slashed to death," cries the ha'penny pamphleteer at the execution of Styles. The film's producers evidently decided that a knife was more photogenic than a ligature, and the script was amended accordingly. But this produced the anomaly that the so-called Haymarket 'Strangler' now required to operate to two different *modi*, simultaneously. The onscreen action skirts around this problem for the most part, but it has since become accepted that Jack the Ripper also strangled his victims before cutting their throats, so *Grip of the Strangler*, in consequence, unwittingly emulated his actual *modus* more accurately than many of the films which purport to portray the real events.

As well as its other similarities to the crimes of Jack the Ripper, *Grip of the Strangler* offered up an unusual take on how such 'mysteries' might remain unresolved: the Haymarket Strangler has supposedly been hanged 20 years before the series of murders around which the film revolves; Karloff is eventually revealed to be both past *and* present murderer but as his character has officially been 'laid to rest' once already, his latest exploits have therefore to remain 'unsolved'...

Grip of the Strangler touched upon the period and the place, if not the person, of the Whitechapel monster, but had it been screened, *The Veil*'s 'Jack the Ripper' would have brought audiences closer to the reality of the Murders than anything that had gone before. "Our story tonight concerns the dark and violent circumstances surrounding one of the most famous criminals in history," Karloff teases, before introducing Niall MacGinnis' character of Walter Durst as 'George' – a continuity slip of the kind that is only possible when the parenthetical musings of a host are filmed in advance of the shows for which they are intended.

In the tale, clairvoyant Walter Durst discovers that he is able to predict events relating to the Ripper murders. He informs the police, who suspect him of the crimes and throw him in jail. Two more murders are committed while Durst is locked up and Inspector McWilliam (Evans) releases him. Durst then leads him to the home of a surgeon in the West End of London. However, the surgeon has died that very day and even now lies in his coffin awaiting burial. But the coffin is shown to be empty. The family doctor reveals that he has faked the death of the surgeon as a cover for having him committed to an insane asylum. The Whitechapel Murders cease, as a result.

Boris Karloff as the Haymarket Strangler in *Grip of the Strangler* (1958)

"He's here; I can feel it. Somewhere quite near. Jack the Ripper. He's here on this bus!"
Walter Durst (Niall MacGinnis) in *The Veil: 'Jack the Ripper'* (1958)

The script for this story has its basis in a fanciful article which appeared in the Chicago *Sunday-Times Herald* in 1895 and which has since become part of apocryphal Ripper lore, up to and including its incorporation – along with much else – in Alan Moore's *From Hell*. 'Walter Durst' was, in fact, a self-proclaimed clairvoyant and leader of a group of Christian Spiritualists named Robert James Lees who, at the time of the murders, lived at Peckham Rye in South London. Lees, it was said, had "seen" the murders and even encountered a man whom he was convinced was Jack the Ripper on a London omnibus at Shepherd's Bush. He offered his help to Scotland Yard but was turned down; eventually, the police relented and he led them to a large house in the West End, in which he maintained they would find their man. There are varying accounts of what then transpired, though none of them can be substantiated. It was subsequently suggested that the house to which Lees had led the police was 74 Brook Street, the home of eminent surgeon Sir William Withey Gull – of whom, more later – and diaries kept by Lees himself confirm his claim to have contacted the police on at least three occasions, only to have his offers of help declined. But there is doubt as to the authenticity of even these diaries.

Niall MacGinnis in
'Jack the Ripper'
(1958)

All the incidents of the Lees story – his snub at the hands of the police; the sighting on the bus; the trail leading to the surgeon's house – are faithfully recreated in 'Jack the Ripper'. Only Lees' incarceration and the outcome at the house were further fictionalised for dramatic effect, though they remained true in spirit to their source. Like so much else to do with the Whitechapel Murders, Robert James Lees was real enough; whether he had any involvement in the case beyond a willingness to offer 'psychic assistance' in solving it, however, is a matter for debate.

"On that night, over 70 years ago, ended a reign of terror unlike any before or since," Karloff summarised. It also ended *The Veil*'s attempt to bring authentic tales of premonition to network television, and although 12 episodes of the series were shot both here and in the States, the show failed to find a sponsor and remained unsold.

"Two women, murdered within an hour. One in a yard at the back of Berner Street; the other in an archway off Mitre Square. Both of them... hacked to pieces... Every man available was on duty in the East End last night. Every suspect we had was under lock and key. Impossible! And yet it happened..."
Inspector McWilliam (Clifford Evans) in *The Veil: 'Jack the Ripper'* (1958)

The *Veil* offered no solution to Inspector McWilliam's dilemma, other than to suggest that the killer originated in the suspicion-free West End of the city, instead of the East. Implicit in the thinking of 'Jack the Ripper' screenwriter Michael Plant, who also penned several first-season episodes for *One Step Beyond*, was that such a person would not have been stopped or questioned with the same degree of alacrity as would less respectable residents of the local area.

There is some substance to this: on the night of the 'double event' – the murders of Stride and Eddowes – the police were under orders to stop any man and woman seen walking together, but not to stop men who were out on their own. There is anecdotal evidence from constables 'on the beat' of their wariness in apprehending anyone whom they perceived to belong to more prosperous sections of society. The ordinary 'copper' considered himself a servant of the State, if not the people, and those who embodied the ideals of the State were treated with due deference. In addition, the police in general were convinced that Jack the Ripper was some form of Whitechapel lowlife, so it was a lowlife for whom they were looking.

Time and again, questions arise as to whether one man, acting alone, could have encompassed all the disparate elements that appear to feature in the so-called 'Ripper' murders. These doubts become particularly acute on the night of the 'double event', when two women – Elizabeth Stride and Catherine Eddowes – were murdered within three quarters of a mile and less than an hour of one another.

Two men were seen with Stride, one of whom acted in such a way as to have afforded cover for the other. A second man then asked after a man and a woman in Mitre Square, minutes before the murder of Eddowes. And at the inquest on Mary Kelly, Sarah Lewis testified that she saw a man standing opposite Miller's Court in Dorset Street, and "looking up the court as if waiting for someone to come out." The same could have been true for Chapman and Nichols, but in each of their cases, no witnesses were present at the time.

Did Jack the Ripper act alone? Or were at least some of the murders an orchestrated plot by more sinister forces? Fenian terrorists were active at this time and had long been engaged in bombing campaigns in the capital. Other radical groups were operating to their own agendas. On the Establishment side of the fence, there were demoralised elements in the 'Secret' or Special Branch of the Home Office Crime Department, who were charged with the defence of the realm. None of this leads into the area so feverishly occupied in later years by such as Stephen Knight, but it is worth noting in passing that the Ripper scare, and the house-to-house searches which were conducted as a result, allowed the police ingress to areas of the East End which hitherto had been denied them. Not only that, but they were welcomed with open arms.

The myth of the phantom killer had grown to such proportions by the time of the 'double event' that few doubted the ability of one man to murder and mutilate two women in a single night, under the noses of hundreds of patrolling policemen from two forces, and somehow manage to escape undetected. By the morning of 30 September 1888, Jack the Ripper was no longer an 'ordinary' murderer – he was an immortal monster, destined to live on in legend even if his human host had, eventually, been placed under arrest.

Detective Constable (later Chief Inspector) Walter Dew, who had found himself attached to Whitechapel's 'H' Division at the time of the murders, told in his 1938 memoir, *I Caught Crippen*, of the bafflement which was to remain with him all his life as to how Jack could have evaded so extensive a cordon of police as was visited upon the area during the Ripper scare: "With all the furore over the murders, with the heightened awareness of all strangers, with the numerous Vigilance Committees roaming the streets, after Nichols' death why were Chapman, Stride, Eddowes and Kelly so easy a target? Was there something about their attacker that put him above suspicion in their minds? Why was he so *invisible*?"

Boris Karloff plays Host to *The Veil* (1958)

The possibility that others might have colluded in the commission of the Whitechapel Murders eluded the new breed of criminologist – amateur sleuths who specialised in writing about true crime, and who had begun to spring up in the wake of the public's interest in detective fiction (just as its interest in ghost stories had produced a rash of 'ghost hunters', or psychic investigators, like Elliott O'Donnell and Harry Price) – but it did not escape the attention of English author Thomas Burke.

Burke had grown up in Poplar, a parish to the east of Whitechapel, and as an orphan had become eternally fascinated by its lowlife ambience and curious mixture of itinerant cultures. He developed a particular affinity with the nearby district of Limehouse, with its indigenous population of Chinese and Oriental immigrants, its tea-shops, drinking parlours, opium dens and easy ways with life, sex and death. *Limehouse Nights*, published in 1916, was the first of a number of collections of his short stories, delineating the strange and often supernormal aspects of this exotic dockside underbelly, and it was followed by *The Pleasantries of Old Quong*, *The Golden Gong* and others of similar ilk. Several of his tales found their way to the screen; his uncompromisingly titled 'The Chink and The Child' (from *Limehouse Nights*) became *Broken Blossoms* for D W Griffith and Lillian Gish in 1919. The same story was remade in Britain in 1936 by John Brahm, later to direct Fox's version of *The Lodger*.

Burke's interest in crime was as no more than a dispassionate observer of that part of the London scene to which he was instinctively drawn, and which for his literary endeavours became a lifelong attachment. But in his 1931 short story, 'The Hands of Mr Ottermole' (part of the collection which formed *The Pleasantries of Old Quong*, or *A Tea Shop in Limehouse* as it was retitled in the US), Burke touched upon the Whitechapel Murders in a way that was guaranteed to stop a reader dead in his tracks, just as surely as if he had been struck from behind by Jack's own knife.

"*Many minds of finer complexion than my own have discoloured themselves in seeking to name the identity of the author of those wholesale murders which took place last year. Who that man or woman really was, I know no more than you do, but I have a theory of the person it could have been; and if you are not pressed for time I will elaborate that theory into a little tale.*"
Thomas Burke, 'The Hands of Mr Ottermole'/The Pleasantries of Old Quong (1931)

The omniscient narrator of 'The Hands of Mr Ottermole' is Old Quong, a ubiquitous Chinese sage in the same mould as Orczy's 'Old Man in the Corner'. Quong's theory relates to the 'invisible' killer who perpetrates the so-called London 'Strangling Horrors' in the fictional district of Mallon End. The tale is one of Burke's less humorous fictions and its real purpose, like Edgar Allan Poe's *The Mystery of Marie Roget*, was to posit a solution to a different set of murders to those with which it notionally deals. As such, it does more than suggest that a killer can 'hide in plain sight'; it comments directly on the events in Whitechapel in 1888.

Unfettered by the constraints of alleged evidence which hampered (and continues to hamper) the investigations of criminologists interested in the case, Burke, as a fiction writer, was free to speculate about what kind of killer might appear silent and unseen in the streets of Whitechapel. His solution was as simple as it was surprising: a policeman. Not a policeman of Burke's day – an amiable 'bobby' on the beat – but the kind of policeman who had fired on unarmed demonstrators in Trafalgar Square in 1887, the year before the murders, in the kind of force that operated along military lines, whose senior officers were all drawn from the ranks of the army and with combat experience in the field; the kind of policeman whose first duty was to Queen and Country, rather than to the upholding of law and order, and whose second was to quell dissent. In Burke's brilliant fiction, it was Police Sergeant Ottermole, to be precise.

The left-wing *Daily News* of October 1888 had previously advanced the notion that the Ripper was a policeman: "Two theories are suggested to us, that he may wear woman's clothes, or he may be a policeman..." Only three years before, campaigning journalist W T Stead, in the third of his 'The Maiden Tribute of Modern Babylon' articles for the *Pall Mall Gazette*, had accused the Metropolitan force of complicity in the white slave trade. (Stead served three months in prison over these articles, though not as a consequence of that particular accusation.) Thomas Burke changed the names, the place, and even the modus of his murderer, but at the heart of his story was a potential solution to the mystery of the Whitechapel Murders along these same lines.

Burke's prose is spare but lyrical, his wit barbed, and his approach to his material oblique but matter-of-fact. His facility for atmosphere and ability to evoke mood is reminiscent of Poe, to whom many contemporary critics compared him: 'The Yellow Imps', in *The Pleasantries of Old Quong*, is an alternative reading of Poe's 'The Tell-Tale Heart'. His sardonic asides and world-weariness make him more like Poe crossed with Dickens, but he is funnier than Poe; more terrifying than Dickens. His stories often border on the surreal and can seem to meander down disassociated byways, the like of which Burke himself was wont to travel for real. But there is real precision in the crafting, the more so for its being disguised, and nowhere in his many books is intrigue spun so well as in 'The Hands of Mr Ottermole'.

Five murders, or rather sets of murders, take place within the space of a few weeks in Mallon End (the body-count is actually eight). The killer is never seen, yet the murders are committed in conditions which make such a circumstance well-nigh impossible. All are victims of strangulation, and one is even a constable on his beat. The final victim is the reporter covering the case. In typical style, Burke produces his solution out of the blue and through a metaphysical muse about a ham sandwich. The one person who could move 'unseen' through the populace to murder an unsuspecting policeman is *another* policeman. Heedless of the danger, the reporter alerts the sergeant to his suspicions. Ottermole obliges him with an admission of guilt, then strangles him.

So effective is this yarn that it has more than once been incorporated by anthologists into various lists of the best mystery stories of all time, and it was duly picked up for adaptation, first for radio in a *Suspense Theatre* broadcast of 2 December 1948, starring Claude Rains and Vincent Price, and then as an episode of the long-running MCA television series, *Alfred Hitchcock Presents*.

The curious thing about *Alfred Hitchcock Presents* is that it was not at all representative of the Hitchcock that filmgoers of the time thought they knew and loved: the mischievous maker of *To Catch a Thief* (1955), *The Man Who Knew Too Much* (1956) and the upcoming *North by Northwest*. It was more illustrative of the Hitchcock of *The Trouble with Harry* (1954) or some of his darker outings in the forties, such as *Strangers on a Train* (1951) or *Shadow of a Doubt*, and it was certainly the Hitchcock who was to shock audiences with *Vertigo* (1958) and, more traumatically, *Psycho* (1960), for which the crew of the television series was used. Part of the reason was that 'Hitch' himself had little to do with the series which bore his name, and less to do with the choice of stories that occupied its 26-minute slots.

The concept of the show had come from Lew Wassermann, then head of MCA, and production was put into the hands of long-time Hitchcock collaborators, Joan Harrison and Norman Lloyd. 'Hitch' was handed around 100 scripts a season, out of which he picked the 40 or so to be shot. Beyond delivering his trademark monologues, Hitchcock's interest in the series can be gauged by the fact that he directed a mere 18 of the 268 episodes which spanned seven years of prime-time television (ten years, if you append another 93 episodes of the *Alfred Hitchcock Hour*). The show may not have meant that much to Hitch, but Hitch meant everything to the show: It turned him into a star in his own right and forever associated him in the public eye with a Micawber-like profile (culled from a self-portrait), a lugubrious demeanour, a taste for sardonic witticisms, and 'The Funeral March of the Marionettes' one of the most famous themes in the history of television, which was composed in Hitchcock's home city of London in 1873 by Paris-born Charles Gounod.

From October 1955 to June 1962, *Alfred Hitchcock Presents* offered a high-profile showcase for the adaptation of a great many macabre short stories which otherwise might have been lost to history with the passing of the Golden Age of Radio. Among them were Stanley Ellin's 'The Speciality of the House', Ambrose Bierce's 'An Occurrence at Owl Creek Bridge' and Michael Arlen's 'The Gentleman from America'. Pulp magazines were the first and most obvious source of stories for the series, and 'The Hands of Mr Ottermole' had been published in *Ellery Queen's Mystery Magazine* in January 1950.

Screenwriter Francis Cockrell set the tale in 1919 (whereas Burke had penned it during the First World War), and he invests Burke's anonymous reporter with a name: Summers. In other respects, the teleplay strays little from Burke's narrative. There is a minimum of dialogue in the short story, so that in the film had therefore to be fabricated; to Cockrell's credit, most of it is drawn from Burke's prose and keeps faith with his thesis. When a nephew of the killer's initial victims remarks that there can be no reason for the apparently motiveless murder, the so-far-unnamed police sergeant reprimands him in true Burkian manner: "Oh, there's a reason all right. Must be. They're dead, aren't they?" Only at the climax – a 'happy ending' which sees the reporter rescued from the sergeant's vicelike grip at the critical moment – does the dialogue collapse into banal summary.

Theodore Bikel in 'The Hands of Mr Ottermole' (1957)

This climax is taken almost word-for-word from the original: "As man to man, tell me, Sergeant *Ottermole*, just why did you kill those inoffensive people?" Summers asks, revealing the policeman's name and the hitherto concealed connection with the story's title for the first time. "Couldn't it be that parts of our bodies aren't really us?" the sergeant considers, moving into a realm of metaphysics previously explored by Maurice Renard's *The Hands of Orlac*, as well as in for the kill. "And ideas could come into these parts all of a sudden. Like ideas come into... *my hands!*" Burke's story, and the life of his reporter, end at this point. The teleplay moderated this grim resolution, and the fate of the foolhardy Summers is gainsaid at the eleventh hour by a douty constable who has been taken into the reporter's confidence prior to the confrontation. Ottermole's ravings are speculated upon in resumé, but Summers ultimately settles on insanity as the likeliest explanation of events.

In his adaptation of one of the very best of the sadly neglected works of writer Thomas Burke, Cockrell had missed the sentence which would have furnished Summers with the most apposite exit-line: "Satan may enter into man by many doors, but in the hands alone can he find the servants of his will." A year later, Cockrell supplied a story called 'The Dark Room' to the first season of the supernatural series *One Step Beyond*, in which actress Cloris Leachman also found herself up against a mysterious strangler, but within the confines of a French hotel.

> "This is a singular man, a man who comes along once in a lifetime, probably. This one man,
> with one pair of hands, has held the entire police force – and Scotland Yard – helpless, with nowhere
> to turn."
> Mr Summers (Rhys Williams) in *Alfred Hitchcock Presents: 'The Hands of Mr Ottermole'* (1957)

The film was directed by journeyman Robert Stevens and graced with a clutch of seasoned professionals: Rhys Williams played the journalist and Theodore Bikel gave his sergeant a Hebridean accent as polished as the French one that he was to effect for Stanley Kramer in *The Pride and the Passion* the following year, if less explicable. Network sensibilities saw to it that Ottermole's murder of a child was changed to that of a flower-seller, and reference to the Whitechapel Murders comes only in an anachronistic surmise from Torin Thatcher, as his police constable speculates upon who might be responsible for the mysterious series of slayings: "One of those foreign johnnies," he offers, contemptuously.

A muse in Burke's narrative mentions several historical counterparts to Ottermole, such as William Palmer (a poisoner hanged in 1856), Hawley Harvey Crippen (hanged in 1910 for the murder of his wife, Belle Elmore) and George Joseph Smith (the 'Brides in the Bath' murderer, who claimed at least seven victims before going to the gallows in 1915), and Cockrell's inclusion of these in a discussion between the protagonists added Thomas Neill Cream, another poisoner and sometime suspect for the Whitechapel Murders. Jack the Ripper himself is noticeable by his absence from both, but his silent footsteps are as omnipresent in Thomas Burke's 'The Hands of Mr Ottermole' as they were in Marie Belloc Lowndes' *The Lodger*.

A period comedy-thriller called *The Hour of 13* (1952, based on a novel by Philip MacDonald) had been posited on the opposite premise to that in Burke's story: a mysterious killer known as 'The Terror' is murdering *only* policemen, by means of a sword-stick and after issuing warning notes. His motive is revealed to be revenge on the police for a long sentence handed down for a previous crime, although the Terror's fog-bound activities were very much subordinated to the adventures of a trio of jewel thieves led by Peter Lawford. *The Hour of 13* was nevertheless a lively and entertaining tale, interesting on two counts: the Terror himself was played by Richard Shaw, the original 'Sladden' in BBC television's memorable adaptation of Nigel Kneale's *Quatermass and the Pit*, and the film – though British-made through MGM – represented the last gasp of the Hollywood Gothic noir which had begun over a decade earlier with Victor Fleming's *Dr Jekyll and Mr Hyde* (1941).

Rhys Williams' near-fatal encounter with the hands of Theodor Bikel's Sergeant Ottermole may have been thought-provoking, but it was no more than a fascinating byway in the event. Unlike the various versions of *The Lodger*, up to and including *Man in the Attic*, the 'Jack the Ripper' episode of *The Veil* had drawn on a supposed real-life incident from police files on the Whitechapel Murders to provide itself with a basis for drama. By 1959, with censorship restrictions being eroded weekly in what *ABC Film Review* christened "the year of the horror film," filmmakers found themselves freer than they had ever been before to deal with the Ripper's crimes at source, and without having to resort to the euphemisms of fiction.

The result, not surprisingly, was a film called... *Jack the Ripper*.

Chapter Three
The Red-handed League

I have fully appreciated the distinction between fact and theory, and for this reason I present in the first part everything that is material to the story of the crimes, and reserve to the second part all that is a matter of opinion.

Leonard Matters, *The Mystery of Jack the Ripper* (Hutchinson; 1929)

In 1928, Australian journalist Leonard Warburton Matters wrote *The Mystery of Jack the Ripper*, the first serious case-study of the crimes in English. The book enlarged on a newspaper article which Matters had published beforehand, purporting to identify the Ripper as a society doctor who had once lived in Buenos Aires, Argentina.

Matters was no mere opportunist, looking to make a commercial killing. Born in Adelaide in 1881, he had fought in the Boer War and travelled the world widely as a journalist, spending several years as managing editor of the *Buenos Aires Herald*. When he eventually settled in England, he wrote *The Mystery of Jack the Ripper* before standing for Parliament as Member for the Kennington ward of the London Borough of Lambeth, which he won for Labour and held until 1931. Twice married, he also wrote short stories and translated Argentine texts, as well as chairing a number of newspaper societies. He died aged 70 in 1951, the same year as Ivor Novello.

Matters' book, in its numerous printings through a variety of different publishers, remained the only comprehensive overview of the Whitechapel Murders for nearly two decades before being comprehensively trashed by succeeding contemporary experts. Its closing arguments, however, are no more or less far-fetched than those of the authors who decry it. His prose is often archaic, his psychological assertions debatable and his solution

Screenwriter Jimmy Sangster

unsupported, but a man so prominent in public life had no need to sully his hard-won reputation on a piece of hackwork, and there is certainly nothing in *The Mystery of Jack the Ripper* to indicate that it was undertaken in a rush of commercial blood. On the contrary, his evident fascination with the case appears genuinely to have come about from something he may have learned by chance. Be that as it may, no writer since has been able to convey the sense of locale so well; at the time Matters wrote his book, all the murder sites were still as they had been in 1888.

According to Matters, Jack the Ripper was a surgeon who went in murderous pursuit of 'Marie' Kelly after she had caused the death of his son through the transmission of an unspecified disease, implicitly syphilis. This is possible but unlikely, given the time-scale involved: Kelly was 26 when she met her death and for Matters' theory to hold water, any such disease would have had to be highly contagious and fast-acting. 'French pox', as it was known (somewhat ironically, in light of a trip Kelly reportedly made to France), is certainly the former but not normally the latter. The autopsy on Kelly found no evidence of disease, which is but one example of the potential flaws in the Matters version of events.

Where *The Mystery of Jack the Ripper* falls down is in its eschewing of any corroborative material which might lend support to its contentions, in which regard, it should be read as a product of its time. Current fashion in books of this sort is to leave no detail excluded, however insignificant, and extensively to footnote every scrap of information utilised in the texts; a sound enough principle, but one which has tended to obscure, rather than clarify, the *relevant* facts. Matters, for his part, presents a clear and concise picture of the events as they were perceived at the time and only deviates from good journalistic practice when he finally postulates his suspect in the book's closing chapters. Not only – by his own admission – does he present no evidence to back up his claim, but he inexplicably seeks to preserve Jack's identity further by employing a *second* pseudonym: 'Dr Stanley'. It seems not to have occurred to Matters that other writers could do likewise and create an equally valid, if no less elusive, solution to "the mystery."

"Damn you, and all your kind! I want Marie Kelly!" exclaims the fictitious Dr Stanley at a critical juncture in the Matters narrative. It was a battle-cry which was picked up with gusto by Hammer's Jimmy Sangster when he was hired by Tempean Films to turn the story idea of actor-turned-director Peter Hammond into a screenplay called *Jack the Ripper*.

Arrow edition of *The Mystery of Jack the Ripper* (1964)

The movie was produced through Mid-Century Films, a subsidiary of the Tempean parent of Robert Baker and Monty Berman, and shot on standing sets at Shepperton Studios. Baker and Berman shared directing duties, with Berman acting as cinematographer besides. The connection with Hammer extended to the casting as well: actors Ewen Solon and John Le Mesurier had hotfooted it here from *The Hound of the Baskervilles* (Eddie Byrne and Dennis Shaw would do the reverse, moving on to play in *The Mummy* at Bray), while Sangster's next writing assignment for the old firm – a remake of the Barré Lyndon play, *The Man in Half Moon Street* – would echo his association with the Ripper through the inclusion of a killer who first slaughters prostitutes, then removes their pituitary glands. (To avoid unflattering comparisons with *Jack the Ripper*, the location for Hammer's Paramount-backed *The Man Who Could Cheat Death*, as it came to be called, was switched to Paris, an edict that Sangster chose to reflect in his original title for the film: *The Man in Rue Noire*.)

"You drove my boy to suicide... Like some foul malignant virus, you and your kind contaminate the gutters you inhabit, the very air you breathe! Nobody's safe... I've been sweeping the streets, looking for you, Mary Clarke..."

Sir David Rogers/Jack the Ripper (Ewen Solon) in *Jack the Ripper* (1959)

By this time, Jimmy 'Frankenstein' Sangster was a horror icon in his own right. He had been in the film business since 1946, working his way up through the ranks of low-budget exploitation specialist Exclusive – later Hammer – Films. He was variously production manager and assistant director for Hammer when he decided to try his hand at screenwriting, and he wrote several scripts for the company before the success of Hammer's *The Curse of Frankenstein* in 1957 turned everyone who was involved with the film into a hot property almost overnight. Sangster remained with Hammer until 1961 and was instrumental in consolidating its new-found reputation as the leading purveyor of Technicolor horror films, but *The Curse of Frankenstein* had enabled him to branch out, as well.

Between 1958 and 1960, Sangster wrote almost as many scripts for the producer-director team of Robert S Baker and Monty Berman as he did for Hammer (*Dracula, The Revenge of Frankenstein* – both 1958; *The Man Who Could Cheat Death, The Mummy* – both 1959), under the banners of Tempean, Mid-Century or Regal Films. Before *Jack the Ripper*, Sangster was responsible for *The Trollenberg Terror* and *Blood of the Vampire*, and after it, he wrote *The Siege of Sidney Street* and *The Hellfire Club*.

His long years of experience in B-feature production for Hammer meant that Sangster wrote to a strict formula. This is not to disparage his abilities with narrative or to underplay the many original concepts that he brought to the films in his charge, but whether he was dealing with Count Dracula, the Mummy, Callistratus or Jack the Ripper, Sangster's approach to the narrative dynamic of such material was much the same on each and every occasion.

In essence, Sangster operated to the three-act edict that had long been the established practice of his mentor, Hammer producer Anthony Hinds. The first act set the scene and established the protagonist (ie, monster); it also introduced the various antagonists – the 'heroes' who provide the oppositional force of good – as well as the main suspects in the drama. The second act was dedicated to elaborating on the monster's devilish work, disposing of a number of sundry players in the process and expanding on the culpability or otherwise of those who remained. This led towards a third and last act, wherein the villain of the piece was finally revealed or tracked to his lair, and events were brought to a suitably dramatic conclusion.

The construct served Sangster well with Hammer, and it does so here. But its very nature required that almost the entire plot of *Jack the Ripper* had therefore to be fabricated, since real events tend not to unfold with such neat narrative conformity. As a result, the film is a fictionalised and iconic rendition of the case which reinforces existing preconceptions, and where no facts are allowed to intrude which could undermine the suspense element of the tale. "I was always frightened that the facts would get in the way of the story," said Sangster. Previous films about the Whitechapel Murders, most of them originating with *The Lodger*, had revealed the killer in a preamble. *Jack the Ripper*, while deferring to the 'Dr Stanley' theory of Leonard Matters, nevertheless opted to unfold as a 'whodunit', or more precisely, a 'which doctor did it'.

The plot of the film is simple enough: London is being terrorised by Jack the Ripper. Sam Lowry (Lee Patterson), on leave from the New York Police Department, joins Inspector O'Neill (Byrne) in the hunt for the killer. A number of red herrings surface during the course of their inquiry, but they eventually discover that the Ripper is searching for a woman named Mary Clarke and determine to find her. 'Jack' finds her first, but in the ensuing melée, he leaves his bag behind. Lowry recognises the bag and confronts its eminent owner. In panic,

Endre Muller in *Jack the Ripper* (1959)

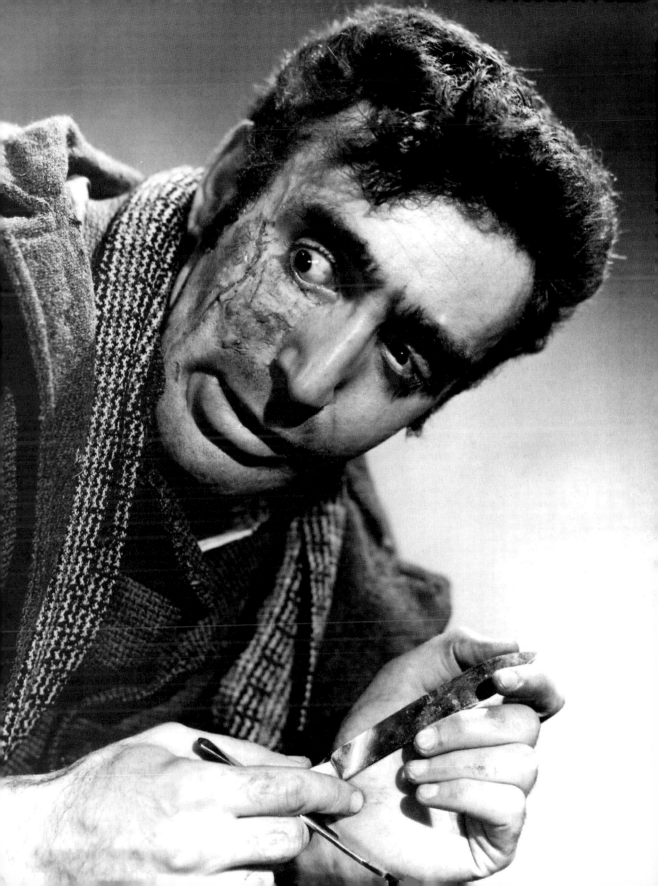

the demented surgeon takes refuge in a lift-shaft, only to be crushed to death by the descending elevator.

The film is much in the manner of the Matters book: an acceptable primer on the basics of the Whitechapel Murders, with a preposterous explanation for the killings which appears to hold considerable attractions if taken at face value. *Jack the Ripper* holds to Matters' thesis in general terms, but cleans it up in accordance with prevailing sensibilities: in the book, Dr Stanley's son Herbert has died as a result of having contracted syphilis; in the film, Sir David's son has killed *himself* after finding out that his lover, Mary Clarke, is a prostitute.

Having established at the outset that the Ripper is to be a doctor, the screenplay naturally directs suspicion onto the staff of the Mercy Hospital for Women, but it loses no opportunity along the way to consider any man who carries a bag, makes an ambiguous statement or casts a sideways glance. Three suspects are eventually proposed, as well as a scar-faced, hunchbacked orderly, who is pitched into the mix to provide the requisite fifties' chamber-of-horrors thrills, in the style of Tempean and Sangster's own *Blood of the Vampire*. 'Louis Benz' is a red herring in this instance, however, and the film, if not the redoubtable American detective, narrows the viewer's focus onto Dr Urquhart (Garard Green) who looks suspicious, Dr Tranter (Le Mesurier) who behaves suspiciously, and the governor of the hospital, Dr Rogers (Solon), who appears to be above suspicion. In the way of these things, the least likely contender turns out to be the culprit. (To mask the identity of Jack the Ripper for as long as practicable, a stand-in was deployed in the street attacks.)

The film fulfils its undemanding brief: it is suspenseful, often eerie, and it keeps the viewer guessing. It also offers a respectably plausible solution to the crimes for a popular audience. Production design is excellent at times, even though the fog machine works overtime, and one of the key sets recalls Gustave Doré's famous engraving of Devil's Acre, Westminster. Perhaps the most curious feature of *Jack the Ripper* is in its casting of Barbara Burke as the pseudonymous Mary Clarke; Burke looks strangely like an old photograph from the 1880s come alive.

The Ripper's appearances are expertly choreographed. His victims find themselves alone on fog-shrouded streets; as if by magic, Jack appears behind, in front, or by the side of them; he whispers an admonition – "Are you Mary Clarke? Where can I find Mary Clarke?" – the litany of a driven obsessive; instinctively, they sense themselves to be in mortal danger; an attempt at escape follows, but they are overcome by supernormal cunning and superior strength. In all of this, the script is aided by Stanley Black's eerie score and Baker and Berman's simple but effective trick of tilting the camera by an angle of 30° to herald the onset of each assault.

These encounters are crafted to make the most of the opportunities for shuddersome effect. Ann Tranter (Betty McDowall) enters a lodging-house in search of an absent Mary Clarke; as she does so, the camera pans to the Ripper's hat and bag resting on a nearby table. An old man walks past a couple who are standing in a doorway; when he subsequently retraces his steps, the man has disappeared and only the corpse of the woman remains to his gaze.

"I didn't see 'im properly 'cause it was dark... But 'e was a posh fella. 'Ere... he was carrying a little black bag!" exclaims the father of Mary Clarke, when quizzed by Inspector O'Neill. Dozens of individuals typifying that description – whether by accident or design (to 'tease' the girls) – were questioned by the police following the rumour that spread throughout the district after the Chapman inquest that the Ripper might be a doctor. According to the East

Off-set shot from
Jack the Ripper (1959)

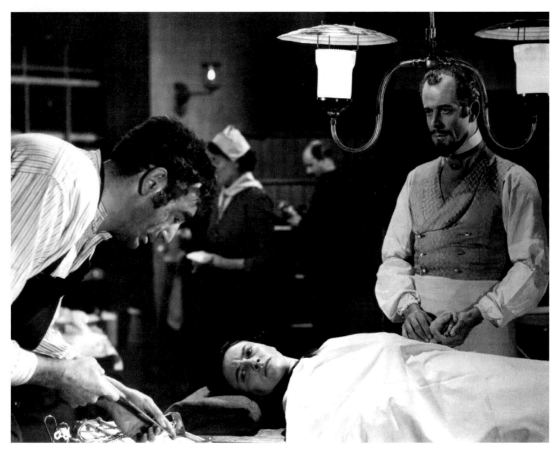

Endre Muller and
Garard Green in *Jack
the Ripper* (1959)

London Advertiser for 13 October 1888, an Albert Bachert had drunk with a man in the Three
Nuns Hotel in Aldgate, whom he described as wearing "a black felt hat, dark clothes,
morning coat, black tie," but who had been paid special attention because he "carried a black
shiny bag". By "doctor," George Bagster Philips had meant *surgeon*, as the killer had seemed to
him to exhibit some "basic surgical skill" in terms of aptitude, as opposed to acumen. But this
proved of no consequence to Leonard Matters, let alone Jimmy Sangster.

Before it was widely accepted that the Ripper strangled his victims prior to using his knife,
Jack the Ripper had to deal with the problem of the Gladstone bag. The film does this by
inserting a cutaway of Jack dropping the bag to the ground, having first pinned his quarry to a
wall with his free hand, then fumbling inside it for the appropriate weapon. The notion works
acceptably enough on screen, with a suitably compliant victim; it is unlikely to have worked so
well in reality, if at all.

Elaborating on his self-created image of the Ripper as a silent, stealthy killing-machine
in top hat and opera cape, Matters had quoted a passage from an unspecified journal
for 3 October: "The awe-stricken dread of this mysterious being who strikes and vanishes is
deepening." The producers of *Jack the Ripper* might have taken this as a design brief. Their
Ripper is the epitome of the professional Victorian gentleman, out for a night on the wrong
side of the tracks. But in crafting the film as a mystery, he is seen only obliquely or half in
shadow, his voice no more than a whisper, his movements swift, silent and deadly. The

combination of the two created a killer in elegant attire who was tantamount to a phantom.

From this film on, Jack the Ripper would be a monster in the classic mould, sporting a high top hat and opera cloak, clutching a black bag full of sharp instruments and looming out of the London fog like the Flying Dutchman of legend; at one, in effect, with the previously established screen image of Dr Jekyll's alter ego, Mister Hyde.

Historical veracity (and the fact that its killer is ultimately unmasked and apprehended) aside, *Jack the Ripper* did more to entrench the myth in the popular mind than anything before or since.

> *"Ladies and Gentlemen… You are about to see a masterpiece of mystery that has baffled even the experts. Try and match your wits against theirs. Watch every move… Listen to every word… Can you guess the identity of… Jack the Ripper?"*
>
> Opening narration (Paul Frees) from *Jack the Ripper* (1959)

American showman Joseph E Levine picked up the film for distribution in the US and provided it with saturation advertising, a teaser prologue, more contemporary title-cards and a new and equally effective (if faintly asynchronous) jazz score by Jimmy McHugh and Pete Rugolo. American audiences were also treated to a brief shot which had been excised from the

Jack the Ripper (1959)

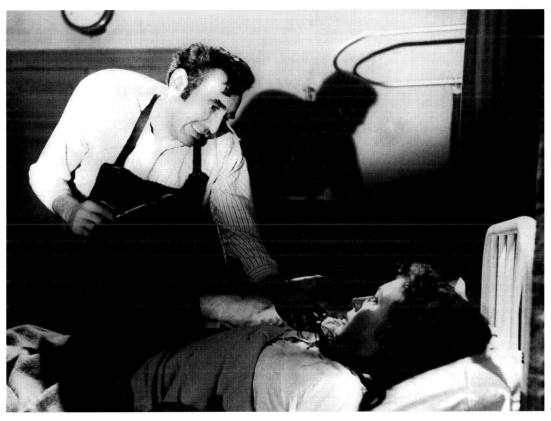

British release print, in which two gobbets of blood are seen to ooze up through the floorboards of the lift at the climax.

In this, Baker and Berman had adopted the short-lived fad of inserting a colour sequence into a monochrome film, as had American International at the end of *I Was a Teenage Frankenstein* (1958) and William Castle at the halfway mark of *The Tingler* (1959). Leftover ends of Eastmancolor stock from *Hello London!* (1958), the Regal-produced last screen appearance of ice-skating diva Sonja Henie, had provided the impetus, but it was ruled out of order by the BBFC, as was a close-up in the film's pre-credits sequence of Jack's blade slowly being withdrawn from the abdomen of his victim before being thrust home a second time; the sexual overtones proved too much for the British censor.

Notwithstanding these embellishments, promotional expenditure in the US failed to produce the level of return to which Levine had become accustomed after the successes of his Italian imports *Hercules* (1959) and *Hercules Unchained* (1960), where he had employed similar tactics.

All the gimmicks that Levine employed to sell *Jack the Ripper* were undone by the more inspired campaign with which the most famous film director in the world, Alfred Hitchcock, chose to accompany a production of his own about the machinations of a knife-wielding maniac in 1960: only one scene from the film was featured in the trailer, and no one was allowed into the theatre once a screening was underway. To add insult to injury, the murderer in the story had been created by a writer with a perennial fascination for Jack the Ripper. The character in question was called Norman Bates (played by Anthony Perkins), the film was *Psycho*, and the author of the original novel on which it was based was Robert Bloch.

> *"We'll never be able to prove it... The most infamous murderer since Bluebeard, and the files will always be marked 'unsolved'."*
>
> Inspector O'Neill (Eddie Byrne) in *Jack the Ripper* (1959)

"...The Ripper, Harry? – You saw the Ripper?" inquires the police inspector at one point in *Jack the Ripper*. In fact, the Ripper was seen for certain twice, possibly three times. Both Annie Chapman and Catherine Eddowes were observed talking with men immediately prior to their being murdered and on a timeline which virtually precluded their killer from having been anyone else. The third, less categorical sighting was that of a man spotted assaulting a woman in Berner Street, approximately 15 minutes before the body of Elizabeth Stride was found in Dutfield's Yard.

In Chapman's case, a neighbour saw her talking with a man only minutes before her death and described him thus: "He was... dark complexioned, and was wearing a brown deerstalker hat. I think he was wearing a dark coat... He was a man over 40... a little taller than the deceased. He looked to me like a foreigner... He looked what I should call shabby genteel."

From a description given in the *Police Gazette*, here is the man who, in all probability, murdered Catherine Eddowes: "a man aged 30... moustache fair, pepper-and-salt colour loose jacket, grey cloth cap with peak... appearance of a sailor." The witness himself said at the inquest, "He had a cloth cap on, with a peak..."

Here, also, is the man who was seen with Elizabeth Stride shortly before her murder, as reported in the *Star*: "...about 30 years of age... and wearing a brown moustache. He was dressed respectable in dark clothes and felt hat." According to the Home Office files on the

Anthony Sagar in
Jack the Ripper (1959)

case, the witness described him as wearing "dark jacket and trousers, and a black cap with a peak."

The witnesses who provided these accounts – Mrs Elizabeth Long, Joseph Lawende, a cigarette salesman, and Israel Schwartz, a Hungarian immigrant – were all thought to be unimpeachable sources by the investigating police. Of the three, the descriptions provided by Mrs Long and Joseph Lawende are almost certainly those of the murderers of Chapman and Eddowes.

Then there is this: an hour after the death of Chapman, a man entered the Prince Albert public house only a few hundred yards from the scene of the crime and ordered a half-pint of ale. The landlady, Mrs Fiddymont, eyed him with a suspicion that bordered on outright terror. His shirt was torn and there were streaks of blood on his neck and between his fingers. He wore a brown hat, pepper-and-salt trousers and a dark coat. He was middle-aged, with a ginger moustache, and his appearance was 'shabby genteel'. When he was subsequently followed from the pub, he seemed nervous and disorientated. Joseph Taylor, the builder who followed him, described him as "Wild-looking and staring... everything about his appearance was exceedingly strange."

Ewen Solon in *Jack the Ripper* (1959)

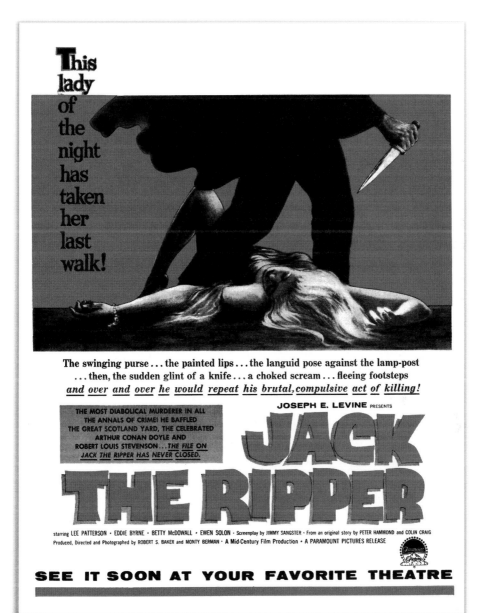

There are clear similarities between these descriptions; in particular, those of the men who were seen with Chapman, Eddowes and Stride (though they would not match those of men who were later seen with Mary Kelly). Two or more of these sightings may well have been of the same man. But one – *any* one – of these men was undoubtedly Jack the Ripper.

Despite the smoke screens which have been raised by conspiracy theorists in the intervening years, this simple fact disposes of 'Jill' the Ripper, Prince Eddy, Sir William Gull, Francis Tumblety, and a dozen others, at one fell swoop. It also disposes of the popular view that the Ripper was a tall man in a top hat and cloak, carrying a black bag, and elegantly

Anthony Perkins in
Psycho (1960)

cruising the streets of Whitechapel in search of his next victim.

Cops and Rippers

Psycho may have mitigated the impact of his first starring role, but it gave the image of Jack of the Ripper a whole new lease of life. The notion of a knife-wielding assailant began to be viewed as a viable means through which to enliven the lower echelons of that old staple of the crime genre: the police thriller. It, too, had almost had its day – despite several excellent late examples (Sapphire; 1959, Jigsaw; 1962, The Informers; 1963) – and was rapidly being overtaken by slick 'private eye' movies, where hip sub-Bond beach cops like Tony Rome (1967) solved all manner of murder mysteries off their own bat, with no need of help from any quarter as lowly as the local police force.

There were two advantages to this: any new series of murders would resonate with the same pre-sold horror as the 1888 prototype, and the scene of the crime could be moved into the present day. For novelists, this circumvented time-consuming research and enabled 'their' Ripper to be sited closer to home; for filmmakers, it meant a considerable saving on cost. The trend can be seen germinating in Fredric Brown's The Screaming Mimi (filmed as Screaming Mimi by Gerd Oswald in 1959), but the first film to overtly reference Jack the Ripper in the setting of a contemporary police thriller was a West German krimi called The Monster of London City in 1964 (released in Britain and the US in 1967). A more appropriate title might have been drawn from the way in which the killer is referred to in its closing moments: "Jack the Ripper number 2".

> "Another girl of the streets murdered – same as on the stage of the Metropole Theatre – a new Jack the Ripper..."
>
> Newsvendor in The Monster of London City (1964)

The Monster of London City (Das Ungeheuer von London City) was the kind of cheap continental import which cropped up with depressing regularity in 'flea-pits' across Britain throughout the 1960s in their attempts to stave off the inexorable decline in attendance figures brought about by television.

The film's origins lay in a novel by Bryan Edgar Wallace, son of Edgar Wallace, creator of King Kong and Sanders of the River, and a phenomenally popular – as well as prodigiously prolific – dime novelist, whose more than 180 novels (with their 150 film adaptations) and innumerable short stories secured him a loyal following from the early 1900s right up to the late 1960s. Wallace senior was particularly esteemed in Germany, where his tales of villainous masterminds, mysterious killers and double-dealing – often employing the whole panoply of Gothic horror effects, but in a contemporary setting – were viewed as thematically wed to the criminal conspiracies of Fritz Lang's Dr Mabuse.

Rialto Film had specialised in adapting Wallace's work for the screen throughout the twenties and thirties, until it was proscribed by the Nazis, but a revival of interest on both sides of the channel after the war saw others enter the field. *The Four Just Men* had played for 39 episodes on British television in 1959, and Merton Park Studios produced a series of second-feature Wallace mysteries from 1960 on (with titles such as *The Clue of the New Pin* and *The Malpas Mystery*), while in Germany, Rialto was joined by CCC Filmkunst in producing new versions of old Wallace war-horses.

Even the work of an author as voluminous as Wallace was not infinite (he died in 1932), and producers were eventually forced to turn to the less fertile output of his son for alternative material. *The Monster of London City* and its companion-piece on release, *The Phantom of Soho*, both came from the pen of the lesser Wallace, whose stories were similar in style to those of his more industrious father, but less original and intricately woven.

> "*In the early hours of last Monday morning, the horribly maimed body of a young woman was discovered in a park near Osbourne Street. The victim had been stabbed and then mutilated in a truly horrifying manner. The methods used by the killer are almost identical with Jack the Ripper's, as presented every evening in London's most talked about play...*"
>
> News broadcast in *The Monster of London City* (1964)

When a killer with the same MO as Jack the Ripper stalks modern London, suspicion falls on Richard Sand (Hansjörg Felmy), the lead actor in a play about the Whitechapel Murders at the Edgar Allan Poe Theatre. Sand, a former drug-addict, comes to doubt his own sanity as evidence mounts to implicate him, until the real murderer is revealed to be Dr Michael Greeley (Dietmar Schoenherr), a police surgeon and Sand's rival for the hand of Ann Morley (Marianne Koch). Greeley's father had caught syphilis from a prostitute and, having inherited his madness, the son set out to conduct a proxy (or poxy) revenge.

The Ripper themes are already too familiar to warrant repetition, save to say that the murderer's given motive has now moved one generation down the line (a notion which resurfaced in *Hands of the Ripper*). More inventive is the stratagem of contrasting a supposed real event with its dramatic counterpart, as represented by the staging of a play about Jack the Ripper in which Sand stars as a fang-toothed killer. Blurring the distinction between fact and fiction by means of a play within a film harks back to Marcel Carné's *Les Enfants du paradis* (1945), and was later employed in *Theatre of Death* (1966) and *The Murders in the Rue Morgue* (1971). Here, its purpose is to cast suspicion on the psychologically disturbed Sand, who is actually the victim of an elaborate plot, but its worth in context is in pointing up a parallel with the charge that was levelled against actor Richard Mansfield in 1888, for daring to play the role of a monster on stage while a real one stalked the Whitechapel streets. "Murder in the theatre, murder in the streets," Sand muses at one point. On 2 October 1888, Mansfield dropped *Dr Jekyll and Mr Hyde* from the season of plays which he had been engaged to perform at the Lyceum and replaced it with *A Parisian Romance*; after that, he was no longer considered a suspect.

The Monster of London City boasts of the accuracy of its fictional play, from which the extract featured in the film depicts the "faithfully reconstructed" murder of Mary Kelly, after a row with her pimp. It proves to be an idle boast. "Left-handed? Like the original Jack the Ripper," the thespian police inspector remarks, based on the fact that several of Jack's victims had their throats cut from left to right. This myth has persisted for decades, and it arose out of the unfeasible premise that the killer stood in front of his victims when attacking them (an idiosyncrasy which looks better in films, and is perpetuated in From Hell). Place him behind them to inflict the fatal blow, where he is less likely to become saturated with blood as a result, and the left-handed killer immediately becomes right-handed, re-engaging with the majority of the population in the process. More sanguine in this respect is the film's deference to a killer who skulks about in galoshes, a salient factor that the police in 1888 advised the attaching of rubber soles to hobnailed boots to combat.

In exploring the misconceptions which might result from drawing a parallel between a real event and its representation in fiction, The Monster of London City connected with a contemporary debate about stage and screen censorship in general. The film's other red herring is Sir George Edwards (Fritz Tillman), a reactionary Member of Parliament who considers the play "dangerous" and desires to have it banned because of its potential to deprave and corrupt. Sir George is ultimately revealed to be pursuing an agenda of his own, but it is one which involves the medical welfare of Greeley senior, and not the carving up of prostitutes.

> "Jack the Ripper is dead. It's all over. He said he would kill 12 women and 12 women are dead. The monster who has terrorised all of London is dead."
>
> Speech from the play-within-a-film in The Monster of London City (1964)

Unlike Jack the Ripper, The Monster of London City made no pretence to be a horror film per se, and the Gothic elements are mainly confined to what takes place on its fictitious stage. This provides a neat transition between the period-piece horrors of The Lodger and what, from here on, were more often to be modern-day re-enactments of the Whitechapel Murders by other hands. "You'll go on discovering more and more murders, all of them committed by Jack the Ripper, night after night..." Sand admonishes his police persecutors. Five years later, his words were used as the title of another copycat thriller in which the censorious motives of its Establishment protagonist would prove to be much less altruistic than those of Sir George.

The mad USAF general portrayed by Sterling Hayden in Stanley Kubrick's Dr Strangelove, or How I Learned to Stop Worrying and Love the Bomb (1964; from a novel by Terry Southern) was famously named Jack D Ripper. Given that by the end of this apocalyptic drama, General Jack has unleashed World War III upon the nations of the earth for no better reason than that he holds the Russians responsible for the onset of impotence, he could conceivably be regarded as a mass-murderer. In real terms, any connection to the Whitechapel mystery went no further than the pun on the killer's notorious sobriquet. (A 16mm Canadian short of 1999 called Captive Audience also used 'Jack the Ripper' as the on-air signature of a radio jock held hostage in his own studio.)

Kubrick's film did, however, maintain Jack's profile in the public mind, and the next move was to pit him against a foe of equal and opposite merit, like Dracula and Van Helsing. The idea was not a new one, but it was soon to become par-for-the-course as a means of sustaining contemporary cult heroes in long-running television series. For it to work with Jack the Ripper, he was required to battle an adversary every bit as recognisable to the public at large as he now was himself.

Jack's own real-time frame of reference fortuitously coincided with the first appearance in print of the most famous detective in fiction: Sherlock Holmes. The methodology that Holmes employed owed much to the detective skills of Edgar Allan Poe's C Auguste Dupin, a debt that his creator acknowledged in the first Holmes story to see print – 'A Study in Scarlet' – albeit in backhanded form. (Marie Belloc Lowndes' own creation of Hercules Popeau served as a similar model for Agatha Christie's Poirot, but without any credit at all in her case.) Doyle never pitted his hero against Jack the Ripper – although he sited Holmes' rooms at 221b Baker Street, off Marylebone Road, where Mrs Lowndes had domiciled the Buntings – but he was occasionally vocal on the subject, offering outlandish suggestions to the press of the day about the Ripper's possible identity.

If anything, Doyle was as studious as the rest of his class in ensuring that even his fictions came into contact with the East End as little as possible. In 'The Adventure of Black Peter' (*The Return of Sherlock Holmes*; 1905), Dr Watson notes in passing that an unrecorded adventure saw Holmes remove a "plague-spot" by name of Wilson, the canary trainer, from the East End of London, while in 'The Adventure of the Cardboard Box' (*His Last Bow*; 1917), a maiden lady is sent a package in the post containing two human ears, as the Ripper had promised to do to the police in the second of his 'Dear Boss' letters. Doyle also made use of mysterious lodgers in several Holmes stories, prefiguring Mrs Lowndes, 'The Case of the Veiled Lodger' in *The Casebook of Sherlock Holmes* (1927) being the most obvious of them. Minor allusions aside, though, the most famous murder inquiry in the annals of Victorian crime was significantly absent from the case-files of its most illustrious detective.

> "Look out of this window, Watson. See how the figures loom up, are dimly seen, and then blend once more into the cloudbank. The thief or murderer could roam London on such a day as the tiger does the jungle, unseen until he pounces, and then evident only to his victim."
> Sir Arthur Conan Doyle, 'The Adventure of the Bruce-Partington Plans'/His Last Bow (1917)

In 1965, exploitation producers Michael Klinger and Tony Tenser made a documentary called *Primitive London* for their Compton Cameo outfit, which had featured a 'reconstruction' of one of the Ripper murders. Through this came the idea of doing something more ambitious along these lines, and the pair arrived at an ingenious and original solution: pit super-sleuth Sherlock Holmes against Jack the Ripper.

Directed by Arnold Louis Miller, *Primitive London* promised scenes of "the jungle behind the bright lights," but the jungle as it *was* was more in evidence in a similar documentary released by British Lion two years later. *The London Nobody Knows* was directed by Norman Cohen and based on a book of that name by London historian Geoffrey Fletcher. One sequence shows the real Hanbury Street site where 'Dark Annie' Chapman met the Ripper, before the area was demolished soon after the film was made. The 53-minute featurette may not have led to an opus about Sherlock Holmes and Jack the Ripper (although it was narrated by James Mason, who starred in one), but its timely focus was longer lasting: it is now a historical document in its own right.

The idea of franchising the Holmes character, divorced from the canon of stories to which he is usually affiliated, was one that had already suggested itself to American accountant

Henry E Lester, executor of the Doyle estate and head of Sir Nigel Films, its media arm. Having gone the rounds with Hammer, Lester now allied with Compton, ideas were pooled, and the project was passed to Donald and Derek Ford to develop. As the budget rose in line with the ambitious subject-matter, the proposed film acquired the services of an American co-producer and a prestigious director in the person of James Hill, who went on to make *Born Free* immediately afterwards.

A *Study in Terror* was shot at Shepperton Studios at a cost of £165,000. The film played its part in helping to catapult ex-Bridlington cinema manager Tony Tenser into the mainstream from out of the twin cul-de-sacs of foreign language imports and skin-flick sexploitation. He soon left Compton to form his own company, Tigon, from which base of horror-accented operations he then set out to rival Hammer for real.

> "*You wish me to intercede with my brother, that he may come to the aid of Scotland Yard and apprehend the Whitechapel murderer.*"
>
> Mycroft Holmes (Robert Morley) in A Study in Terror (1966)

The film's co-producer at the American end was Herman Cohen, the man responsible for such teen delights as *I Was a Teenage Werewolf* (1957), *Horrors of the Black Museum* (1959), *Konga* (1960) and most recently *Black Zoo* (1962). A *Study in Terror* benefited from an English cast of theatrical pedigree and the production values which were accorded it by Columbia's involvement. In Herman Cohen's case, it was the exception which proved the rule; after this, he returned to low-budget dross of mind-numbing banality: *Berserk!* and *Trog* in 1967 and 1970 respectively (both with Joan Crawford); *Craze* in 1973 (with Jack Palance). Cohen had wanted 'Fog' as the title of the film but was overruled by the Doyle estate, who preferred the allusion to 'A Study in Scarlet'. Either choice would have fitted the bill, but as little fog is in evidence in the end-product, the Doylists win by a hawk-like nose.

For the first time in a screen career which stretched back to the turn of the century, the casting of the great detective was less important than the plot in which he was involved; thus the aquiline profiles of Basil Rathbone (in a long-running series of films for Universal in the forties) and Peter Cushing (in Hammer's *The Hound of the Baskervilles*; 1959) gave way to the less Sidney Paget-inspired, more Stan Lee-like, jut-jawed physiognomy of Shakespearean actor-manager John Neville, while Donald Houston was also less of a Dr Watson and more a plain Dr Houston. Rathbone's portrayal of Doyle's enigmatic detective had majored on the haughty intellect and steely reserve of the man and supplanted all previous depictions of the character for several generations of fans. Cushing had added a mercurial temperament, but was given little opportunity to move beyond the bounds of a restrictive screenplay. John Neville looked the part, but a softness of expression weighed against the sense of inner strength which is so essential to any successful characterisation of Holmes.

The obligatory aphorisms were sprinkled liberally about the script, but the sheer horror of the murders (no matter how sanitised, even with a British 'X' certificate) submerged the Holmesian motifs and secured a film that was not so much an adventure for Sherlock Holmes as another attempt to provide a solution of sorts to the identity of Jack the Ripper.

Holmes did not survive this latest duel to forge a new career in feature films, as the producers intended. Instead, it was Jack the Ripper who found himself up against a variety of

John Neville as Sherlock Holmes in A *Study in Terror* (1966)

different foes over the next two decades (including a return match with Holmes), and not Doyle's detective.

> Lestrade: *"He's written to us, written a letter."*
> Holmes: *"Try to be coherent, Lestrade. Who's written?"*
> Lestrade: *"Jack the Ripper."*
>
> Frank Finlay and John Neville in A Study in Terror (1966)

After the murder of two prostitutes in Whitechapel, consulting detective Sherlock Holmes is sent a surgical instrument case in the mail. His inquiries lead him to the stately home of the Duke of Shires, where the case is found to belong to the Duke's eldest son, Michael, a former medical student now thought to be dead. Other murders ensue, and Holmes discovers that Michael's marriage to a prostitute named Angela was used by her and her lover, publican Max Steiner, to blackmail his father. A falling-out among thieves left Michael brain-damaged but not dead, and Holmes traces Angela's whereabouts, revealing *her* to have been the one who sent the case, thinking Michael was the killer. It turns out not to be Michael but his younger brother, Edward, who has been working his way to Angela by a process of elimination, in an insane attempt to protect the family name. Holmes confronts him when he is about to strike again. During their struggle, Edward sets the pub on fire but perishes in the resulting conflagration, as do Angela and Steiner. Holmes somehow manages to escape, and he and Watson agree to keep the good name of 'Jack the Ripper' to themselves.

The promise in the film's premise of pitting Doyle's ace detective against Jack the Ripper is never quite realised by a script which sees its first duty as providing a solution to the crimes, albeit a fictional one. Much effort is spent on developing updated screen personae for Holmes and Watson (a mistake which the wily Peter Bryan avoided in his script for Hammer's *The Hound of the Baskervilles* seven years before), while none at all is spent on advancing the Ripper as an adversary worthy of special attention, like Doyle's Professor Moriarty or Colonel Moran. Nor is it a battle of equals in other respects: aside from the lengthy cutaways to garish murders (the dispatch of Polly Nichols is especially effective: half-drowned in a horse-trough before she is stabbed to death, her blood turning the churning waters red), Holmes and Watson hold centre stage for the whole of the first half, while Jack is not mentioned by name until after the murder of Elizabeth Stride, number four in the film's list of five victims: Smith, Nichols, Chapman, Stride and Kelly, in that order.

This oversight could be seen as an attempt to maintain historical veracity (though the idea of a 'monster' abroad on the streets of London is given little weight in a film which treats Jack as just another killer on the loose), but the reason behind it was a desire to downplay the Ripper and re-establish Holmes and Watson as series characters at a time when cinema was in the grip of others of that ilk: James Bond, Derek Flint, Matt Helm, Bulldog Drummond, even Batman. Neville's Holmes goes equipped with pistol and sword-stick, and he is not averse to employing a bit of jujitsu to lay low the local bully-boys, but the overly effeminate characterisations of both the film's leading players were out of tune with the hard-drinking, easy-laying, fast-acting hedonism of mid-sixties super-spies. As a result, *A Study in Terror* did moderate business at the British box-office through the strength of its plot and the appeal of its villain, rather than any new-found vigour on the part of its protagonists.

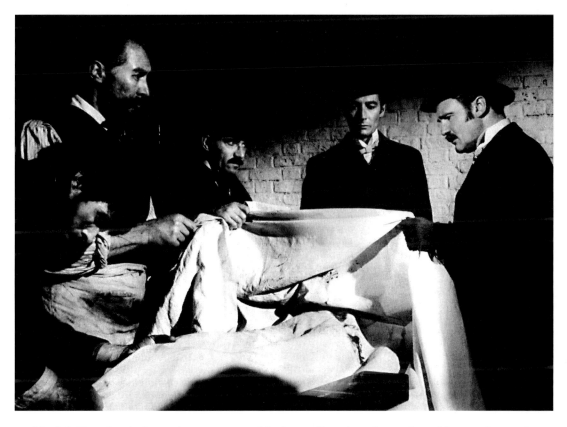

A *Study in Terror* does its best to integrate some of the known facts about the murders with what is otherwise another wholly fabricated scenario. The famous letter to Central News is given prominent attention, so as to allow Holmes to exercise his graphological expertise (he comes to all the wrong conclusions), and there is talk of a bayonet being used as the murder-weapon, which nods to the case of Martha Tabram (albeit that Tabram fails to feature in the film's body-count). But a distinct air of superficiality hangs over the story whenever it ventures from Baker to Dorset Street. "Annie Chapman's purse was found with her body," Inspector Lestrade somewhat incongruously remarks to a police constable at the scene of her murder, a bald statement promoting the idea of documentary precision in the screenplay. Untrue, as it turns out: Chapman's meagre possessions were found with her body (placed by her side in a conscious 'arrangement', according to Dr Bagster Phillips), but she had *no* purse and was left with no money by her murderer. Combine this with the curious circumstance that the murders are plotted out of sequence, and the film's take on the crimes can be adjudged to be sketchy, at best.

Was it always so? According to producer Herman Cohen, the original script was redrafted: "I hired Harry Craig, a writer that Adrian Conan Doyle and Henry Lester liked very much. He worked very closely with me and James Hill, the director, on the final screenplay, which was based on the original story and screenplay of Donald and Derek Ford. Harry Craig didn't want a credit on *A Study in Terror* because he was doing a big film for Columbia at the time."

Be that as it may, the heavy hands of Mr Cohen are all too evident on the end product. The final film was deprived of the murder of 'Cathy' Eddowes, who had been cast as the Ripper's

Anthony Quayle, Frank Finlay, John Neville, and Donald Huston in *A Study in Terror* (1966)

fifth victim. Part of the reason for this was the late inclusion of a 'teaser' pre-credit sequence, in which a streetwalker is accosted by an unseen client who stabs her; as she lies dead on the ground, Jack's knife is seen to be embedded in her throat. This murder made up the numbers and substituted for the loss of Eddowes, but while the sequence is trashily effective in itself, it is illustrative of the tampering which cut the heart out of *A Study in Terror*.

The victim is subsequently named as Emma Smith (an unlikely candidate for the Ripper, in truth), while the first in the film proper is Polly Nichols, even though the murder of Tabram actually preceded that of Nichols. Given that the script is otherwise accurate in its overall frame of reference with regard to the Whitechapel Murders (as already noted, it even has Watson quote the 'Dear Boss' letter in full), its inability to unfold them in the correct order can be directly attributed to the removal of Eddowes and the addition of Smith, after the event, by one less well-versed in the history of the crimes than the original writing team. The image of a knife protruding from a girl's throat is itself reminiscent of the schlock-horror scenes familiar from *Horrors of the Black Museum* (1959) and *Circus of Horrors* (1960). Were such an item to have been left by the Ripper in the original story, it would have presented Holmes with an obvious port of call for his famously touchy-feely forensic skills.

"Then I warn you. Put every available man you have on the streets of Whitechapel."
Sherlock Holmes (John Neville) in A Study in Terror (1966)

A Study in Terror was the first film about Jack the Ripper to use the real names of the victims; fine in principle, but not so clever if someone decides to tamper with the structure of the story after the event. The film was re-cut on completion to reduce its overall length and improve a slow middle section. Veteran performer Kay Walsh, who played Eddowes, saw her role reduced to a couple of extraneous scenes at the beginning of the film. Having Eddowes survive the knife of the Ripper defeats the object of using the correct names in the first place.

The murder of Elizabeth Stride was then moved forward a reel, to space out the killings more evenly, but the narrative pace of Holmes and Watson's investigation had to remain unchanged. This leads to Stride's death passing unnoticed by the principals, and the viewer is left to gauge its impact on the tale from the fact that Mycroft Holmes (Robert Morley) is immediately thereafter asked by the government to engage the services of his brother. Mycroft was originally intended to enter the fray after the murder of *Chapman*.

What follows is equally anomalous. The Holmes siblings share a sherry and discuss tactics, at which point Lestrade enters with the Ripper's letter and Sherlock delivers his warning about imminent murder. The next sequence sees Sherlock (belatedly) attending the mortuary to view the body of Stride; there is a fade-out and Mycroft is back in Baker Street, all bluff and bluster on the second occasion (in which he is reacting to a murder that no longer features in the film) and demanding of his brother that he *act*. "Go to the scene of the crime. Use your powers. Interview the people concerned. What was it mother used to say? Stir your stumps!" The trouble is that Sherlock already *has*, in the scene immediately before.

When the supposedly dead Michael Osbourne is found to be alive, Dr Murray, his paternalistic guardian, tells Holmes that he was the unwilling victim of a blackmail plot concocted by Angela and her lover, Steiner: refusing to go along with the plan, Michael was embroiled in a fight in which he was beaten into imbecility and Angela was accidentally scarred with acid. But the film then turns this around. Holmes traces Angela to a room over

Barbara Windsor as Annie Chapman in A Study in Terror (1966)

Steiner's pub, where she reveals what really happened: the blackmail plot was Michael's idea, with Steiner acting as go-between. When Angela wanted out, Michael – a "vicious, worthless libertine" according to his wife – threw acid in her face, as a result of which he was beaten by Steiner.

It is when Angela discloses her tale to Holmes that he finally realises who the Ripper must be: Edward, Lord Carfax, believing Murray's version of events, has been looking for Angela Osbourne in revenge for what she did to his brother. Holmes lays a trap for Carfax, and confronts him in a struggle to the death in Angela's bedroom.

This is how the story was meant to have played. It is not, in the event, how it actually does.

In a revision to the script, Holmes takes his leave of Angela and promptly rejects her version: "I'm afraid, Watson, you're not probing deeply enough. Her scars extend far beyond the surface..." "What do you mean?" Watson asks, understandably in the circumstances. "She may well believe her strange story to be the truth..." the detective responds in part, before losing the thread completely. The implication is that Holmes still believes Murray's version, and the purpose was to retain the sympathy for Michael which the film has been at pains to build. Consequently, Angela and Steiner take the fall and the Osbourne family is vindicated, rehabilitated, and becomes the beneficiary of a cover-up initiated by Holmes.

The actors saw things differently. Barry Jones, as the Duke of Shires, is plainly in denial of the fact that *both* his sons have inherited the insanity that has run through four generations of his family, as Holmes makes clear. Only at the close of the film does denial turn to acceptance,

Peter Carsten and
Adrienne Corri in A
Study in Terror (1966)

resignation, remorse. The give-away is the role of Max Steiner. As played by German-born Peter Carsten (a genuine villain in *The Mercenaries* in 1968), Steiner is the most sympathetic character in the film. Despite his superficial air of bully-boy bravado, his devotion to Angela is total and he dies trying to save her from the climactic fire. Not the kind of man who would beat somebody to a pulp just for the hell of it, as Murray infers. He and Angela are victims of circumstance; as such they pay the time-honoured price. The rewrite reversed this concept and confirmed Angela as embittered harridan and Max as pimp, blackmailer and foreign thug.

John Fraser as Jack the Ripper in *A Study in Terror* (1966)

Thanks to these alterations, the film is incorrigibly schizophrenic: it feigns sympathy for the underclass of the East End, yet ultimately condemns it as the agent of its own undoing. In the original draft, one mad brother seeking revenge on a whore for what has befallen the other mad brother was to have been a case of two wrongs making a Ripper. As things turned out, Lord Carfax was afforded some justification for his actions, in seeking warped redress for an act of violence committed against his sibling: less of a madman and more a moral avenger. And with the help of Sherlock Holmes, his family is allowed to keep secret this rather eccentric notion of natural justice.

The original had intended the fault-line to run with the British aristocracy, cosseted in regal splendour while the poor lay destitute on the streets. After Herman Cohen had fallen for the lure of ermine, the aristocracy – barring one demented exception – was given a clean bill of health, with the prostitute and her protector becoming the villains of the piece.

> "This butcher-boy has the government – has all of us – on the edge of a knife. Only this morning, three more men were attacked on the streets of London... carrying Gladstone bags!"
> Mycroft Holmes (Robert Morley) in *A Study in Terror* (1966)

A Study in Terror never quite manages to blend its contradictory styles of the typically cerebral Holmesian investigation with the brutal pseudo-reality of true-life crime. Doyle was shown to be wise in having avoided the conflict. Herman Cohen's influence on the production can also be seen in distractions like an unnecessarily prolonged tour of the Duke of Shire's stately home early in the proceedings, while Holmes is given to disporting himself like the conscienceless West Enders whom he is meant to disparage, casting handfuls of coin at local waifs as though he were on the streets of Bombay or Calcutta. For all its pretensions to the contrary, *A Study in Terror* is firmly on the side of the Establishment.

There is, however, *some* effort to relate the killings to the conditions prevailing in the East End at the time, along the lines of an argument first put forward by George Bernard Shaw, and the film's mere passing acquaintance with the rudiments of the Whitechapel Murders is more than made up for by a pleasing familiarity with the Holmes stories: Neville may utter the obligatory but erroneous "Elementary, my dear Watson" in their opening exchange, but a subsequent spot of fraternal banter with his brother Mycroft is lifted almost word-for-word

from a passage in 'The Greek Interpreter' (in *The Memoirs of Sherlock Holmes*; 1894), while a later commentary on the London fog is drawn from *His Last Bow*. "Fog to the murderer is what the jungle is to the tiger, Watson. It conceals him from all until he pounces, and then he is evident only to his victim," Holmes paraphrases, in one of the few scenes to actually feature the stuff. Other asides lay claim to the same literary provenance, as does Holmes' proclivity for firing his revolver indoors.

An 'Ellery Queen' mystery novel, also called *A Study in Terror* and written by Frederic Dannay and Manfred B Lee, accompanied the film on release in the US; while notionally based on the Fords' script, the novelisation offered an alternative ending: the Duke of Shires is the Ripper, not his son. The fact that such a reading was possible shows the sparsity of clues in the narrative and how, in *A Study in Terror*, the great detective arrives at his conclusion as much by intuition and guesswork as he does by deductive analysis.

> *"You know, don't you? You know who Jack the Ripper is."*
> **Dr Watson (Donald Houston) in** *A Study in Terror* **(1966)**

How successfully *did* Jack the Ripper elude the police? In principle, he was 100 per cent successful; he was never officially apprehended. In practice, certain officers may have been convinced of the guilt or likely guilt of particular suspects, but were unable to proceed against them for a variety of reasons. Foremost among these was the total lack of forensic science, so felons had virtually to be caught in the act: literally 'red-handed', in Jack's case.

Before Jack the Ripper, most murders in London were either perpetrated in the commission of a crime or they were of the 'Saturday night' or domestic variety. With regard to the first two, good intelligence on the ground provided the suspects and very often the culprits; the latter was usually concluded by the discovery of a body under the floorboards, an empty arsenic bottle in the cupboard, a forged will, or other evidence of nefarious activity behind closed doors. The police were not so much baffled as to who Jack the Ripper was, or how he managed to evade capture, but about how to bring him to justice.

Detective Inspector Harry Cox of London's City Police recalled the sense of bewilderment felt in all quarters in an article published in 1906: "I can well remember the sensation which the first of the horrible crimes caused among those whose duty it was to investigate the untoward happenings of the East End. The murder of Martha Turner (Tabram) was an amazing puzzle to each of us. Never in the course of our experience had such a case occurred. It was clearly no ordinary East End crime." A more contemporaneous reflection in the *Evening News* of 23 July 1889, quoting an anonymous CID source, pronounced: "There has been nothing like these murders in the history of crime." A parallel need only be drawn with random acts of terrorism in our own age.

The Whitechapel Murders were a catalyst in bringing about change in the policing of the capital which was long overdue. Not only were the last of the rookeries (made famous by Dickens in *Oliver Twist*) swept away in the years that followed, but street-lighting was increased, police communications were improved and the art of detection was turned into a science.

Fingerprinting was but one of the techniques which were now brought into play, after reports on its potential efficacy had spent years shuffling between the desks of those in authority. (The first criminal conviction using fingerprint evidence came in 1902; the first for a murder case in 1905.) Blood-grouping was another. Jack the Ripper, or one at least of the murderers

A Study in Terror
(1966)

whose deeds became enmeshed in that all-embracing net, may have been known to police; doing something about it was another matter. If their suspicions had been made known to him, or if the killer himself had begun to suspect that they knew, this might account for the cessation of the murders after 9 November. Police inquiries continued until 1891, which makes it plain that no single officer knew the Ripper's identity for sure. They may not have been certain, but they may well have been close.

"My job is not unlike yours, doctor. I may not be able to remove a cancer from the body, but I can remove it from society."
Judge Charles Lomax (Jack May) in *Night After Night After Night* (1969)

Jack May in
*Night After Night
After Night* (1969)

In 1969, independent producer-director Lindsay Shonteff was offered the director's chair on a four-week exploitation quickie called *Evil Is...*, the title of which was modelled on Lindsay Anderson's *If....* (1968). The story was that of a modern-day Jack who also targets vice girls, but for a different and more up-to-the-minute reason. The film was financed by Butchers Films (a second-feature outfit run by John Philips and Henry Fisher) in association with Dudley Birch, the business partner of its underrated cinematographer Douglas Hill, and it was initially geared for Soho's 'cinema club' market.

Shonteff rewrote Dail Ambler's teasing screenplay as shooting progressed to give the film more depth but, in shades of *A Study in Terror*, the completed print was re-cut by producer James Mellor – himself an editor and occasional director – to bring it back more in line with the premise of Ambler's original script. It was also invested with the more sexually suggestive title of *Night After Night After Night*. Shonteff had his name removed from the credits, substituting the pseudonym 'Lewis J Force' that he kept up his sleeve for such occasions. Years after the film had effectively bombed, Birch confided to Shonteff that, in his opinion, it would have fared better in its former version, which by then was small comfort to its Canadian-born director.

Night After Night After Night is *The Monster of London City* without the association of a fictional stage play about Jack the Ripper to provide a frame of reference. Shot on the lowest of low budgets, it features a copycat Ripper ('Ripper killings youth sent for trial', cries a news-sheet) who stalks the streets of the West End of the city, around Soho night-spots and among the streetwalkers of Hyde Park. The climax takes place in Shepherd Market, Mayfair, a notorious red-light district at the time of the film's production.

High Court Judge Charles Lomax (Jack May) suffers a mental breakdown when the Victorian values that his office is expected to uphold are brought face to face with the seamier aspects of the swinging sixties' sexual revolution, day after day after day. In response to this dichotomy, he takes to donning black leather and a Beatles wig (in place of his judicial one) and prowls the capital with a switch-blade – one minute feeding birds, the next minute slaughtering them. He fails to be apprehended by the effortlessly stupid Inspector Rowan, whose own wife has fallen victim to the killer and who spends most of his time 'leaning' on the wrong suspect, but eventually succumbs through betrayal.

On the face of it a seedy exploitation piece, *Night After Night After Night* is a remarkable film in more ways than one. The non-existent budget stretched to neither courtroom nor police cells (Shonteff worked around the lack of key sets by shooting low-angle for the most part), but favours were clearly called in to stage scenes inside restaurants, sex shops and strip clubs. As a result, its depiction of the milieu of the sixties sex industry is second to none. In its vibrant use of extant locales, *Night After Night After Night* captures a sense of period and place that is now long gone, matching the films of Ealing Studios in their pioneering use of location shooting in and around post-war London.

Jack May, fresh from MGM's *Goodbye Mr Chips*, delivers a powerful and thoughtful performance as the judge. Menacing yet piteous, he extracts a considerable measure of sympathy for the man, despite the violence of his actions. (Only in the murder of Rowan's wife does motivation jar and the catchpenny nature of the original surface.) It was a brave role to tackle, especially in the closing scenes where Lomax has to walk real streets in near-farcical drag. It is to May's credit that he manages to pull this off, his agony at his plight only too real. The film bears a passing resemblance to Michael Powell's *Peeping Tom* (1960), and had it been given more of a budget and distributed in venues other than those which it set out to disparage, its polemic against the corrosive effects of the sex trade might not have gone so neglected.

Night After Night After Night is more noteworthy now than it was perceived to be on release, when a preoccupation with nipple-gazing blinded critics to its real value. As a social document it deserves respect; as a piece of honest filmmaking against the odds of a criminal lack of funds, it is a small triumph in its own dedicated way. If anything, it moves at rather too stately a pace, but it is May's performance which turns it from a conventional psycho-shocker into a case study of an individual incapable of coming to terms with the changing world around him. Clever writing constantly undermines the very audience to whom it was first designed to appeal, which is presumably how it managed to attract the services of May to begin with. "I blame the women, walking about the streets half naked. They ask for it," opines the judge's clerk-in-chambers, before poring over porn magazines on the sly. "Some things die more quickly than others," Lomax reflects, in reference to a sex life that has been made to seem unwholesome to him. The film suffered some minor cuts in release, though most of its plentiful nudity remained surprisingly intact.

"Please help me," Lomax pleads as a police marksman puts an end to his torment on the Thames embankment by Albert Bridge. It is an entreaty which takes us back to *Pandora's Box*, suggesting that society at large is to blame for the ills which befall it, not just one man with a knife.

One-eyed Jacks

Author William Stewart, in his now largely redundant *Jack the Ripper: A New Theory* (Quality Press; 1939) which postulated a mad midwife instead of a mad doctor, 'Jill' as opposed to Jack the Ripper, wrote: "Could a Jack the Ripper today evade the police as easily as in 1888? If Jack the Ripper was the sort of person I imagine, there can be only one answer: 'Yes.' Apart from all the arguments which can be put forward to support this contention, there is the disturbing fact that since 1927, there have been several murder mysteries in London which still remain unsolved, and none of these contained those factors which make such crimes as the Ripper committed unsolvable. Writing in the June of 1938, there have been in the last 30 months, in Soho alone, three murders of women of the same class from which Jack the Ripper chose his victims... Scotland Yard turned Soho inside out in its fruitless attempts to discover the murderer or murderers."

Taking Stewart at his belated word, the next police thriller to tack Jack the Ripper onto its plot-excuse for lingering over voyeuristic sex murders was *Jack the o of London* (*Jack, el* destripador de Londres; 1971), a hybrid which obligingly switched Jack's action from Whitechapel to Soho but failed to gain much of a release outside Spain, its chief country of origin, even under that linguistically challenged come-on title.

The sex trade that played such a prominent part in *Night After Night After Night* also provided the backdrop for this Spanish/Italian co-production, which was filmed under the less assuming title of *Seven Bodies for Scotland Yard*. Conceived as a copycat thriller, this modern-day Ripper variant was a change of pace from werewolves, mummies and other Universal-inspired monsters for Paul Naschy, a former professional wrestler – real name Jacinto Molina Alvarez – and now a one-man Spanish horror industry. "They're calling me the new Jack the Ripper," observes the anonymous Mangler in a note to Scotland Yard. "I'm not criticising the old Jack; he was great for his time. But since then man has actually walked on the moon." If it was comparisons that the screenwriters were after, then the turkey had landed.

> "Dear Commissioner Campbell – As you see, the circle is getting smaller; from the prostitute to the princess, everybody's paid their dues. Regarding the princess I just wanted to see if her blood was red or blue. But her eyes were so blue, I kept them for myself... With best regards, Jack."
>
> Letter from the Mangler in *Jack the Mangler of London* (1971)

Naschy – an icon of sorts in his home country but an actor of little range beyond an ability to growl effectively (in the guise of Waldemar Daninsky, his werewolf alter ego), throw punches, and roll about in a convincing tussle on the floor – plays Peter Dockerman, a crippled ex-trapeze artist resident in Soho when a spate of Ripper-style slayings of prostitutes breaks out. When Dockerman's wife joins the list of victims after a spot of 'night work' to keep her husband's head above water, Dockerman becomes prime suspect. Dockerman himself is led to believe that investigating Police Commissioner Campbell is the real culprit; an unlikely scenario on the face of it, but only three players feature in the drama. The *commissario* suspects

Italian poster for *Jack the Mangler of London* (1971)

someone else again: his best friend and professor of psychology, Winston Damery-Christi, who also happens to be impotent.

The killer, needless to say, is the third of these, whose motive is to possess women in death in a way that he cannot in life: "They were all mine. Mine forever. Because their last breath was all mine. Even if I couldn't possess them like everyone else, I possessed them with the kiss of death forever." Campbell and Dockerman each pursue the Mangler to his 'castle in Sussex', the basement of which is filled with trophies from his kills, and after a fight, he dies on the point of his own knife.

Jack the Mangler is a throwaway item, amateurishly directed by José Luis Madrid and notionally set in London only by virtue of a day or two's location shooting in which Naschy looks all at sea in the environs of Piccadilly Circus. Few of Naschy's juvenile horror efforts ever saw release in Britain for want of a distributor foolhardy enough of take them on, *Hell's Creatures* (*La marca del hombre lobo*; 1967) and *Shadow of the Werewolf* (*La noche de Walpurgis*; 1970) being among the exceptions.

"Every time Scotland Yard investigates a serial killer we get lots of crazy people writing letters claiming to be the killer," observes the Commissioner. True to form, a sackful of mail from Jack promises a wealth of gory delights: no sooner has a newspaper headline announced

'Another crime of Jack the Mangler' than the police receive a head in a hatbox (shades of *Night Must Fall*), a sight which is greeted as though it were an everyday occurrence at Scotland Yard.

Mexican lobby card for *Jack the Mangler of London* (1971)

The plotting is nonsensical and contrived on a similar level of believability to Naschy's Gothic escapades. Why Jack removes organs and appendages from his victims and stores them in pickling jars in the basement of his castle goes without explanation. The film has its novelties, though: Scotland Yard is depicted as a provincial police station, and how the Commissioner arrives at the aforementioned castle in Sussex by taking a train from Piccadilly to the West London borough of Chiswick and walking the remainder of the way is a mystery in itself. "Stop at the first emergency clinic you see," Campbell tells his driver at the close, suddenly recalling that he has a bullet in his shoulder, courtesy of Jack. "I don't want to be the last victim of Jack the Mangler." No fear of that, as any who have watched the film could testify.

Jack the *Mangler* was moved to murder and mutilate through his inability to 'possess' the women to whom he is attracted in the normal way, but Jack the *Ripper* was not a sex-killer in the commonly understood sense of the term, in that there is no evidence to support the notion that his crimes were sexually motivated, any more than the crimes of Yorkshire Ripper Peter Sutcliffe were sexually motivated.

An interesting aside is that while writers tend to treat Jack as the first serial sex-murderer, films have continued to cast him in the form decreed by Leonard Matters, as a deranged killer out to avenge himself on whores. This may in part be due to the attitude of the British censor, pre-1970, with regard to the portrayal of sexual violence on screen, when stabbing a woman of the streets with a long-bladed knife was considered acceptable but penetrating her with a more fleshy instrument beforehand was not. Nevertheless, this concept has persisted, and those on the receiving end of Jack's wrath are rarely depicted as the victims of lustmord.

Serial strangler John Reginald Christie was shown in Richard Fleischer's 10 Rillington Place (1970) as only being able to achieve orgasm by choking the unfortunate recipients of his amorous advances to death, a sexual kink in itself. Similar notions have rarely applied to Jack. In this respect, filmmakers appeared to have their fingers on the button of the Ripper's psychopathology more assuredly than many commentators on the case. It was the exceptional film which proved the rule, as well as the exceptional filmmaker: if sex was to marry violence at some point in Jack's cinematic career, then Spanish sleaze-merchant Jesús Franco was almost guaranteed to be the one who would preside over the ceremony.

> "Ladies and gentlemen, we've called you together to help us employ a new method of police detection which we believe may aid in our search for the sadistic killer popularly known as Jack the Ripper."
> Inspector Selby (Herbert Fux) in Jack the Ripper (1976)

If Jack the Mangler was Paul Naschy's view of the Ripper's crimes, then Jack the Dismemberer was Jesús Franco's. In Jack the Ripper (1976), Klaus Kinski plays an anonymous doctor, demented son of a prostitute, whose idea of 'ripping' his victims is to chop them up into small pieces and dispose of the body parts in the Thames. As this methodology would have resulted in few of them being discovered – beyond the occasional hand dredged up on the end of a fishing line, as here – it is difficult to imagine how it might have engendered the panic among the London populace that is in evidence at the start of the film.

Where John Brahm's 1944 version of The Lodger identified Jack through the anachronism of fingerprinting, Jack the Ripper achieves the same end by employing the services of a sketch artist, a technique which was in use at the time of the original murders: "A small black goblin" is one witness' opinion of Kinski's Ripper, which is an elegant allusion to Stevenson's description of Mr Hyde as a 'Gothic gnome'.

A particularly bestial sequence has the doctor pursue his quarry into a woodland glade, where he stabs her repeatedly in the abdomen before raping her; carrying the now half-dead girl to his lair, he bloodily amputates both her breasts and her right hand. It is a dubious compliment to advance gratuitous violence as a high point in an otherwise tepid piece of exploitational schlock, but the episode does capture the charnel horror of the original crimes.

The 'Whitechapel' scenes are set around a music-hall venue called Pike's Hole (echoing the Judas Hole of Grip of the Strangler), but atmosphere and ambience are so reminiscent of 1930s Berlin that one expects the first victim to be named Sally Bowles, not Sally Brown. Franco's film is not without merit, but the plotting, dialogue and dubbing are quite atrocious, while characterisation and quality of performance are in a league of their own. Several lines have to be heard to be believed – "We can wait a bit longer to get well, Doctor", says one of Jack's unfeasibly patient patients – and there are times when it seems as though the script for the English version has been put together by the Python team out of discarded pages from The Life of Brian. Against that, the film is sensuously photographed and contains some evocative touches: a carriage glides silently into the fog with Jack and his victim aboard, in shades of Gray's in Robert Wise's The Body Snatcher (1945).

Klaus Kinski as Jack the Ripper (1976)

KLAUS KINSKI in
JACK THE RIPPER
DER DIRNENMÖRDER VON LONDON

This Ripper is caught red-handed in the final reel, in the most anticlimactic finale since Franco's last outing as a director. "It's over... You're a prisoner of the Crown. Scotland Yard has hooked a shark this time: Jack the Ripper!" declares Inspector Selby. "You'll never prove it," Jack replies as the cuffs are put on his wrists, a nod to the fact that the real murderer was never brought to justice. Given that the doctor has been apprehended at the scene, with the tools of his trade about him, having just confessed all to a potential victim who has survived his latest onslaught and is therefore able to testify against him, this parting shot is clearly more bravado than boast.

"Every woman in London is in danger as long as he's out there..."
Jack Hyde (Anthony Perkins) in *Edge of Sanity* (1989)

No cinematic CV of a killer as exploitable as Jack the Ripper would have been complete without the intervention of the ubiquitous Harry Alan Towers, a 40-year industry veteran of colourful second-feature fare, who has had a hand in adapting the works of every marketable author from Sax Rohmer to De Sade. Towers was deprived of a literary source when he finally came to tackle the Ripper in the centenary year of 1988, so he decided to find one for himself. His uninspired choice was, of course, *Dr Jekyll and Mr Hyde*, served up in the unappetising form in which Brian Clemens also abused it on behalf of Hammer – Jekyll turns first into Hyde and then into 'Jack' – but inspiration there was in the casting of Anthony Perkins in a role that had waited patiently for him ever since he uttered the cry of "Mother... Blood!" to his Oedipal alter ego in the Freudian laboratory of the Bates Motel in Hitchcock's *Psycho*.

Accidental dope-fiend Dr Jekyll turns not so much into Mr Hyde as into an antithetical expression of his repressed self, who looks like a raddled refugee from *Reefer Madness*. In this guise, he indulges in masturbatory fantasies of voyeurism and murder, which lead the police to surmise that a 'Ripper' is on the loose. The British-Hungarian co-production was directed by French porn filmmaker Gérard Kikoïne (his first of three features with Towers). As such, it is nothing more than a softcore sex film with pretensions to the mainstream; a plotless parade of peek-a-boo imagery, with its action confined to brothels, bagnios and bars; elegantly photographed but utterly devoid of wit or style.

Perkins was diagnosed with AIDS soon after playing the role of Jack Hyde in *Edge of Sanity* (in place of Robert Vaughn) and it might have helped to put money in the bank for his dependants. No other motive for his participation in the project seems possible. "The Ripper's in *Hyde Park*... The Ripper's on *London Bridge!*" the frustrated inspector remarks during the futile hunt for the killer; if this punning line was intended to refer to some of Jack's parallel escapades on screen, it would easily have been the sassiest thing in the film. Judging by the level of literary expertise in the rest of the thin script, these were merely place-names picked at random.

"I'm working with a very special patient, a man who can only visit me at night. He has a strange sort of sleeping sickness..."
Dr Henry Jekyll (Anthony Perkins) in *Edge of Sanity* (1989)

By the time the gaunt and ghostly Perkins had struggled gamely through a grotesque caricature of the persona with which he had been saddled for nearly 30 years in *Edge of Sanity*, Jack the Ripper was all too clearly an empty vessel without the added substance of a more feasible suspect on which to hang his cloak and hat.

Jack the Ripper (1976)

Chapter Four
Light-hearted Fiends

"There's a man who walks the streets of London late at night
The Ripper, Jack The Ripper
With a little black bag that's oh-so tight
The Ripper, Jack The Ripper..."

Screaming Lord Sutch and the Savages, *Jack the Ripper* (1963)

Where writers and filmmakers in Britain and Europe had been undeviating from the first in terms of the relative respect that they had shown for the Ripper in a fictional context – retaining him, at the very least, in the period to which he properly belonged and adhering to the broad tenets of the associated history – such was not the case in America.

Technological innovation, and the forging of the nation from 1892 on, left the migrant peoples of the United States bereft of the historical and cultural baggage to which the ghosts and vampires of their faraway homelands owed allegiance. The ephemera of the European Tale of Terror came in piecemeal through the crowded portals of Ellis Island, but the fabled creatures of Gothic nightmare remained umbilically chained to their native soils; having beached near Whitby's Tate Hill Pier, the good ship Demeter, with Dracula aboard, could make no port further west.

The New World had severed the cord to its own Gothic traditions in the bloody cataclysm of civil war, and the purgative fires of unification had all-but swept away the superstition-haunted backwaters explored and immortalised by the likes of Hawthorne, Poe, Bierce and Twain. The whimsical frights of 'The Legend of Sleepy Hollow' (1820) and *The Adventures of Tom Sawyer* (1876) – even the outright horrors of Bierce's *Can Such Things Be?* (1893) – were supplanted by the more contemporary concerns of Theodore Dreisser and Frank Norris. Whatever remained of America's Puritan past to lure the literary dreamer into darker byways was sacrificed on the altar of modernity, or buried beneath dispossessing towers of concrete and glass. With only the present to draw on for inspiration, American fear fiction set about creating an entirely new myth-structure of its own, and in this multicultural environment of social experiment and free marketeering, the most prevalent neurosis was readily identified as crime.

'Pulp fiction,' with its slick, mass-produced and easily digestible diet of westerns, mysteries, romances and tales of foreign intrigue, was soon industrial America's equivalent to the Penny Dreadful. With the continuing influx of European immigration, the consequent growth of ethnic ghettos, the transplanting of cultural divides, the formation of 'lodges' and secretive societies, and the installation of religious creeds and practises alien to the indigenous citizenry, crime became the stuff of the pulps, and it was not long before crime fiction began to embrace the half-remembered folk tales which had once been their creators' birthright.

Villains appeared in ever more exotic guise, resonant of a lore which had no root in native American iconography but which was nonetheless deployed with rapacious speed across the

Dr Jekyll & Sister Hyde
(1971)

whole spectrum of popular entertainment. If the real hoodlum had only to turn up the collar of his trench-coat, tug at the brim of his fedora and jab a 'gat' into a ribcage to gain respect, his fictional counterpart needed to be garbed in the ritual cloth of a pantheon of monsters whose influence had somehow managed to span an ocean. No sooner did the new century dawn and the 'jazz age' beckon than America began to swarm with arch-criminals operating under chimerian aliases like 'The Gorilla', 'The Phantom', and 'The Bat'. In 1923, these and other, more supernatural creatures of the new pulp order found a home from home in *Weird Tales*.

The world of the pulps, to which nothing was sacred, knew little about the Ripper killings that was not erroneous or exaggerated out of all proportion as a result of the sensational newspaper reports which had crossed the Atlantic both during and after the murders. In this triumph of imagination over a need to maintain some sort of historical perspective, the Whitechapel monster was perceived as a character whose nickname became a catch-all, like Gilles de Rais or 'Bluebeard', for a particular type of atrocity. As such, the Ripper was fair game for any time period – past, present or future – where he might usefully be deemed to add cachet, or provide shock value, to another narrative entirely.

In 1943, Jack had been made the subject of a short story in *Weird Tales* magazine which had freed him from the constraints of time and place and opened the way for others to do likewise. It had meant the abandonment of certain basic principles in the cause of populism, but the young Robert Bloch's first excursion into Ripper territory (herein represented by the streets of Chicago rather than Whitechapel) was thought to be worth it. 'Yours Truly, Jack the Ripper' is a story still regularly anthologised and fondly referred to today by those with a low threshold for narrative originality, but its combination of title value and trademark 'surprise' ending made it perfect for adaptation on radio throughout the 1940s and 50s.

Bloch's obsession with the Ripper killings never waned in his 60-year career as a writer of weird tales, just as his knowledge of, or insight into, the crimes never improved. This deadly combination eventually produced *The Night of the Ripper* in 1984, a novel so bad, so miserably uninformed, as to defy analysis. *The Night of the Ripper* opens as follows, courtesy of *Macbeth*: "Hell is Murky. That's what Shakespeare wrote, long ago, but he might have used the same words to describe London. Beneath the black pall of smoke shrouding the city the gaslights flared and flamed as the lost souls stumbled down the streets of Inferno. Demons dwelt here – drunken navvies reeling into suckcribs, mucksnipes lurking before netherskens, square-rigged swells prowling in search of buors."

Victorian London might have seemed like an alien place to Chicago-born Bloch, but it was not *that* alien: explanation of these terms is offered in the next paragraph, but they are drawn in their entirety from the glossary of slang which is provided by author Kellow Chesney in his *The Victorian Underworld* (1970). Chesney's book deals with the period to 1860, however, not that of the 1880s.

> "Mr Carmody," he said, "Have you ever heard of Jack the Ripper?"
> "The murderer?" I asked.
> "Exactly. The greatest monster of them all. Worse than Springheel Jack or Crippen. Jack the Ripper. Red Jack."
>
> Robert Bloch, 'Yours Truly, Jack the Ripper' (1943)

In 'Yours Truly Jack the Ripper', Bloch boiled Jack down to base icon in the style beloved of the pulps. The story stripped the killer of his humanity and reduced him to an 'ageless pathological monster'. Such rampant fundamentalism was a feature of pulp fiction throughout the forties and fifties, as it was of cold-war politics with its talk (as recently as the 1980s) of 'evil empires'. Bloch re-crafted Jack as an alien invader, an entity like those of his mentor H P Lovecraft; a great Satan, in other words, which had to be subdued before it hacked the world to destruction.

Just as the killer in Bloch's 1959 novel *Psycho* turned out to be Norman Bates and not his mad mother, so the title character of 'Yours Truly, Jack the Ripper' proves to be the narrator of the piece and not the protagonist. So far, so original. The Ripper is an eternal fiend who murders at regular intervals to seed his immortality; so theorises Sir Guy Hollis, British Ambassador. Enlisting the help of psychiatrist John Carmody, Hollis sets out to track down the fiend among the Bohemian inhabitants of Chicago. Their quest proves fruitless and they retire to a seedy bar. Here, the hitherto sceptical Carmody finally becomes convinced of Hollis' determination to pursue the Ripper until he is captured or killed. They exit into the street, and Carmody stabs Hollis to death: "'John!' he screamed. 'Never mind the "John",' I whispered, raising the knife. 'Just call me Jack.'"

The story is typical of the author's output. There are no shades of grey in Bloch's simplistic view of the universe; there is good (occasionally) and there is evil incarnate as represented here by Jack the Ripper, Bloch's very own Old Testament devil. Nowhere is this better exemplified than in the nickname which Bloch coined for his killer. Before 'Yours Truly, Jack the Ripper', the anonymous assassin had been known as the Whitechapel murderer, Leather Apron, even Saucy Jacky, but nowhere in the historical record was he tainted with a political hue. Thanks to Robert Bloch, and those who followed him in adopting the same pseudonym, the East End killer became an even bigger enemy of Western civilisation than was previously thought. Now, he really *was* a monster. He was *Red* Jack.

Pulp frictions

In 1960, veteran horror star Boris Karloff was still being shunted from one television series to another as either host to, narrator of, or participant in weekly adaptations of 'weird' tales. *Thriller*, set in train by NBC producer Hubbell Robinson, turned out to be the perfect format.

Essentially a weekly adaptation of short horror stories, with no remit other than that promised by its title, *Thriller* enjoyed the modicum of success that had eluded *The Veil*. During two seasons from 1960 to 1962, the series was beset with production problems, but it managed to attain a respectable total of 67 episodes before eventual cancellation. Among the writers who contributed to the show were Richard Matheson, Cornell Woolrich, Charles Beaumont, Barré Lyndon and Robert Bloch. Among the stories chosen for televising was 'Yours Truly, Jack the Ripper'.

Bloch provided three scripts for the first season of *Thriller*, each based on short stories of his own, but the adaptation of 'Yours Truly, Jack the Ripper' was entrusted to *Lodger* adapter Barré Lyndon. But Lyndon was chosen for another reason as well: he had written a play about an immortal killer, *The Man in Half Moon Street*. What Lyndon had striven to rationalise in both of these earlier treatments – the motivation of the murderer – he was now called upon to subvert for the sake of a rabid display of pulp-mentality paranoia.

The troubles that afflicted *Thriller* arose because none of the producers engaged to oversee the series could agree on how its title should relate to the material on offer. A compromise was arrived at, whereby crime stories would alternate with more conventional horror fare. Bloch's story was duly adapted with this diversity of approach in mind. By the time 'Yours Truly, Jack the Ripper' reached the small screen, it was a perfect marriage of the contradictions going on behind the scenes.

> Captain Jago: "But it can't be Jack the Ripper. If he's still alive, he'd be 90 or more."
> Sir Guy Hollis: "He is alive. And he's in this city."
> **Edmon Ryan and John Williams in *Thriller*: 'Yours Truly, Jack the Ripper' (1961)**

'Yours Truly, Jack the Ripper' begins with a brief prologue set in 1888. A woman walks home through the fog in what by then was time-honoured tradition; once indoors, she turns to camera to face an unseen killer; a knife rises, phallus-like, into shot; a hand is clasped over her mouth and she sinks out of frame, as the eye of the camera remains fixed on the wall behind her head, where hangs a portrait of a mother and child. This leads into a music-hall turn, performed under the light of a street lamp by J Pat O'Malley, which puts the famous rhyme to song:

> "I'm not a butcher,
> I'm not a *kid*,
> Nor yet a foreign skipper.
> But I'm your own *dear loving* friend,
> Yours Truly, Jack the Ripper."

The change made to the second line was explicable in terms of network sponsorship and Jewish sensibilities, but that to the fourth was directed by Bloch's story, in which he misquotes. The sequence was filmed to provide a trailer at the close of the previous week's instalment of the show; it has nothing whatsoever to do with the tale that subsequently unfolds.

'Yours Truly, Jack the Ripper' (1961)

The real entrée features Guy Hollis attempting to convince a squad of Chicago detectives that the Ripper is at large in their city. Hollis is supported by John Carmody, a police psychologist equally convinced of the theory of an immortal murder-monster stalking down the ages. (In the original story, Carmody remains cynical throughout.) The rest of the film then alternates between the action dictated by Bloch's story and new scenes of the Ripper stalking victims while police stakeouts attempt to catch him in the act.

In the story, Bloch provides Hollis with a rationale for his extraordinary hunt: his mother was murdered by the Ripper. He describes the killer thus: "He took my mother's life and the lives of hundreds to keep his own hellish being alive. Like a vampire, he battens on blood. Like a ghoul, he is nourished by death. Like a fiend, he stalks the world to kill." The turning point comes when Carmody is made aware of Hollis' motive, and the fact that he will never relinquish the chase; there is then only one thing to do. All of this is lost in translation to the screen.

The Lodger's John Brahm directed more than his share of the episodes commissioned for *Thriller*, but not the one that might best have suited him. Bloch's story was placed in the unrewarding hands of Oscar-winning actor-turned-director Ray Milland. His directorial style was flat and functional and better tuned to realist pieces like *The Safebreaker*, which he shot in 1958. As such, the scenes of police stakeouts in 'Yours Truly, Jack the Ripper' are efficiently staged; the horror elements and long expository exchanges are less well handled. Worst of all is the hash that Milland makes of Bloch's surprise ending.

Prior to killing Hollis, Carmody leaves their table at the strip joint (which the latter has reasoned will be the site of the next murder) to check on the welfare of the girls. He makes his way to a dressing-room door: "Are you all right?" Carmody inquires. "Well of course, I'm all right. Why shouldn't I be?" Miss Beverly Hills replies. "I just wanted to make sure, that's all," comes the rejoinder. "Well, now you've made sure." Carmody closes the door again and returns to his table. The scene was included to point the finger at the psychiatrist in the final stages of the drama, only for it to be withdrawn again when the girl remains unharmed and thus make the switch back to Carmody the more unexpected. In Milland's ham-fisted staging, the incident pans out like so much padding.

"Not John... Jack," says Carmody, sheathing his knife and strolling away in the studio fog. The final sequence is so badly choreographed as to be almost independent of what has gone before. Nothing leads to it, even indirectly, and nothing is alluded to in the teleplay that might make sense of it, as in Bloch's story: "I believed him then. He wouldn't give up. He wasn't just a drunken babbler any more. He was as determined, as relentless as the Ripper himself. Tomorrow he'd be sober. He'd continue the search. Perhaps he'd turn those papers over to the FBI. Sooner or later, with such persistence – and with his motive – he'd be successful. I'd always known he had a motive," Carmody narrates. Any of this could have been turned into dialogue in the adaptation. None of it was.

Carmody was played by Dana Andrews lookalike Donald Woods, best known to genre fans for *The Beast from 20,000 Fathoms* (1953) and *13 Ghosts* (1960). His cynical smirk and plasticated features were well-suited to Bloch's concept of the Ripper as an abhuman entity. They were the only elements of 'Yours Truly, Jack the Ripper' which were. Bloch found himself better served by *Thriller* in his own adaptation of 'Waxworks', an episode that *was* directed by John Brahm, expressionistically, and which featured an extraordinary performance from Oscar Homolka.

> "He disappeared from the scene as suddenly as he had come, but similar murders followed at intervals in other countries. There are many who believe that Jack the Ripper still walks the earth, still continues his diabolical activities. That's a chilling thought..."
> Boris Karloff introducing Thriller: 'Yours Truly, Jack the Ripper' (1961)

Presumably for reasons of personal antagonism (if the caricatures in the story are anything to go by), Bloch had located his killer among the 'subterraneans', the narcissistic north-side Bohemian community of Chicago, and this was maintained in Lyndon's teleplay. As Sir Guy is at pains to explain: "Soon after Jack the Ripper disappeared from London, an artist – said to be an American – vanished from his lodgings and left some bloodstained clothing behind. Later on in Dusseldorf, after similar murders, the police learned of a man who spent all his time studying in art galleries. In Cleveland, a man who had vanished was said to be an art dealer. And in Bordeaux, France, they discovered an artist who always destroyed his pictures, which is what the man in London had done."

All this was added by Lyndon, as Bloch had relied on cheap jibes at the expense of the "so-called intelligentsia." Why the Ripper should have been accorded a measure of artistic skill is not made clear in either story or film, unless it was merely Bloch's way of scoring points, but the embellishments which Lyndon supplied have some merit to them:

After the 'double event', a man lodging at 22 Batty Street, which runs parallel to Berner Street where Stride was killed, vanished from his rooms, leaving behind him a bloodstained shirt. Some newspaper reports alleged that he was an American, but none that he was an artist, nor was he the only suspect sought for being in possession of bloodstained clothing at the time. In 1967, however, a Polish serial killer named Lucian Staniak (whose sobriquet – 'Red Spider' – would have warmed Bloch's heart) was arrested for the murders of more than 20 young girls over a three-year period. Staniak was a painter, and he earmarked his victims from fellow attendees of the Art Lovers' Club in Krakow. Staniak's paintings were as lurid as his crimes, which echoed those of the Ripper in the poetic missives penned in red ink which he was wont to send to the police and which earned him his nickname: "There is no happiness without tears; no life without death. Beware, I will give you cause to weep."

Staniak's motive was vendetta, with perhaps dozens of women paying the ultimate price for the actions of a single one, which rather vindicates the Matters theory. But the conflation of life and art that was represented by the 'Red Spider' was to find its way into Ripper lore, when a much more talented painter than the insane Lucian Staniak suddenly began to appeal to a new clutch of writers on the case, and the resonant colour motif of an inspirational neckerchief produced a real 'Red' Jack as suspect for the Whitechapel Murders.

An interesting aside relates to the picture that hangs on the wall behind the victim in the prologue of the film; it depicts a mother and child, and its purpose in the scene is to elicit audience sympathy. In chronological terms, it is fair to assume that this woman is meant to be Mary Jane Kelly, and it is enticing to think that either Lyndon or Milland might

'The Widow' by
Evariste Luminais

have employed the portrait to provide resonances of the real murder: one of the few items recorded as being found in the dead woman's room was a framed print on the wall – a picture that is referred to as 'The Fisherman's Widow'.

Kelly was said to have spent some time in France around 1884 – in the Paris of Rodin, Charpentier and Henri Rousseau – which, if true, is likely to be where she picked up the affected forenames of 'Marie Jeanette' by which she was alternatively known (notably by her lover, Joseph Barnett). Paris is also where she could have found a print of 'The Widow (A Fishing Family)' by Evariste Luminais, a Nantes-born painter of the realist school, with which she might have felt an affinity had she been widowed at 16, as she apparently claimed, and with which her meagre squat in Miller's Court was subsequently adorned.

When Kelly returned from France, the story goes, she was engaged in a West End brothel before a sudden downturn in her fortunes found her in lodgings off Ratcliffe Highway, St Georges-in-the-East. From here, she is reported to have made a last trip to the brothel to collect some items of a personal nature, and the next thing known for certain about her is that she was cohabiting with Barnett at a number of addresses in Whitechapel, on a downhill slide all the way to Miller's Court.

The print in question could conceivably have been part of the fixtures and fittings, always assuming a slum landlord like Jack McCarthy, despite his Gallic ancestry, had the taste and beneficence to kit out his 54-pence-a-week 'rents' with copies of French paintings. But if the print *did* belong to Kelly, and it was retrieved from the brothel in addition to articles of clothing, then it can be seen as circumstantial evidence (along with her French names) of both her trip to France and, given its subject matter, her notional bereavement. The fact that it remained in place after the murder lends no weight to the idea that it was *not* Kelly who died in Miller's Court, for were she to have fled the scene in haste, rather than been butchered, that print, in its frame, would not have featured among items which had to be taken along for the ride. It may be significant, poor as she was, that no personal possessions of Kelly's were found in the room after the discovery of the body. And Kelly was not as poor as some of those slain by Jack the Ripper, most of whom were found to have trinkets on their persons at the time of their deaths.

If the above is speculation – and it is! – it merely adds to much that is speculative about the Kelly case. Whether the set designer on 'Yours Truly, Jack the Ripper' was aware of the relevance is another matter, as only the cognoscenti would have recognised the reference; more likely is it that the presence of such a picture was a coincidence, along with many others that relate to 13 Miller's Court.

Thriller was effortlessly usurped in the hearts and minds of fantasy fans by the long-running science fiction anthology series, *The Twilight Zone*, a less grim, doomy, and foreboding foray into the far reaches of imaginative fiction, whose legacy was already in place even before the first episode of the Karloff show had aired.

The Twilight Zone was the brainchild of Rodman Edward 'Rod' Serling, the New York-born Emmy award-winning writer of the 1956 'Playhouse 90' production, *Requiem for a Heavyweight*, starring Jack Palance. An astute and original talent of compassionate concerns and persuasive prose, Rod Serling had numerous run-ins with American television's very own Ministry of Fear, the network sponsors, whose institutional unwillingness to offend potential consumers was not only diluting the very essence of his work but creating the imposition of corporate censorship on a totalitarian scale.

By 1959, Serling had come to realise that the only way to present challenging ideas about the human condition on the anodyne airwaves of America was through the medium of science fiction, where subtext passed by unnoticed and therefore unchallenged. Rather than consign his writing to the twilight zone of compromise and cop-out, he made virtue of a vice by literalising his disillusionment in that famously ironic title and, in turn, was able to launch a subversive showcase for social comment that proved acceptable to all. Against the odds, *The Twilight Zone* debuted in November 1959, to run for five successful years on CBS, and ever after in repeat syndication.

During its fourth season in 1963, an episode of *The Twilight Zone* drew on both 'Yours Truly, Jack the Ripper' and 'Waxworks' from *Thriller* for its inspiration. By this juncture, the moral and ethical considerations of earlier and better shows had taken a back seat to more clichéd stories with either a macabre bent or conventional sting in the tail. Serling himself had tired of the format by then, and the Ripper's belated appearance left the host of the series unable to provide any of the pithy polemic with which he might otherwise have enlightened viewers about the nature of serial killing.

> *"Now here we have another soul in torment: Jack the Ripper. Who was he? And which – of all the faces that moved about London's Whitechapel district – which one was his? And why did he feel driven to kill those pathetic drabs with one sweep of the knife you see here? ... I'm afraid we shall never know."*
> Martin Senescu (Martin Balsam) in *The Twilight Zone*: 'The New Exhibit' (1963)

Jack the Ripper was one of five murderers to feature as 'wax' models in a *Twilight Zone* episode entitled 'The New Exhibit', the other four being William Burke and William Hare, the Edinburgh-based 'resurrectionists', Albert W Hicks and Henri 'Bluebeard' Landru.

Martin Balsam and David Bond in 'The New Exhibit' (1963)

In a plot derived partly from *Mystery of the Wax Museum*, Feguson's Wax Museum is threatened with closure and mild-mannered curator, Martin Senescu (played by Martin Balsam), opts to store his favourite pieces – the five killers in the museum's 'Murderer's Row' – in the basement of his own home for safe keeping. Senescu's fondness for the exhibits slowly turns to obsession and when his wife, brother-in-law and former employer attempt to intervene, they are subsequently found dead in his basement. It appears to Senescu that the wax figures are somehow responsible – "You sure these ain't alive?" asks the gas man; "Not altogether," Senescu replies – but in typical *Twilight Zone* style, he is deluded: it is *he* who has been committing the murders all along. An epilogue shows the five figures housed in another museum, where a wax effigy of Senescu is now the newest exhibit alongside them.

The episode aired on 4 April 1963 and was directed by John Brahm. Brahm makes the most of the opportunities presented him to feature grim close-ups of the wax figures (all of which are played by actors). One shot in particular is eerily effective, as the five step off their podia in unison to threaten Senescu at the finale. However, Brahm is hampered throughout by witless lighting and cramped set-ups, due to speed of execution and the need for the piece not to play too dark on television. Script credit for the episode went to genre specialist Charles Beaumont, although 'The New Exhibit' was actually ghost-written in its entirety by Beaumont collaborator Jerry Sohl, and padding is evident for much of its length.

James Doohan in 'Wolf in the Fold' (1967)

The first two murders are implied, using camera angles and cutaways, in keeping with the premise that Senescu is responsible, but Brahm forgets himself on the third occasion: the film shows Landru springing to life to throttle the owner of the waxworks, whereas only a shot of the garrotte would have been required to maintain contextual integrity. This slip of the directorial whip has the effect of creating a 'trick' ending, and it betrays the rules of the genre.

As modelled by David Bond, Jack the Ripper comes with 'Joker' make-up and a long scarf thrown over his shoulder, harking back to the Spring-Heeled version of Leni's *Waxworks*. It is Jack who 'perpetrates' the first murder (that of Senescu's wife), but the episode as a whole was originally inspired by the mutinous exploits of axe-murderer Albert Hicks (a pirate hanged in New York on 13 July 1860), rather than those of the Ripper himself.

"I point out that Jack the Ripper slew at will in the heart of the most populous city of old Earth, and was never identified. I suggest the possibility of a hypnotic screen, which blinds all but the victim to the presence of the killer."

Mister Spock (Leonard Nimoy) in *Star Trek*: 'Wolf in the Fold' (1967)

A galactic retread of 'Yours Truly, Jack the Ripper' had Jack boldly go where no Ripper had gone before in producer Gene Roddenberry's groundbreaking sci-fi series *Star Trek*. Robert Bloch had reworked his original in techno-speak and sent it into space to challenge the crew of the Starship Enterprise, in a 1967 episode entitled 'Wolf in the Fold'.

Again, the question is posed as to how the killer was able to commit the atrocities and yet remain undetected. *Star Trek* offered up another answer in the jargon of science fiction, but it was not one which might have helped the police of Jack's day in their inquiries.

Stardate 3614.9, and Captain Kirk and company are partaking of some much-needed rest and recuperation on the fog-planet Argellius II, when someone or something starts to kill off its women with a knife. The finger of suspicion points to the good ship Enterprise's chief engineer, as he is habitually to be found hovering over the corpses with bloodied hands, clutching said knife. Nothing is ever that simple on *Star Trek*, though, especially where the wholesome motivations of its morally unimpeachable crew are concerned.

The stage-bound plot soon devolves into a prolonged courtroom scene, with an all-knowing computer presiding over the proceedings as judge and jury, while Kirk and first officer Spock act as counsels for both the defence of 'Scotty' and the prosecution of the real killer, which turns out to be the immortal entity of Bloch's original and which on this occasion has adopted the guise of Argellius administrator, Hengist (John Fiedler). From here the story descends into farce, as the entity leaps invisibly from body to body in an attempt to find a new host (an idea which would find its way into *Fallen*, in 1997), until its path is conveniently 'blocked' by the tranquillising effects of a sedative administered by ship's doctor 'Bones'. The entity finds itself trapped inside the corpse of the now-dead Hengist, with whom it is then beamed into the far reaches of space.

The episode is of marginal interest as an allegorical attempt to explore the concept of 'evil' in psychological, as opposed to philosophical, terms, but, as ever with *Star Trek*, any resolution of the moral complexities raised comes down to battling amorphous globs in studio space. *Thriller*, *The Twilight Zone* and *Star Trek* had all played their part in entrenching Jack the Ripper as an iconic villain for hire, and he continued to make guest appearances in similar series throughout the 1960s and 70s. The high point of these guest-spots was not reached until the 1990s, but as the sixties neared its end, the low point was less than a rubber-soled footfall away.

> Tipton: *"I believe that Jack is here."*
> Crown: *"That's insane."*
> Tipton: *"You have death to prove it. Here in the fog… Just like London fog. Watching, waiting… with his knife sharp and his eyes bright. Here…"*
> **Patrick Horgan and Stuart Whitman in *Cimarron Strip*: 'Knife in the Darkness' (1968)**

Venerated author Harlan Ellison eventually disowned the script that he had supplied to the western series *Cimarron Strip* in 1968, as he had a disconcerting habit of doing when the powers that be failed to treat his work as holy writ, so the impression is gained that had it been shot to his original, the resulting episode would have been that much better. It was a clever tactical ploy that anyone might have been tempted to make had 'Knife in the Darkness' appeared on screen with their own name attached to it.

"Strange weather," observes Stuart Whitman's US Marshall Jim Crown as fog descends over the Christmas festivities of *Cimarron Strip*, a television show in the *Bonanza* tradition that ran for only 23 episodes during 1967-8. The portent is realised within minutes, as a floozy from Pony Jane's bordello is stabbed to death in an alley and the cast begin to eye each other with suspicion.

Cimarron Strip was peopled with the expected clutch of regulars: a female innkeeper, a dependable Scot and, conveniently in the case of 'Knife in the Darkness', a newspaper editor who turns up a copy of the London *Times* to deduce that the killer in their midst is none other than Jack the Ripper.

Tom Skerritt and Jill Townsend in 'A Knife in the Darkness' (1968)

Minor red herrings are expeditiously disposed of as more murders ensue and the suspects narrow to two: an émigré from George Lusk's Vigilance Committee, allegedly hunting the Ripper, and a dreamy-eyed vagrant looking for "peace and fulfilment" out west. No prizes for guessing which of them it turns out to be. Crown's incisive line of inquiry comes down to asking all and sundry what exactly they are doing in Cimarron City, a cunning ploy that fails to reveal the killer only because the place is uncharacteristically filled with oddballs who either own, sharpen or appear to be conspicuously handy with

knives. With Crown content to wander the streets in futile search, discovery of the Ripper falls to a secondary character and a suitcase full of bloodied clothes.

Ellison, like Robert Bloch, is noted for dabbling in Ripper territory in the short story field and 'Knife in the Darkness' was original in following up the suggestion that the real Ripper may have fled to America after the last of his murders, a line of inquiry developed by Stewart Evans and Paul Gainey in their book *The Lodger: The Arrest and Escape of Jack the Ripper* in 1995. Ellison's Ripper has killed seven women in England, beginning with Martha Tabram, but by the time of his arrival in Cimarron City, he is reported to have killed *another* seven (in New York, Washington, Philadelphia, Chicago and Kansas City). This puts his ten-week record in London to shame, and to show what a fast worker he really is, he not only notches up three more victims in the space of a single night but has time to pen Marshal Crown a 'yours truly' letter, as well.

The Ripper turns out to be a man on a mission of 'social reform' and is climactically brought to book by a trio of Indian braves who, with a little incongruous help from the Great Spirit, manage to succeed where the entire police force of London signally failed. Canonical references are dotted about to smooth the story along but bent to suit the plot. Mention is made of the Thames drowning of Montague Druitt, a one-time Ripper suspect himself (although Druitt's connection to the crimes was not made public at the time), while an anomalous interjection has the newspaper editor telegraph the Vigilance Committee's George Lusk personally, to verify a matter of detail.

Five more episodes of *Cimarron Strip* followed 'Knife in the Darkness', after which the show was cancelled. "Are you sure he was Jack the Ripper?" Crown asks the young editor at the finale, oblivious to the mass of evidence which has been accumulating around him but not, apparently, to the need for the case to remain unsolved. He was right to doubt: as Whitman headed into the sunset, Jack turned up back in England in more jocular vein.

> "Fine steel this, sir, yes... Very fine. Like a surgeon's... scalpel."
>
> Knife grinder in *The Avengers*: 'Fog' (1969)

The working title of *A Study in Terror* did not go to waste for long: in 1969, an episode of the long-running ABC Television series *The Avengers* picked it up for a tale about the 'Gaslight Ghoul', who murdered nine women in 1888 and now seems intent on doing much the same to members of the World Disarmament Committee, on a visit to London under the protection of tongue-in-cheek British agent John Steed (Patrick Macnee) and his sidekick Tara King (Linda Thorson). There was certainly plenty of 'Fog' around on this occasion, enough to obscure the city's entire population, save the motley of stock characters, as well as the increasingly tired modish humour of a show that already was past its prime.

'Fog' (1969)

'Fog' has a cartoonish feel to it; it is neither slick, scary, sardonic, nor even as sartorially elegant as earlier *Avengers* episodes. In keeping with the whimsical approach of the series as a whole, the low-camp London streets are deserted except for the anachronistic presence of peasants playing barrel-organs, selling 'lucky white heather' or sharpening knives, and members of the delegation take to wandering about in the fog pursued, in short order, by the Gaslight Ghoul.

John Hough's direction is appropriate to the light-hearted style of the film, but it is also repetitious and over-reliant on deep-focus set-ups where hands, feet and assorted bric-à-brac bob in and out of frame at the beginning or end of each shot. This was a technique brought to *The Avengers* by Robert Fuest, who directed many of the series' best episodes and went on to helm *The Abominable Dr Phibes* (1971). In Hough's hands, it was beginning to look like pastiche.

Guy Rolfe, as the Ghoul, plays the role to the hilt – which is more than can be said for the rest of the cast – and he turns in a respectable villain who quotes Poe's 'For Annie': "And the fever called 'Living' is conquered at last." The show's writer, Jeremy Burnham, clearly had aspirations to higher things, but Hammer's *The Horror of Frankenstein*, which he wrote the following year, could not have been among them. Nigel Green, a red herring in 'Fog' but another actor who could chill the marrow when he chose, also went the way of Hammer Horror in the wake of *The Avengers* but, by 1972, his long career as a featured player in some of the fantasy genre's best-remembered films was over, when he was found dead from an overdose of barbiturates.

Of passing interest is the location chosen for the Ghoul's fictitious crimes: Gunthorpe Street is the contemporary name for the alley that was formerly known as George Yard, where Martha Tabram was stabbed to death by an unknown assailant, possibly Jack the Ripper.

Hammer attacks

If an opportunity was lost to genre cinema in the 1960s, it was that Jack the Ripper never managed to feature in a Hammer horror film.

Hands of the Ripper (1971)

To some extent, Hammer's thunder in respect of Jack had already been stolen by Mid-Century's film of 1959, especially as it had been written by Hammer protégé Jimmy Sangster. Hammer's rivals in the field of Technicolor terror, Tigon and Amicus, were also remiss in their lack of attention to Jack. In Tigon's case, chief executive Tony Tenser could be forgiven for thinking that he already had paid his dues in that regard by co-producing, with former partner Michael Klinger, *A Study in Terror* in 1966, a film which itself had attempted to emulate the Hammer style. The Amicus Productions of Milton Subotsky and Max J Rosenberg, on the other hand, had enjoyed an intimate relationship with writer Robert Bloch in the same period, and many of Bloch's short stories had been used to form the basis of Amicus films: *The Skull* (1965), *Torture Garden* (1967) and *The House That Dripped Blood* (1970). Notwithstanding, Amicus side-stepped the chance of delving into Bloch's regular literary excursions into Ripperdom, such as 'A Toy for Juliette' or the 1954 novel, *The Will to Kill: Was He to be Jack the Ripper All Over Again?*

Tigon and Amicus preferred to play their horror films in modern dress for budgetary reasons – unlike Hammer, which benefited from a relationship with costumier Monty Berman.

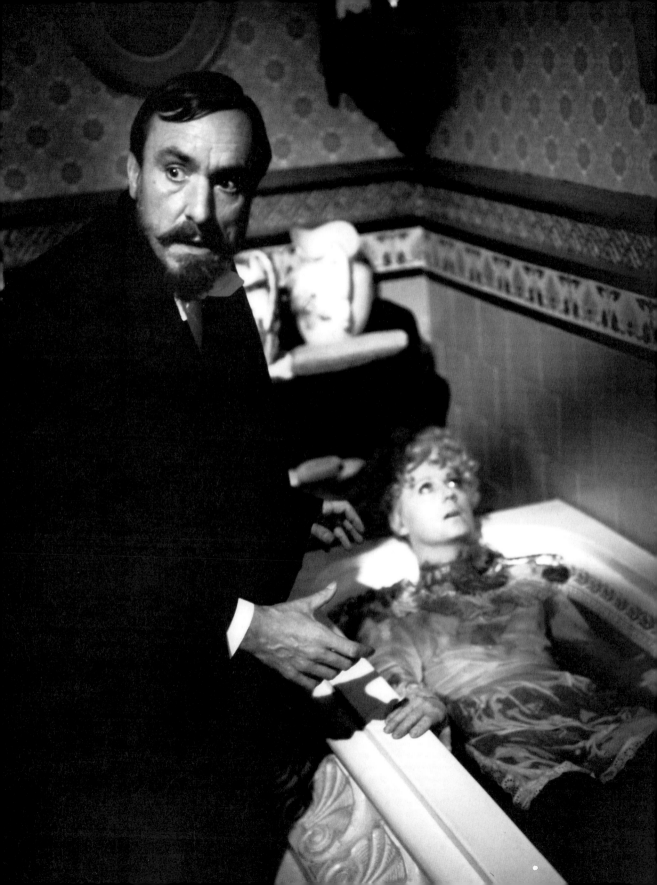

Amicus, in particular, fought paradoxically shy of any overt bloodletting on screen. Hammer was the supreme master of the period horror film and its creative personnel had a natural bent for all things Victorian, as they had proved time and again since *Dracula* in 1958, but an executive tendency to opt for the safe bet constantly precluded more diverse deployment of this unique facility.

All this conspired to leave Jack floundering in the backwaters of an occasional feature, usually foreign in origin, for much of the sixties. By 1970, however, Hammer, and the British film industry as a whole, was in trouble. Frankenstein and Dracula had run their respective courses as viable series characters; key personnel had upped and left the company; new ideas were in short supply. These factors, coupled with the easing of the censorship restrictions that had reduced the number of knife thrusts permissible to Mid-Century in its attempt to deal with the Whitechapel Murders, encouraged Hammer to make up for lost time. Early in 1971, Jack the Ripper was suddenly flavour of the month – not once, but twice. And nearly the *same* month, at that.

The films in question were *Hands of the Ripper* and *Dr Jekyll & Sister Hyde*, both of which were appropriately released during October-November of that year. Produced three weeks before its thematic stable-mate but released to theatres three weeks after it, *Hands of the Ripper* was by far the better and more original of the two.

Jack's role in the film is restricted to a pre-credits sequence, cribbed, in part, from *The Son of Dr Jekyll* (1951). The Ripper is pursued to his lair in the West End of London by a mob out for his blood. Inside the sanctuary of his home, he is revealed as having a wife and daughter. "There was another murder. They're looking for Jack the Ripper. It's you… It's you they're looking for!" screams the wife, before finding herself on the receiving end of Jack's knife as the daughter looks innocently on.

To the archetype created by Jimmy Sangster, *Hands of the Ripper* added a collodion scar on Jack's cheek. He plays no real part in the story, other than to sire the film's killer. In the prologue, and in typical Hammer style, only his eyes feature prominently, which adds an element of monster chic to the character. This striking sequence opens the way to a succession of set-piece murders, all of them committed by Jack's unwitting daughter, now grown to womanhood, whenever she becomes entranced by twinkling lights, though none of them are committed with a knife (in fact, everything but: a poker, a vanity mirror, a clutch of hat-pins, a pair of lorgnettes and finally the 'hands' themselves, in an Ottermole-like strangulation attempt), the Ripper's genetic blueprint having apparently been confined to temperament alone.

> Madam Bullard: *"Blood… A man has murdered the mother of his child, and that child… that child… is Anna."*
> Pritchard: *"Who is this man?"*
> Madam Bullard: *"Berner Street… Berner Street. Why it's… Oh, my God! He's the Ripper!"*
> **Margaret Rawlings and Eric Porter in Hands of the Ripper (1971)**

Hammer's familial brand of horror invariably kept death within domestic environs, and *Hands of the Ripper* was no exception. The daughter of Jack the Ripper is unwittingly adopted by a kindly physician and follower of Freud (Eric Porter), intent on using new-fangled psychoanalytical techniques to get to the bottom of her murderous seizures. Mayhem

Eric Porter and Marjie Lawrence in *Hands of the Ripper* (1971)

Eric Porter and
Angharad Rees in
Hands of the Ripper
(1971)

unsurprisingly results from his actions and Anna (Angharad Rees) murders both his maidservant, a matronly whore and a society clairvoyant before fatally wounding the good doctor himself. Trailing her with the aid of painkillers to St Paul's Cathedral, where she now threatens the welfare of his prospective daughter-in-law in the Whispering Gallery, the dying Pritchard urges her to jump from the balcony and join him below. She obliges, and a 200-foot plunge puts paid to both their careers.

The film's theme of congenital madness is conveyed by the visual marker of a Ripper who is clearly ravaged by a virulent skin-disease, which erupts to stigmatise Anna's hands when she is overcome by the desire to kill. Through this simple mechanism, the idea of a syphilitic avenger again raises its head and gives substance to Pritchard's otherwise prurient 'investigation' into the psychology of murder. It is an original concept, and consistent with Victorian thinking that nothing was beyond the reach of science. "You can't cure Jack the Ripper and that's who she is," he is admonished by a libidinous politician. This being a Hammer film, Pritchard's detractor is proved to be correct.

Time and place are actually Hammer-Victorian, in spite of the story having been set in the Edwardian period of 1903: when Pritchard decries the truth of Anna's genesis as "a lot of mumbo-jumbo about Jack the Ripper being her father," he adds obligingly, "He's been dead for 15 years." Little seems to have changed in the East End in the meantime, though, despite the demand for 'Votes For Women' scrawled on a Whitechapel wall. Fleeing from Pritchard's home after nearly decapitating his maid, Anna is taken to the ample bosom of a blowsy tart named 'Long Liz' (the real-life nickname of Elizabeth Stride), whose charity she repays by stabbing her in the eye with the aforementioned hat-pins.

Ex-television director Peter Sasdy's handling of the horror elements in the film veers dangerously close to parody at times: a medium is speared to a door with a poker, and remains pinned to it as it swings open in front of the astonished doctor; Pritchard relieves himself of a sabre through his midriff by hooking it onto the handle of another convenient door and heaving himself to the floor, in a variation on the sore-tooth-and-length-of-string model. A mock-operatic score attempts to supply the climax with a transcendent quality, but for all its superficial appearance to the contrary, only a vestige of old-time Hammer style remains attached to a film that should, by rights, have been called 'Blood' and not *Hands of the Ripper*, to avoid the trap into which *Grip of the Strangler* had fallen, which was not about strangling either.

If Jack provided little more than the inspiration for *Hands of the Ripper*, at least his presence was integral to the story, something that could not be said for Hammer's second offering

Eric Porter at the climax to *Hands of the Ripper* (1971)

along the same lines. Any good that *Hands of the Ripper* may have done for Jack was quickly counteracted by the treatment meted out to him in *Dr Jekyll & Sister Hyde*.

Although similar in incident, the two films borrowed little from one another. Each came from a separate source: a story by Edward Spencer Shew in the case of *Hands of the Ripper*, and the quirky and novelettish pen of television scriptwriter and *Avengers* co-creator Brian Clemens in that of *Dr Jekyll & Sister Hyde*. Nor were they stylistically a pair: *Hands of the Ripper* had been shot on the expansive stages of Rank's own Pinewood Studios, whereas its companion in crime was unceremoniously shoehorned into the cramped and expeditious hangars of Elstree.

> *"You've heard of the murders in this area? Well, I have been involved in them in an official capacity. There's a terrible similarity about all the victims. About what he does to them…"*
> Prof Robertson (Gerald Sim) in Dr Jekyll & Sister Hyde (1971)

Into the mix that Brian Clemens concocted for *Dr Jekyll & Sister Hyde* went one part Robert Louis Stevenson, one part Burke and Hare and one part Whitechapel Murders, the whole spiced with a liberal dash of the company's own *The Man Who Could Cheat Death* (1959).

For no reason relevant to the plot, other than the excuse that it provided for the removal of body parts in the style of *The Man Who Could Cheat Death*, Dr Jekyll is chemically seeking the Elixir of Life. The ensuing potion produces a sex-change instead, and he transforms into 'Sister Hyde'. To return to his former self requires additional doses of serum, which in turn necessitates the extraction of female hormones. Jekyll acquires the services of a pair of body snatchers to provide the appropriate corpses, but when they are put out of business by a baying mob, Jekyll takes to stalking the streets himself, scalpel in hand. As word of the outrages spreads through Hammer's standing-set on the Elstree lot, Jekyll is again 'transformed', this time into Jack the Ripper. All ends predictably. If *Hands of the Ripper* had borrowed its opening scene from the prologue of *The Son of Dr Jekyll*, *Dr Jekyll & Sister Hyde* does likewise with its closing one: Jekyll/Hyde falls to his death from the top floor of his own house.

Jekyll is suspected of being the killer when Professor Robertson, a former colleague, establishes which organs have been excised from the victims and equates them with Jekyll's experiments. "There's no point in offering him this one," he informs the mortuary attendant whose dealings with the doctor have involved the sale of dead bodies "What he wants has already been taken." Though no direct mention of it is made in the film, it would be fair to assume that Jekyll has removed the women's ovaries, which places him closer to the real Ripper's activities in this area than any previous screen incarnation.

Closer still is the set-piece murder which forms the centrepiece of the film. Roy Ward Baker was always a better director than the material that came his way in the later stages of his career, but in the killing of Betsy (Virginia Wetherell), *Dr Jekyll & Sister Hyde* rises out of its self-ploughed rut. Tart and doctor repair to a sparsely furnished room. She undresses by the light of an open fire while he sits opposite her contemplating the impending deed. She asks him to help her with her corselette; he stands behind her, slits the fastenings with his knife and hurls her onto the bed. A frenzy of violence ends the encounter.

The point about this sequence is its uncanny resemblance to the killing of Mary Jane Kelly. The room is bare but for bed and chair, the former sited in approximation of Kelly's own. At some time during the early hours of 9 November 1888, a 'blazing' fire was lit in number 13. Kelly was slaughtered on her own small bed. Whether by accident or design, Baker comes

Ralph Bates and Virginia Wetherell in *Dr Jekyll & Sister Hyde* (1971)

Ralph Bates in Dr Jekyll & Sister Hyde (1971)

nearer than any director before or since to a real sense of the Miller's Court murder, not only through his staging of the action but through his filming of it in the flickering firelight and against an eerie blue-green glow from studio lamps, which plays on a deeper level to intimate the presence of death. Taken in isolation, this episode ranks as one of the high points of Ripper cinema.

Unfortunately, the merits of the scene have to be tempered by the vehicle in which it found itself. Writer Brian Clemens – British television's answer to Robert Bloch – was a dab hand at contrived thrillers and his way with plotting matched that of Jimmy Sangster, evidenced in Dr Jekyll & Sister Hyde by the neat dovetailing of all the disparate elements in the story. His approach to such material left no room for anything as unpredictable as verisimilitude, however, and whatever might be good about the film is offset by a medley of stereotypical

Dr Jekyll & Sister Hyde
(1971)

images of Victorian street life, imported from 'Fog' and a slew of old Christmas cards. "Tall man wearing a tall hat and a dark cloak," advises a poster warning of the killer; "He is tall, bearded and has been seen carrying a carpet bag," said an identical handbill in *The Avengers* episode.

Two monsters for the price of one in a single film was a sign of the decline of Gothic horror subjects by the early 1970s. Before long, a half-dozen feature players were required, as well. Ray Milland's second encounter with Jack the Ripper came on the other side of the camera, as one of a number of former star-names no longer able to command an audience on their own, but who together were still thought to be capable of rustling up paying customers.

Terror in the Wax Museum borrowed the plot of Patrick Hamilton's stage play *Gaslight*, dipped it in a glaze of *House of Wax* and 'The New Exhibit' episode from *The Twilight Zone*, and relocated it to a museum in the London borough of Westminster in Tudor England of the 16th century if the set design was to be believed – but just before the turn of the 19th, according to the dating in the script. Milland, still with his trademark toupée and puckish grin despite his 66 years, led a similarly aged troupe of ex-leading actors in a flamboyant throwback to more innocent times. Alongside him were John Carradine (*House of Frankenstein*; 1944 among more than 400 others!), Patric Knowles (*Frankenstein Meets the Wolfman*; 1943), Elsa Lanchester (*Bride of Frankenstein*; 1935), Louis Hayward (*The Son of Dr Jekyll*; 1951), and Broderick Crawford (perhaps best-known for his stint as Dan Matthews in the long-running television show *Highway Patrol*). Some contemporary resonance was provided by Mark Edwards, last seen in *Blood from the Mummy's Tomb* (Hammer; 1971), while Maurice Evans (slumming it after a long stint in the *Planet of the Apes* franchise) and Shani Wallis (Nancy in the film version of Lionel Bart's *Oliver!*) completed the eclectic mix.

If its cast dated from the 1930s, its plotting from the 40s, and its look from the over-saturated 50s, *Terror in the Wax Museum* was an antique in every respect: a nostalgic wallow in matinée monsterdom. The fact that it surfaced in 1973 is proof of the parlous state of the industry in general at that particular time.

"And there he stands – Jack the Ripper – this fiend, with the skill of a surgeon, who has committed at least 20 murders in the city of London. And only this morning, another foul murder was committed in this very museum…"

Harry Plexner (Ray Milland) in *Terror in the Wax Museum* (1973)

Claude Duprée (Carradine), owner of Duprée's Wax Museum in London, is murdered with the knife that is clutched in the hand of a wax figure of Jack the Ripper. A prospective purchaser of the museum's exhibits is also killed. Duprée's niece, now 'living over the shop', imagines that she sees the figure of the Ripper come alive. The police investigate, but the solution to the puzzle is more mundane: Tim Fowley (Hayward), landlord of the tavern next door, has been insinuating himself into the museum at night dressed as Jack the Ripper, in order to search for Duprée's hidden treasure; murder was an expedient in the pursuit. A climactic set-to with the virile Sergeant Hawks (Edwards) sees Fowley impaled for his trouble.

The film's utilisation of the Ripper is no more revealing than Leni's original *Waxworks*. Jack is merely a convenient bogeyman, whose hat and cloak provide the appropriate shadow-fall in supposedly spooky scenes. "We found out he had once been an actor," Maurice Evans' police inspector says of Fowley at the close. The remark might equally have been applied to any of the participants. For those who have not guessed the identity of the killer by the end of the film, there is a novel fade-out to clarify matters, but there are no obvious suspects prior to this denouement, therefore no suspense, and spilt blood is in tragically short supply.

Marred by a ridiculous 'X' certificate in Britain, no doubt at the insistence of the distributor, *Terror in the Wax Museum* is lacking in every virtue which might otherwise have encouraged the paying public to part with the price of admission. It is mannered and tedious, its ponderous narrative leavened only by the inclusion of two faddish dream sequences, and any pleasure that is to be gained comes from watching the clutch of seasoned pros go through their paces. Milland himself fares better here than he did a decade earlier with 'Yours Truly, Jack the Ripper', and his new-found confidence was a sign of the career revival which followed his appearance in the top-grossing *Love Story* (1970). His tongue-in-cheek style and flippant manner were ill-suited to serious horror programmers, however, and they were better employed in *The House in Nightmare Park* (released the same year), which was at least intended to be funny.

Ripper motifs also found their way into a film called *Knife for the Ladies* in 1974, a risible western romp shot in Arizona's Old Tucson, which appeared to be directed more towards rustling up some buddy-appeal between the ornery sheriff (Jack Elam) and the young detective from back East (Jeff Cooper) than it was towards invigorating the tired rash of Ripper-style killings that are decimating the working girls of Mescal. The similarly titled episode of *Cimarron Strip* provided the theme, as well as the sub-plot about the lynching of the wrong suspect, but the real killer turns out to be town matriarch Ruth Roman, who keeps a syphillis-ravaged son locked in an upstairs room. (A similar story, but with a different setting, turned up in Tyburn's *The Ghoul* the following year.) Roman's motive is the predictable one of revenge against the town's whores, but rationale goes out of the window when she climactically attacks a pretty young pianist whose only crime appears to be that she plays Chopin's Étude in E major in the wrong place at the wrong time. Thwarted in her murderous intentions by her deformed offspring – "Don't you appreciate, my son? I killed them for you!" – she then turns the knife on him before Elam pops her clogs with his trusty six-shooter.

Nicole Shelby and Broderick Crawford in *Terror in the Wax Museum* (1973)

Ray Milland in *Terror
in the Wax Museum*
(1973)

In the early seventies, it was plain for all to see that genre filmmakers had not only run out of ideas, they had run out of the talent to put whatever ideas they still had into practice. Like the rest of his kind, Jack the Ripper had been homogenised into another standby for the fantasy factory, a mass-produced monster-suit which could be tailored to fit any occasion.

"*I've finally been processed. They made me adjust to modern times. This is 1888, isn't it? I'm Jack. Cunning Jack. Quiet Jack. Jack whose sword never sleeps. Hats off, I'm Jack. Not the good shepherd. Not the Prince of Peace. I'm Red Jack, Spring-Heeled Jack, Jack... from hell. Trade name? Jack the Ripper!*"

Jack Gurney (Peter O'Toole) in *The Ruling Class* (1972)

What humour there was on the satirical stage by the end of the 1960s was of a strictly black variety. Where previous Rippers had railed against the evils of modernity, Jack Arnold Alexander Tancred Gurney, 14th Earl of Gurney, was encouraged positively to embrace them by his analyst and a kangaroo court of literal peers in *The Ruling Class* (1972), the screen adaptation of a savage attack on the mores of the British Establishment by playwright Peter Barnes, which was originally staged in Nottingham in November 1968 before transferring to London in February 1969. Barnes followed *The Ruling Class* with his own interpretation of Wedekind's *Lulu*.

By 1969, student protests over tacit European support for the Vietnam war were followed by troops being despatched to Northern Ireland after a flare-up in the Troubles. Respect for the British monarchy and government in general had fallen to a new low, similar to that which afflicted the nation at the time of the Whitechapel Murders. The battle of Red Lion Square on 15 June 1974, in which protesters were bludgeoned by mounted policemen, held echoes of the Trafalgar Square riot on 'Bloody Sunday', 13 November 1887.

This mood of dissent contrived to give *The Ruling Class* a vicious cutting edge and Peter O'Toole, still a class act at this juncture, turned in a towering performance in the film version as Jack Gurney, mild-mannered but feeble-minded heir to the Gurney title, whose delusions of grandeur have led him to believe that he is Jesus Christ personified, until 'peer' pressure persuades him to conform to type. He transforms into Tory man, taking up his hereditary seat in the Upper House among the mouldering corpses of the 'hang 'em and flog 'em' brigade, as Lord Jack... the Ripper.

The Ruling Class took its cue from the widespread sense of disenchantment to launch a searing indictment of the upper classes as shallow, self-serving, senile, sanctimonious and seriously out of touch with the prevalent mood. It was timely in suggesting that Jack the Ripper might have been a member of the British aristocracy, when such a notion had only recently been postulated by serious researchers. It was also uncannily prescient in charging that the Establishment invariably closed ranks to protect its own, no matter the nature of the crime. At the climax of the film, love has been replaced by hate as the philosophy to which the Earl adheres and, in a bid to cut the last tie that binds him to his former self, he murders his wife with a Ripper's knife.

Peter O'Toole and Alastair Sim in *The Ruling Class* (1972)

On 7 November 1974, Richard John Bingham, 7th Earl of Lucan, allegedly tried to do exactly the same to his own wife in the basement of his London house at 46 Lower Belgrave Street, though with a bludgeon in his case. The Lucans' nanny, Sandra Rivett, was the tragic recipient of the fatal blows in Lady Lucan's stead, and her assailant was forced to flee. The police investigation into the murder came up against a wall of silence among Lucan's gambling cronies at the Clermont Club and the trail of the missing Earl eventually went cold at Newhaven docks on the Sussex coast. A story was put out that the Earl had committed suicide by drowning somewhere in the English Channel, but it has since come to light that 'Lucky Lucan' was just as likely to have been helped flee the country and start a new life, possibly in Africa, by friends and associates with interests abroad. If *The Ruling Class* appeared to some to be excessively bilious at the time of its making, it soon paled by comparison with the reality that it stood to accuse.

As the world became increasingly entrenched in the polarisations of Cold War politics, and the United States moved further to the Right, so American representations of the Ripper followed suit. Popular media now cast him as a universal force of evil, which had happened to manifest itself in London more than a century before.

The British cultural view of Jack remained unchanged, and does so to this day: interest is spurred by the 'who' and the 'why', a secular and pragmatic approach, typical of the killer's country of origin. The Hollywood machine, on the other hand, settled for the opposite view. Who and why, cause and effect, were no longer relevant. Hollywood opted to formulate its own who and why according to prevalent preconceptions; no excuses, no justifications, no moral grey areas. Jack the Ripper was evil incarnate and would be depicted as such. He was the Devil's Wind, and he could play fast and loose with any story concept in any period; no more a man tied in time by the unbreakable bonds of history, but an anti-man, a demonic entity sent from Hell to test the faith of the faltering and remind the less vigilant to remain on their guard, lest the forces of chaos sweep over them. As Robert Bloch prosaically put it in 'Yours Truly, Jack the Ripper': "'I tell you, a mad beast is loose in this world! An ageless, eternal beast, sacrificing to Hecate and the dark gods!'"

Bloch's sermonising from the pulpit of pulp had come to pass: the Ripper was a Devil god, elevated to the Temple of Terror where fabulous film fiends lurked, each one interchangeable according to mood and moment, and all of them emblematic of the Evil within, or without.

Peter O'Toole as Lord Jack in *The Ruling Class* (1972)

A recent book on the portrayal of the Ripper in popular media subscribed to the theory that he represents the potential for evil that resides in us all; a singular viewpoint, it relates only to Jack on American screens. To the British audience, he has never been anything more than a criminological curiosity, a pathological puzzle. But by the 1970s, American teleseries were dominating the world and, on American television, the Ripper was already auditioning as a killing machine, devoid of rationale, reason and the last vestige of his original humanity. He was steadily being reduced to the level of mechanical monster, garbed in the guise of a bygone age, but prescient of present threat.

In deferring to the demands of television, Jack achieved the schizoid split that commentators had attributed to him from the very beginning. In Britain, he continued to be viewed as a deranged Dr Jekyll – or the insidious agent of an autocratic regime at worst – but in America, he was now an unambiguous Hyde, with no way back to the bottle.

The first series to extrapolate the idea that the worm which had eaten into the Ripper's skull could transplant itself as easily into any susceptible psyche was called *The Sixth Sense*. This short-lived Universal Television show was an attempt to make a drama out of a psychic crisis, and it majored on stories with an edge of extrasensory perception.

> "*Adam's been conditioned to receive extrasensory reception from London, 1880s. The woman who was murdered in the park last night was attacked in the same way as women in London, in the 1880s, were attacked by Jack the Ripper.*"
> Dr Michael Rhodes (Gary Collins) in *The Sixth Sense*: 'With Affection, Jack the Ripper' (1972)

In 'With Affection, Jack the Ripper', two highly unattractive series regulars, by name of Elizabeth (Patty Duke) and Dr Michael Rhodes (Gary Collins), are conducting an ESP experiment on Adam (Robert Foxworth), who through an etching of a Whitechapel street scene and a tune played on a harpsichord, finds himself transported in time into the mind and body of the Ripper. In this trance-like state, he murders – or attempts to murder – several contemporary females, waking afterwards with no knowledge of what has transpired. When realisation dawns on the dull-witted duo who have set this murderous chain of events in motion, Adam is brought back to a semblance of reality, but not before being sufficiently traumatised by the experiment to have to be carted off to a padded cell and promised "the best care available." The incompetent investigators then switch their sights to the next poor sap who will be stupid enough to ask for their help in the following week's episode.

Directed with some panache by *Grip of the Strangler*'s Robert Day, 'With Affection, Jack the Ripper' is constructed like an exercise in silent cinema as Day attempts to convey the confusion in Adam's mind through visual imagery alone. It left the viewer, like Adam, wondering what on earth was going on and only made it more obvious that the film's scriptwriter had no clearer idea of the mechanics of ESP than its recipient in the show. The mood of the piece was so intense that it was beyond the receptive powers of its intended audience to tune in on a regular basis. *The Sixth Sense* folded after 13 episodes. It was re-syndicated in abridged form some years later, itself, by then, having been magically transported into Rod Serling's *Night Gallery*.

The Whitechapel scenes all took place on the obligatory fog-bound street, empty save for victim and victimiser, both of them trapped in an eternal ritual of pursuit. This said more about the narrative dynamic of the dream-medium of cinema than it did about ESP. But the episode had extracted the essence of the Ripper as a swift and silent force of evil and, in so doing, it removed the need to explicate his presence in the drama, which left him free to indulge in the activities for which he is justly notorious. Such reduction of the character was timely and convenient. Another show desperately seeking super-villains for a weekly dose of monster mayhem lost no time in appropriating it.

The inclination of the American news media to demonise serial killers with shorthand sobriquets aped the treatment meted out to monsters in the pulps, from whom the tabloids took their lead. Earle Leonard Nelson, who claimed at least 22 victims in north-western states during 1926-7 (all of them boarding-house landladies advertising rooms to let) was dubbed 'The Gorilla Murderer' because of some physiognomic similarities. In 1948, Martha Beck and Raymond Fernandez were christened 'The Lonely Hearts Killers' when it was discovered that they had sought out their victims through the personal columns of local newspapers. Edmund Kemper became 'The Co-ed Killer' as a result of a series of brutal murders of hitchhiking students in Colorado in 1962. The murders of 13 Bostonian women during 1962-4 created 'The Boston Strangler' in the unlikely form of Albert De Salvo. The unknown killer who terrorised California for five years from 1969 to 1974, taunting the police with a string of cryptic messages as he went, was nominated as 'Zodiac' for the way he signed off his missives.

The Pasadena press added 'Candy Man' Dean Corll to the roster in 1971, while New Yorker David Berkowitz became the 'Son of Sam' during his murder spree in 1976-7. Also in 1977, Kenneth Bianchi and his cousin Angelo Buono were known as the 'Hillside Stranglers' during their series of sex murders in Los Angeles. And Timothy Spencer, the 'Southside Slayer' of Richmond Virginia, joined the list in 1987 after a similar series of murders involving young women. If fame is sometimes the name of the game for serial killers, commentators are not slow in bestowing it.

European sensibilities regarding the separation of fact from fantasy form no part of the cultural consciousness of the United States. In consequence, one of America's most notorious serial killers, Wisconsin necrophile Ed Gein, became the model for Norman Bates in Bloch's novel *Psycho*, while 'Zodiac', who at one point threatened to kill a busload of children, was the inspiration behind the serial killer in Don Siegel's *Dirty Harry* (1971). As art followed life, so the principle applied equally the other way around.

In 1981, a series of murderous gang-rapes was initiated in Chicago by a trio consisting of Edward Spreitzer and two brothers by the name of Kokoraleis, through which they became known as the 'Chicago Rippers'. The prototype for this nickname originated with a 1974 television show called *Kolchak: The Night Stalker*, the premiere episode of which had featured Jack the Ripper at large in contemporary Chicago.

The *Kolchak* series had sprung from an earlier telefilm about an invincible killer terrorising Las Vegas. Three years later, when a 25-year-old drifter and self-confessed devil-worshipper named Richard Ramirez held suburban Los Angeles in the grip of an unholy terror for 14 months through a campaign of rape, mutilation and multiple murder, the inability of police to apprehend him inspired a widespread belief in his invincibility. Accordingly, Ramirez was christened 'The Night Stalker' by an obliging press, after the killer in the film. "I will be avenged! Lucifer dwells within all of us," he was quoted as saying when sentence was eventually passed, in echo of the simplistic platitudes of the pulps to which he, like Ed Gein, was no doubt devoted.

The ABC Television series *Kolchak: The Night Stalker* had its origins in a 1970 novel by Jeff Rice (*The Kolchak Papers*) and two 'pilot' films: *The Night Stalker* (1972) and *The Night Strangler*

(1973), both of which were written by Richard Matheson. The first of these pilots placed a centuries-old vampire in modern-day Las Vegas, while the second set down in Seattle the immortal alchemist of Barré Lyndon's *The Man in Half Moon Street*. Both monsters found themselves up against the wile of hard-bitten newspaper hack Carl Kolchak (Darren McGavin), who managed to dispose of them despite an incredulous attitude on the part of both his superior and the relevant local authorities.

So successful in ratings terms was the first of these pilots that a spin-off series was inevitable. Actor McGavin, smitten with the concept of Kolchak, stepped in to co-produce the show, sidelining Matheson in the process and drafting in inferior talent to pen the weekly instalments, all of which featured a creature on the rampage in Chicago (where the reporter now worked for a wire service). McGavin had firm ideas about the character of the world-weary newsman, veteran of innumerable temporary postings since being fired from 'The New York Journal': "The day he was fired, he was wearing a seersucker suit, a black string tie and a white shirt with a button-down collar. So he's still wearing 'em. He hasn't bought a suit of clothes since." His vision of the show that he now co-owned was less precise. "I didn't want our viewers thinking we were some sort of monster-of-the-week thing," he said, and for a single season in 1974, proceeded to give them exactly that.

Darren McGavin as Carl Kolchak

The problem with *Kolchak: The Night Stalker* was formula; if ever a show adhered to a formula, this was it. The original telefilm had featured a vampire able to fell a bevy of policemen with a single blow while engaging in superhuman feats of agility (a novelty that Matheson saw fit to reprise in his adaptation of *Dracula* for director Dan Curtis, and which Curtis used again in *The Norliss Tapes*; both 1973), with the character of Kolchak presented as a lone percipient of events, permanently at odds with disbelieving city officials. When it came to extending the premise of one man against one monster (or another) into a weekly series, the idea quickly soured. How quickly was clear from the first episode, in which 'The Ripper' returned to haunt the massage parlours of the Windy City.

> Vincenzo: "Now let me see if I understand you. Are you saying that our Ripper is the same man who killed those seven women in London in the 1880s?"
> Kolchak: "1888, to be precise. And there was five, always five women."
> **Simon Oakland and Darren McGavin in** Kolchak: The Night Stalker: 'The Ripper' (1974)

'The Ripper' episode is little more than a pale imitation of the two pilots: Jack is presented as an immortal entity, impervious to bullets, and capable of leaping tall buildings at a single bound. By a process of logic explicable only to writers of cheapskate television shows,

Kolchak figures out that the Ripper's 'Achilles heel' is electricity and, tracing him to his lair in a deserted house, he lures him to a nearby stream into which he thrusts a power-cable which promptly fries him to a crisp. The Ripper dematerialises and the house burns to the ground, leaving nothing to substantiate Kolchak's story.

Along the way, little is divulged about Jack to underpin the threat, beyond his aptitude with the now-ubiquitous sword-stick. "Throat cut. Her head was nearly severed from her body," Kolchak is informed by a colleague, the detail of his having removed his victim's kidneys being saved for a lunch where the imparting of the information affords McGavin the opportunity to mug distaste, and the network censors that of passing it off as humour.

One of the many irritants of *Kolchak: The Night Stalker* was that despite the activities of its various monsters being witnessed by literally hundreds of policemen and bystanders, Kolchak is the only one ever to realise the truth or to have the vaguest insight into the supernatural origins of the various creatures. "How could you explain it? Who could explain it? Who would believe it?" Kolchak muses rhetorically at the close. True to his surmise, nobody in the show seems capable of believing the evidence of their own eyes – let alone the ravings of the annoying little reporter in their midst, even when the killer destroys a police station single-handedly. ("Your superman is upstairs on the maximum security floor," the police chief informs Kolchak as Jack promptly tears the door from its hinges and strides out of the building.) Carl Kolchak invariably shrugged his shoulders and moved swiftly on to the next monster, but the effect on the audience was exhaustion of patience in short order.

Not all the Kolchak episodes were as bad as 'The Ripper', although all of them deferred to the basic maxims which were set out in the pilots. Jimmy Sangster, ensconced in Hollywood at the time, contributed a more original piece about a Rakshasah with the Lovecraftian title of 'Horror in the Heights', while 'The Spanish Moss Murders' was also among the better examples.

Kolchak's tedious wisecracking harked back to Warner Bros dramas of the 1930s, with their feisty female reporters, apoplectic editors and goofy gophers. The Warner lot housed an army of writers to provide the witty lines, whereas *Kolchak: the Night Stalker* appeared to rely on the ad-libbing ability of Darren McGavin alone. A repetitive mumble and pop-eyed stare in time of trouble was no substitute for a sharp remark, as the show found to its cost when it ran out of sponsorship after 20 episodes.

Jack liked a joke himself – as his missives to the police made clear – but in the 'Ripper' episode of *Kolchak*, he was the butt of the humour rather than the one responsible for it. That soon changed with a starring role in which his talent for deadpan delivery and barbed aside was employed to the full. In an attempt to reconnect him with Jekyll and Hyde, the original script for Orion Pictures' *Time After Time* had called for the Ripper to be none other than Robert Louis Stevenson, the idea being that a celebrity villain would complement the film's celebrated protagonist. This misguided notion was abandoned, and the character was renamed John Leslie Stevenson instead. The role remained essentially the same and Jack was still given the best lines. For one who had written to Scotland Yard on 25 July 1889, "You have not caught me yet you see, with all your cunning, with all your 'Lees' with all your blue bottles," it was somehow fitting that the devil should finally be given his due.

"My name is H G Wells. I came here in a time machine of my own construction. I'm pursuing Jack the Ripper, who escaped into the future in my machine... !"
Herbert Wells (Malcolm McDowell) in *Time After Time* (1979)

Transplanting Jack the Ripper to other times and places was fast becoming a staple of science fantasy on television, but the first feature film to attempt it came in 1979 from the pen of Nicholas Meyer, writer of the Holmes spoof *The Seven-Per-Cent Solution* (1976). "You're a regular Sherlock Holmes," David Warner says to Malcolm McDowell in *Time After Time*, but Meyer's new script was no sequel to Herbert Ross' Holmes picture: McDowell is actually H G Wells in the person of his own creation, the Time Traveller, who is forced to set off in hot pursuit of the Ripper (Warner) when the latter flees to the future using the very device that Wells has built for himself.

Time After Time opens in 1889, with the obligatory tart ejected onto the street and into the hands of the waiting Ripper. They repair to an alley where he introduces himself as 'John', before appending a punch-line pinched from Bloch's story: "But my friends all call me Jack." The dawning realisation on the tart's face is followed by a ripping sound low down on her abdomen. The remainder of this bright and breezy exercise in genre crossbreeding never quite lives up to its opening moments.

Jack the Ripper is Dr John Stevenson, "chief of surgery in Whitechapel" according to the Abberline lookalike whose clutches he escapes by whisking himself off in a time machine built by H G Wells (a writer not renowned for his engineering skills). The history of human endeavour in the intervening period is marked by rather too many milestones of Jewish history, reflecting Meyer's native sympathies, and how the protagonists manage to touch down in San Francisco, as opposed to London, is explained away by the presence of the machine as a museum exhibit in a room dedicated to Wells. (One is tempted to ask why no one has since tried it out.) "The world has caught up with me and surpassed me," Jack intones, as he is held in thrall by television news footage of everyday atrocities. "Ninety years ago, I was a freak. Today, I'm an amateur." It sounds convincing, and it is a theme that would find echo in *From Hell*, though even a casual reading of history gives the lie to it: if Stevenson desired to murder and mutilate at leisure, he might have spent his time-travelling hours more profitably as a mercenary in the Hundred Years War than as a man-about-town in the Bay area.

There are some good jokes, though: "You may have been born yesterday, but I certainly wasn't," says a Frisco detective to Wells, who by now has followed Jack to the present day through the cunning ploy that, like a bad penny, the machine is programmed to return to base after use. After his own arrival in the future, Wells falls for a thoroughly modern miss and the real thrust of the plot is forgotten till Jack, desperate to regain some screen time, kidnaps the girl in order to refocus Wells' attention on the matter in hand.

"What time is it?" asks Jack's third San Franciscan victim. "Later than you think," he replies, and a sudden sweep of his knife shoots a red droplet up to his eye, where it trickles as a tear of blood. It is an elegant metaphor, and it is reinforced in the climactic scene, when he gives a tacit nod to Wells to pull the plug on the machine and atomise him into infinity. Both of these insights might have been better placed in a film other than this one, however.

Time After Time fails time and again to exploit to the full the possibilities inherent in its concept, and terminology rather than technology becomes the focus of Wells' perplexity about the 'Utopia' in which he inadvertently finds himself. With its lush Miklos Rozsa score and prolonged romantic interludes, the film, like Wells, was itself out of time in a cultural era that was about to embrace the 'splatter movie' and 'slasher' film. In this one respect, at least, *Time After Time*'s Jack had got it right: he was to find himself more at home in the 1980s than would the science fictional dreams of H G Wells.

David Warner and
Malcolm McDowell
in *Time After Time*
(1979)

"That's the last anyone will hear of Jack the Ripper," Wells proclaims as he climbs into his machine for the journey home. He might have been able to travel into the future, but he was clearly unable to *see* into it.

By the end of the 1970s, fantasy was the dominant force in film and most of the studio blockbusters during the last half of the decade had plots which were fantastic in origin. But, with the notable exception of *Star Wars*, it was fantasy of a less simple-minded kind than before, and realism in terms of sex and violence (in particular) had advanced at a disproportionate rate to the censorious pace of change in the preceding 30 years: the great white shark in *Jaws* (1975), for example, ate men *alive*. *Time After Time* was a novel way to remake Wells' *The Time Machine* with a grittier spin, and the inclusion of Jack the Ripper in its plot was in tune with the mood of a moment in which *The Omen* franchise had made a superstar of the Devil himself. His appearance in *Time After Time* may have done Jack a lasting disservice by entirely removing him from his own time and space, but it did furnish the continuum for his next appearance on screen.

Had *The Lodger* been remade again in the post-1960 era, the role of the homicidal house-guest would most likely have gone to Victor Buono, the natural successor to Laird Cregar's heavyweight crown. Buono shot to (Best Supporting Actor) success in 1963 after stealing Robert Aldrich's *Whatever Happened to Baby Jane* from under the wrinkled noses of its two stars, Bette Davis and Joan Crawford. His career went rapidly downhill from there, as he quickly became typecast in the kinds of roles that myopic casting agents felt befitted his huge girth. Consequently, he was soon guest-spotting as various larger-than-life villains in the likes of *The Man from U.N.C.L.E.*, *Batman* and *The Wild, Wild West*. He had played a *Lodger*-like character named Leo Kroll in *The Strangler* in 1964, but not until 1980 was he given the opportunity to ape the Cregar role and play Jack the Ripper for real in an episode of the aptly titled *Fantasy Island*, one of the many long-running and terminally lightweight weekly teleseries from the decade's self-crowned king of prime-time, Aaron Spelling.

Fantasy Island was endowed with the most puerile premise imaginable: diverse characters arrive on the island to be granted their hearts' desires by a 'wishmaster', the anthropomorphous Mr Roarke (Ricardo Montalban), and his diminutive sidekick Tattoo (Hervé Villechaize). The point of this fable was to exemplify the old adage about being careful what one should wish for, and Roarke is a combination of angel and storyteller, present only to enable the spatio-temporal displacements necessary to literalise the show's premise and ensure that the moral is driven home after the required running-time has elapsed. Many of the tales were transmitted in interleaved pairs that shared a common theme, thus 'With Affection, Jack the Ripper' (as per the episode in *The Sixth Sense*) was complemented by 'Gigolo', both stories being about self-obsessed males who preyed on unsuspecting females.

'Gigolo' arrived at the usual happy ending, with the protagonist learning to respect both himself and the woman whom he is intent on pursuing, but Jack turned out to be surprisingly irredeemable and was climactically dispatched to die beneath the wheels of a coach, thanks to the timely intervention of Mr Roarke. The moral of this story appeared to be that some men simply cannot be reformed.

> "I am very much afraid that Jack the Ripper found your gateway back here and is, at this very moment, loose on Fantasy Island."
> Mr Roarke (Ricardo Montalban) in *Fantasy Island*: 'With Affection, Jack the Ripper' (1980)

Lorraine Peters (Lynda Day George) desires to discover the identity of the Ripper for a book she is writing. After putting up some initial resistance, Roarke consents to send her through a time portal where she finds herself in Whitechapel, 1888. In a matter of minutes, she has her nominated suspect banged to rights and her theory vindicated, but Jack – or Dr Albert Fell as he is here, in a blatant steal of the Ripper's surname from *Room To Let* – has been trailing her all along, and he follows her back through the portal to the island in the present day: "Oh Lord, I was born out of time. There is so much work I can accomplish here," he intones wistfully. (Fell is unnerved by electric light and hearing a voice on the other end of a phone line, even though both inventions were already becoming commonplace by the end of the 1880s; a neater touch is the 1980 calendar displaying the show's transmission date in the US.) Despite this nod in the anachronous direction of *Time After Time*, Dr Fell soon tires of the debauches of modern life – typified by sarong-clad native girls cavorting around palm-fringed studio sets – and he whisks Peters back to the Whitechapel streets. At the critical point, a *deus ex machina* arrives in the form of Mr Roarke, and Jack is doomed to his unrepentant fate.

As with many such series episodes, the germ of a good idea exists at the core of 'With Affection, Jack the Ripper', this one being that someone who sought to establish the identity of the Ripper might themselves become a target for the killer's knife. But that is a side issue soon dispensed with in a prolonged chase that sees Buono do little more than skulk menacingly in bushes, scalpel in hand. Allusions to *The Lodger* go marginally deeper than Buono's shadowing of Cregar's performance in the 1944 film – Peters finds herself in 'Braham' (Brahm?) street when she arrives in Whitechapel – but the episode is only elevated out of mindlessness by Buono's impressive presence, which undercuts the saccharine frivolity of the show's overall format at every turn: his sneering close-ups are often palpably threatening, and his ominous bulk and crooked stance are cunningly etched with chill foreboding.

> "I have a remedy for all your ills, harlot!"
> Dr Albert Fell (Victor Buono) in *Fantasy Island*: 'With Affection, Jack the Ripper' (1980)

Buono is accorded the minimum of dialogue by writer Don Ingalls, but he plays the unrewarding role with conviction. His automaton style as the Ripper derives from the fact that Ingalls was also responsible for the identically-titled episode of *The Sixth Sense* eight years previously, in which Robert Foxworth behaved in similar fashion. Unlike his slim-line counterpart, Buono weighs in as the harlot-hating homicide with such authority as to suggest that, were he to have pursued his quarry along the Whitechapel Road for real, he could literally have bowled her over before setting to work with his knife. No matter the fraudulent context in which the character found himself, and the purely iconic representation to which he was required to submit, *Fantasy Island*'s Dr Albert Fell is one of the great Rippers of the small screen.

By the 1980s, Victor Buono was an actor prematurely out of time, and like Cregar before him, ongoing weight problems contributed to an early demise. A mere two years after his appearance in *Fantasy Island*, Buono succumbed to a fatal heart attack; he was 43. His death robbed genre cinema of its last great post-war heavy, but before the final curtain call, he had at least handed Jack the high point of his career in the pulps so far.

> "Judge Pettibone has ordered us to search for the Ripper. Do you understand? Jack the Ripper."
> Police Inspector (Barry Melvin) in *What the Swedish Butler Saw* (1975)

The low point, on the other hand, was a period sex romp made in Sweden and originally filmed in 3-D, called *What the Swedish Butler Saw* (*Champagne pa Sengekanten*; 1975). The film starred Ole Søltoft (of *Seventeen* fame) as Jack Armstrong, whose wish to become a photographer of Victorian *poses plastiques* has him purchase a studio with hidden passages which Jack the Ripper (Martin Young) uses as a bolt-hole. Not that this is of any consequence in a plot engineered solely to offer up as many scenes of female nudity and softcore copulation as possible. Jack's appearances are mainly confined to ogling flesh from behind a portrait of Queen Victoria. When the police arrive late in the proceedings, ostensibly to search for him but really to give the girls a breathing space, the Inspector remarks, "The next thing you know, someone will have me questioning the Prince of Wales!"

That someone was Thomas Stowell, and it was not the Prince of Wales but his son, Prince Albert Victor Christian Edward (known as 'Eddy'), Duke of Clarence and Avondale, in an article for the *Criminologist* entitled 'Jack the Ripper A Solution?' Stowell later denied having made any such claim, but that was not enough to stop a New York author named Frank Spiering from cobbling together *Prince Jack* in 1978, one of the most specious so-called exposés in the entire Ripper canon, but one which would inevitably provide some equally unprincipled filmmakers with a new suspect to justify another rake over the coals in Mary Kelly's grate.

David Warner as Jack the Ripper in *Time After Time* (1979)

Chapter Five
Not-so-final Solutions

Jack the Ripper is a misnomer. The name conjures up visions of a lone assassin, stalking his victims under the foggy gaslight of Whitechapel. It is just this mistaken notion, inspired almost solely by that terrifying nickname, which rendered the murders of five East End prostitutes in 1888 insoluble. For Jack the Ripper was not one man but three, two killers and an accomplice.

Stephen Knight, *Jack the Ripper: The Final Solution* (1976)

While genre films had come to see Jack in a frivolous or emblematic light, a new generation of researchers now conversely had begun to take him more seriously than ever. These self-annointed 'Ripperologists' were in much the same mould as the amateur criminologists of old, except for the fact that mutual interest was confined to the Whitechapel Murders alone or, less productively, to seeking the identity of Jack the Ripper.

In the six years between the release of *A Study in Terror* and that of *The Ruling Class* in 1972, Jack the Ripper had featured in some eight other films or television series episodes, culminating in the two Hammers. Many more were in the pipeline. This resurgence of interest in the Whitechapel murderer was matched by a number of new books on the subject, begin-ning with Tom Cullen's *Autumn of Terror* (Bodley Head; 1965) and ending – for the moment – with Daniel Farson's *Jack the Ripper* (Michael Joseph; 1972).

A veiled article in the November 1970 issue of the *Criminologist*, by a Dr Thomas Stowell, appeared to implicate Prince Albert Victor Christian Edward (later Duke of Clarence and Avondale), eldest son of the Prince of Wales and grandson of Queen Victoria, commonly known as 'Eddy', in the Whitechapel Murders. The piece was widely disseminated on the strength of the assumption and it brought a new flurry of activity on the Ripper front, as a result. In January 1973, BBC television embarked on an investigation of its own from which the Corporation intended to produce a 'definitive account' of the case, and which it considered might even *solve* the 85-year-old mystery. According to Stephen Knight, a 20-year-old reporter on the *East London Advertiser* at the time but soon to be the author of *Jack the Ripper: The Final Solution* (Harrap; 1976), BBC involvement sprang from "a revival of interest in Jack the Ripper which had started two years before and showed no signs of abatement."

Chosen to head up the investigation on screen were British television's two most popular fictional detectives: bullish Detective Chief Superintendent 'Charlie' Barlow (Stratford Johns) and his more amiable sidekick, DCS John Watt (Frank Windsor), both of whom had begun their careers in *Z Cars* before being promoted to a show of their own called *Softly, Softly*.

Jack the Ripper was transmitted in six 50-minutes episodes, commencing with 'The First Two' and proceeding from 'Double Event', 'Butchery', 'Panic' and 'Suspects' to 'The Highest in the Land?' The show set Barlow and Watt to work on every scrap of information which BBC research could provide and notionally required them to come up with an answer to the age-old puzzle by the application of modern investigative techniques. The running commentary of the two principals was offset by period reconstructions of key events and witness testimonies.

Jack the Ripper (1988)

If viewers lost their way by the second episode, it was no surprise: in order not to miss a trick, the show was so information-heavy that it was constantly disappearing up blind alleys of its own making and digressing into all manner of inconsequential tangents. Foremost among these was the introduction of an alleged link between one of the Whitechapel murders and the supposedly secret rites of freemasonry.

During a search of surrounding streets that was conducted after the discovery of the body of Catherine Eddowes, a piece of material which the murderer had cut from his victim's apron in order to carry away the missing body parts turned up a quarter of a mile away in the entry to Wentworth Model Dwellings in Goulston Street. Chalked on the wall above the bloodstained rag was a message: 'The Juwes are The men That Will not be Blamed for nothing.' Without labouring a wealth of esoteric detail, suffice it to say that this wording was thought to have possible masonic significance, especially in light of the role that Commissioner Warren (himself a prominent mason) played in ordering it erased before it could be photographed. Much debate was given over to the theoretical 'meaning' of this message, and the resultant conjecture that Warren had recognised the writer – Jack the Ripper? – as a fellow mason from the text.

If nothing else, *Jack the Ripper* served to illustrate why the police took five long years to apprehend 'Yorkshire Ripper' Peter Sutcliffe, whose own reign of terror began in 1975, the very year that Elwyn Jones and John Lloyd, the two writers responsible for the show, published their findings in a book. In 1979, the Yorkshire force received a tape-recorded message which it took to be from the Ripper. So convinced were the investigating officers that Sutcliffe was eliminated from the inquiry after the latest in a total of nine interviews because he had a Yorkshire accent, not a Wearside one like that on the tape. After Sutcliffe's eventual arrest, the tape was designated a hoax but one which had wasted two years of police time and directly contributed to the deaths of three more women.

There is nothing to substantiate the contention that the 'writing on the wall' in Goulston Street was the work of Jack the Ripper, let alone to connect it to the mystic lore of masonry, but the consequences which have arisen from its cryptic entreaty bear comparison with those from the much-publicised but ultimately unconnected voice-tape in the case of the Yorkshire Ripper. Fortunately, the time wasted on this occasion was only that of the Ripperologists.

> "Here, we've been beating our brains out for months, trying to find out who was Jack the Ripper – people have been trying for 80 years – and the Director of Public Prosecutions may be sitting on a file, knowing the answer all along... Only he isn't telling."
> Chief Superintendent Charlie Barlow (Stratford Johns) in
> Jack the Ripper: 'The Highest in the Land?' (1973)

After more than five hours of talking heads transmitted during the summer of 1973, the top telly cops of *Jack the Ripper* came to the conclusion that the evidence was inconclusive. To say that this was something of a letdown after the scale of information overkill which preceded it would be to understate the case. Barlow and Watt took another stab at investigating 'unsolved' crimes for a short-lived BBC series of 1976, called *Second Verdict*. As the duo were unable to shed any new light on the Whitechapel Murders, the astonishing thing is that someone should have offered them a second chance.

The show's surprise witness, held back to the last few minutes of the sixth and final instalment, was a man called Joseph 'Hobo' Sickert, illegitimate son of painter Walter Richard Sickert, who had a strange tale to tell regarding his own genealogy. According to Sickert, his mother was the result of a union between *her* mother and the aforementioned Prince Eddy, and she had been looked after in infancy by a nanny named Mary Kelly.

Sickert went on to delineate the ramifications of this alleged royal indiscretion: "Various people high in the government and the royal household became very worried indeed about the possibility of the news getting out that the heir presumptive to the throne of England had married and had a child, and that the child had been born of a Catholic mother. You have to remember [that] it was a time when the possibility of revolution was thought to be a very real one and that the problems and violence surrounding Ireland were at their height. It was decided that Mary Jane Kelly would have to be silenced. The operation was undertaken by the driver, John Netley, and the royal physician, Sir William Gull. To conceal the dangerous motive behind Mary Kelly's death, and the inquiries they were making for her, she was killed as the last of five women in a way that made it look like the random work of a madman..." Sickert neglected to explain why neither mother nor child had been put to death in the same expedient way, let alone Walter Sickert and others evidently privy to the information.

Sickert's onscreen appearance via Super-8 ciné film was self-scripted and carefully rehearsed, and Barlow greeted his intervention in the way that John Neville's Holmes had greeted the tale told him by Angela Osbourne: "Joseph Sickert believes it," Watt remarks when asked for his opinion. "What Mister Sickert believes isn't evidence," Barlow replies. But it was evidence enough to set in motion a conspiracy theory that would reverberate through the halls of Ripper research to this very day, and change the face of Ripper cinema in the process.

Knight after knight

After the televising of the BBC's *Jack the Ripper*, the young Stephen Victor Knight was sent to interview Sickert on behalf of the *East London Advertiser*, in the hope that he had more to tell. This interview and others led Knight to believe that Sickert's father, Walter, had been part of an elaborate plot whose roots lay at the heart of Victoria's government. The premise of the conspiracy was that Prince Eddy (a known bisexual) had sired an illegitimate daughter with a Catholic shop-girl and part-time artist's model named Annie Elizabeth Crook. When this supposed threat to the stability of the monarchy became known, mother and daughter were spirited away and a quintet of Whitechapel tarts, who were also privy to the affair through the employment of one of their number (Mary Kelly) as the child's nanny, and who collectively had proposed a spot of blackmail as a result, were disposed of by a team of assassins comprising Sir William Withey Gull, Physician-in-Ordinary to the Queen, coachman John Netley and Assistant Chief Commissioner of the Metropolitan Police, Robert Anderson. All Knight's alleged conspirators, including Robert Arthur Talbot Gascoyne-Cecil, 3rd Marquess of Salisbury and British Prime Minister since 1886, were said to have been bound together by their oaths of allegiance to the Worshipful Brotherhood of Freemasons, a 'secret' trades society dating back constitutionally to 1723, and a source of fascination for the author in its own right.

Knight turned this into a book, but, not content with the intrigue spun by Sickert, he decided to spring a surprise of his own in the last chapter of what was now called *Jack the Ripper: The Final Solution*. And no one was more surprised than the chief witness in Knight's case for the prosecution, Joseph 'Hobo' Sickert. It was one 'revelation' too many, as it turned out, and it soon rebounded on the young writer in a most unexpected way: when he realised that Knight was contriving to put his father's name more into the frame than was originally intended, Sickert withdrew his co-operation and put it on record that he had made everything up.

A sense of impending crisis can be detected in the pages of the book, as Knight's prose becomes increasingly ardent in its plea to the reader to see things his way. As the rhetorical entreaties mount, the author pitches in with what is, for him, the only possible – nay, *final* – solution: Gull was the Ripper, enticing his victims with poisoned grapes and operating, literally, from inside a coach driven by Netley, while Anderson stood in as occasional lookout. But even this is overturned and replaced by a new and more 'final' solution at the close. "It all sounded terribly unlikely," Knight says himself at the beginning of his tale, before madness prevails. And so it is. But here is not the place to expound the reasons why; others have done that with the attention to detail in which Knight is so remiss.

What begins as a lucid account of a fresh inquiry into the thickening fog of disinformation, with much in the way of new data and clever insights, ends in a frenzy of unsubstantiated assertion and wild conclusions. Knight seems to be unaware throughout that he has fallen victim to a clever hoaxer intent on finding somebody who independently would corroborate his claim to one of the oldest cons in the book: illegitimate heir to the throne of England. Only in the final few pages of the book, as Knight's imagination runs away with him, does he reveal that Walter Sickert, not Robert Anderson, was the 'third man' in the triumvirate of terror that operated under the name of Jack the Ripper. At the selfsame time, the trap is sprung: Joseph Sickert is son to Walter and *Alice Margaret Crook*, bastard daughter of Prince Eddy and Annie Elizabeth, whom his father had subsequently taken as a mistress. Ergo, he is of Royal blood. One can almost sense the air of satisfaction in Sickert's silence at this point, as Knight is allowed to arrive at the conclusion all by himself.

'Hobo' Sickert's self-serving participation in both *Jack the Ripper* and *Jack the Ripper: The Final Solution* aside, Knight was advocating the idea that the Ripper was effectively a collective: Walter Sickert and William Gull to commit the murders, and John Netley to plug the gaps in geography and credibility by driving them to the scenes of the crimes.

It seems not to have occurred to Knight (and others who have trod the same path since, but with a different choice of candidates) that, having failed to find a suspect who could fit all of the canonical crimes, he was merely creating a *composite* killer out of individuals who separately could be made to fit one or two of them. By pairing these, the Whitechapel murderer is revealed.

Walter Sickert had an alleged fixation about the Ripper (he supposedly left 'clues' in his paintings) and had been nominated as the killer by the dubious opinions of contemporaries; he was supposedly involved in the Crook conspiracy, and the fact that he conceivably went about the streets with painterly implements matched witness descriptions of a Ripper who was seen holding a parcel (as opposed to a Gladstone bag). But Sickert was clearly no doctor, and nor did he have any known surgical skills. Knight's solution? Complement him with a doctor who may also have been seen in the area at the time of the murders and to whose house Robert Lees had ostensibly led the police in psychic trance. Sickert and Gull were thus combined to form Jack the Ripper, and the loose ends of the case were neatly tied into place. Apart from the lack of evidence with regard to each man individually, there is no independent support for the contention they were ever known to each other.

Intriguing as Knight's theory was, none of it stood up to close examination once the first wave of excitement washed away. More troublesome was the fact that in 1978, two years after publication of Knight's book, Joseph Sickert renounced his complicity in the affair to the *Sunday Times*, stating publicly that the part relating to Jack the Ripper was entirely a hoax, a "whopping fib" (he subsequently retracted this also). Knight was forced onto the defensive, and he attached an addendum to his book which attempted to explain away the fact that Sickert had recanted his story. What the imbroglio achieved was to put investigators onto *Knight's* trail, who rapidly unravelled the intricate web of deception. "His research is now known to have uncovered evidence which proved that the story was untrue," Philip Sugden wrote in his *The Complete History of Jack the Ripper* (Robinson, 1994). "Yet he shamelessly chose to suppress it."

The counter-evidence is easy to come by, and a point-by-point repudiation of Knight's theory can be found in *The Ripper Legacy: The Life and Death of Jack the Ripper* by Martin Howells and Keith Skinner (Sidgwick & Jackson; 1987), a book which then proceeds to offer a similarly unsupported solution in its stead. But Knight would brook no dissenters from the conspiracy which he had preordained from the fantasising of Joseph Sickert, not even Sickert himself. In terms of tabloid journalism, he was a credit to his profession.

Jack the Ripper: The Final Solution and its more recent variant, *The Diary of Jack the Ripper* (Smith Gryphon; 1993), continue to find favour with those to whom the witchery of *The X-Files* holds more appeal than cold, hard facts. Both have been comprehensively damned as fodder for the gullible by those who know, but that alone is not enough to stop the already converted from continuing to preach to themselves.

Jack the Ripper: The Final Solution became an immediate best-seller at a time when conspiracy theories, especially those which related to government 'cover-ups' (of so-called UFOs, for example) were again exerting a hold on the popular imagination. The book pitched Gull and his cohorts so firmly into the frame for the Ripper murders that after 25 years of house-arrest on suspicion, no amount of counter-evidence has yet been able to exonerate them. And Stephen Knight himself was soon placed beyond the inquisitorial reach of his accusers: nine years after the book's publication, its author died of a cerebral haemorrhage at the age of 33.

When the search for the Ripper notched up a gear as a result of Jack the Ripper: The Final Solution, suspects began to be sought among the celebrity class. The commercial attractions of such a prospect were obvious, but so was a reversal of the old adage that 'where there's muck there's brass', and unfounded accusation quickly became the order of the day. Stephen Knight had opened his book with a quote from Shakespeare's Twelfth Night: "Here comes my noble gull-catcher." He and others might have profited more from an acquaintance with Richard III:

> "Since every Jack became a gentleman,
> There's many a gentle person made a Jack."

While the controversy remained to be settled, screenwriter John Hopkins (a veteran of Z Cars and co-writer of the James Bond film Thunderball) saw in Knight's elaborate conspiracy about the Ripper murders a scenario more suited to the investigatory methods of Sherlock Holmes than the familiar plot which the Ford brothers had generated for A Study in Terror. Here was a case worthy of Holmes' unique talents; one in which he would be required to do more than simply browbeat his way to the most obvious suspect.

The Hopkins take on Knight's hypothesis was called Murder by Decree. It featured Christopher Plummer and James Mason in the roles of Holmes and Watson, was staged at both Elstree and Shepperton studios and directed by Bob Clark, and it saw release in 1979. It was also, to date, the final bow for Doyle's detective on the big screen as he was originally conceived, before big-budget pastiche consigned him to an exhaustive but overly reverential rendition of his familiar repertoire on British television in the effete personage of Jeremy Brett.

To play it safe, the film credited Lloyd and Jones' book as the source of its inspiration, and made only oblique reference to Knight's tale by acknowledging an additional debt to "recent theories on the infamous crimes committed by the alleged 'Jack the Ripper'."

By March 1888 – according to the chronology established by Doyle in The Adventures of Sherlock Holmes – Holmes and Watson no longer shared their famous suite of rooms in Baker Street, due to Watson having married and moved out in the interim. The good doctor now resided with his equally good but entirely invisible wife in Paddington Street, their domestic arrangements incorporating a maidservant with the circumstantially striking name of Mary Jane. No mention is made of this coincidence of names in Murder by Decree, but then the film operates in that parallel universe known only to those who adapt the written word for the screen, where Watson is forever in Baker Street by his mentor's side, no matter what their creator may originally have intended for either of them.

Holmes: *"I understand you know something of the Whitechapel Murders."*
Lees: *"I have seen the man known as Jack the Ripper…"*
Christopher Plummer and Donald Sutherland in Murder by Decree (1979)

James Mason and Christopher Plummer in *Murder by Decree* (1979)

On the Sherlockian side of things, the rapport which Plummer and Mason establish as the famed duo is among the most relaxed since the great days of Basil Rathbone and Nigel Bruce. Their repartee is a joy, much of it ad-libbed by the actors themselves. Like any good marriage, the keynote of this partnership is humour; Watson, in particular, is delivered of a splendid cameo by Mason, a veteran actor of such finely honed technique that he could turn an expression of disappointment when Holmes displays impatience with him ("You squashed my pea…") into the best scene in the film.

Christopher Plummer graciously defers to Mason for the most part, taking centre stage only when his acting partner in crime-solving requires to vacate it. His Holmes has some of the intellectual detachment of Doyle's detective – "I can well imagine that people may be a trifle discouraged," he opines when informed of the impact the murders will have on Whitechapel trade – and, by comparison with John Neville in the first Holmes/Ripper film, he was a star name to boot. But Plummer neither looks, sounds nor acts like Holmes: he weeps openly, untypically attempts to strangle the governor of an insane asylum and is too good-humoured by half. Unlike the character played by Neville and most of his forerunners, he is, in fact, a socialist: when told of the perceived threat to the government by no less a person than the Prime Minister himself, he replies, "I care nothing about that; you're all the same to

Murder by Decree
(1979)

me." If *A Study in Terror* had reduced Holmes to the level of protagonist by any other name, *Murder by Decree* further diluted him to the needs of its complex plot.

> *"The search for Mary Kelly and the plot for her disposal had begun. Oh, they searched... Nothing would stop them. They searched for Mary; they searched for the child. In terror of her own life, Mary shared the secret of the royal indiscretion and in so doing, sealed the fate of her friends. They murdered anyone who might have known of the child. Thus was born the myth of Jack the Ripper..."*
>   Sherlock Holmes (Christopher Plummer) in *Murder by Decree* (1979)

Murder by Decree is not, in any sense of the term, the remake of *A Study in Terror* that it is often attributed to be, particularly in interviews given by the voluble Herman Cohen, co-producer of the latter. Both films feature Sherlock Holmes and Jack the Ripper, but that is where the similarity ends. Part of the reason for this misconception lies with the fact that Frank Finlay repeated the role that he had played in *A Study in Terror*, that of Inspector Lestrade: a "sallow, rat-faced, dark-eyed fellow," according to the literary Watson. In this take on the case, Holmes and Watson are installed to replace Barlow and Watt, not Neville and Houston.

The screenplay takes its cue from the theory that was speculated upon in the BBC's *Jack the Ripper*, whereby the discovery of an illegitimate heir to the throne of England provokes a highly-placed plot to silence all those in the know. The story adheres to the chronology of the crimes without acknowledging the fact on screen, but in disposing of the first four victims by the second reel, the film cleverly slots its action into the period between the murders of Eddowes and Kelly, which provides Holmes with ample time to offer up a solution.

Interestingly, the script serves up *two* Rippers for the price of one through the introduction of a new character named William Slade (whose lack of identity is masked by an expedient nod to *The Lodger*). To all intents and purposes, Slade (Peter Jonfield) is the coachman, Netley, under another name, but he goes much further here than the real Netley is alleged to have done. Slade is not only the prime mover in the plot to kill Kelly, he actively participates in the murders by guiding the hand of an addled and compliant Gull (also renamed as Sir Thomas Spivey), as well as personally assassinating several other cast members who get in the way.

Freemasons acting in concert is central to the plot, but *Murder by Decree* decries Knight's theory of a government conspiracy to kill and substitutes the more feasible notion of a conspiracy to cover up in its stead. Prime Minister Lord Salisbury (John Gielgud) has unwittingly acted like Henry II when faced with the problem of what to do about Thomas à Becket ("Who will rid me of this turbulent priest?"). Slade has taken up the cudgel on his behalf, but when it has subsequently come to light how this knight of "the secret order of Freemasons" has gone about ridding England of Kelly and her turbulent tongue, a higher

Susan Clark and Christopher Plummer in *Murder by Decree* (1979)

Donald Sutherland, Teddi Moore and Christopher Plummer in *Murder by Decree* (1979)

allegiance than Queen and Country has come into play, and the government is deemed guilty by association. The script nods to Knight's tale of a threat to the throne, a blackmail plot and a physician as Ripper by royal appointment, but it roundly rejects it in the final analysis: "There is not now, nor has there ever been, a danger to the monarchy," Holmes tells a rattled Salisbury at the close, laying Knight's farcical hypothesis of constitutional overthrow to rest.

Canadian-born director Bob Clark had shot three low-budget horrors before coming to *Murder by Decree* – *Children Shouldn't Play with Dead Things*, *Deathdream* and *Black Christmas* – so his way with the Rippers is in keeping: Slade dons the top hat and cape and lurks in the shadows, sword-stick at the ready, but the more grotesque Spivey is given the full monty of a first-person camera, contact lenses (in close-ups on his eyes), heavy breathing and a *Jaws*-inspired theme to accompany his attacks. Clark also adds a touch of slow motion to the incursions of the killers' carriage-and-pair, which gives it a hearse-like appearance and proves especially effective in a scene where an authentically mutilated Eddowes is thrown out of the door of the brougham to fall straight towards camera.

With four of the victims disposed of so early in the story, however, 'Jack the Ripper' has also to be put on ice for the best part of the next hour. Whereas the first act of *Murder by Decree* bore all the hallmarks of a film of some distinction, the remainder, by contrast, erases them completely, a downward spiral which is signalled by the entry into the drama of medium Robert James Lees, somnolently played by another expat Canadian actor like Plummer himself, Donald Sutherland.

The Lees episode is a retread of the events depicted in *The Veil*'s 'Jack the Ripper' of 1958, and it serves no purpose here other than to direct Holmes to the chief suspect by clairvoyance, for want of him being able to turn up anything of substance on the ground. Holmes puts two and two together through the untypical combination of intuition, guesswork and the scripted cop-out of foreknowledge of the rites and rituals of freemasonry. He does so little actual detecting, in fact, that the film slows to a standstill in its desperate attempt to make it appear as though something of import is wending its way through the sleuth's incisive mind.

Murder by Decree fades out to the melancholy refrain of the Scottish ballad, 'Will Ye No' Come Back Again?', Lady Carolina Nairne's wistful air to the departed Bonnie Prince Charlie. The allusion to the tragic love affair between Annie and her own wayward prince is poignant, but insufficient to compensate for the tedium that has preceded it.

Conspiracy provides a tangled weave for a detective to unravel, and if the detective in question is to be none other than Sherlock Holmes – a character famous for trapping villains through deductive logic, rather than hot pursuit – the more tangled the weave the better. One of the major failings of *A Study in Terror* was that Holmes was reduced to sleuthing like an ordinary copper on the beat: following up obvious clues, questioning suspects by subterfuge and generally putting himself in harm's way in order to extract a mere snippet of information from an unsavoury character; rarely was he called upon to show evidence of insight into the criminal mind, or to arrive at his conclusions by other than rudimentary means. *Murder by Decree* fared no better when it came to addressing this problem; on the contrary, it presented Holmes with a puzzle which afforded even *less* opportunity for the 'prince of detectives' to exercise his cerebellum, rather than his biceps. Neville's Holmes was at least persuaded to examine a surgical scalpel under his famous magnifying glass; Plummer's Holmes examines nothing more than medical records.

The opinions of those who were around at the time of the Whitechapel Murders drive a veritable coach and horses through the idea of a 'travelling executioner'. Inspector Harry Cox made his own views plain in the interview he gave to *Thomson's Weekly News*: "Many amateur detectives were... advancing strange theories as to the murders. Many believe several of them to this day, specially one to the effect that the murders were committed by some mad medical specialist, and the bodies conveyed in his own conveyance to the East End. An absurd piece of nonsense! In nearly every case, the murders were committed on the actual spot where the bodies were found, or very close to it."

Modern researchers now tend to support this contention, though one is tempted to wonder why the inspector should have chosen to comment on a means of murder in 1906 that to all intents and purposes was only proposed by Elwyn Jones, John Lloyd and Stephen Knight in the 1970s.

Centenary murders

Throughout the 1970s, genre films featured serial killings with increasing frequency, though they were never designated as such. The 'splatter movie' phenomenon, which was begun by *The Texas Chain Saw Massacre* in 1974 (using the same source-material as *Psycho*, namely Ed

Peter Jonfield and
David Hemmings in
Murder by Decree
(1979)

Gein) and expanded to include *Eaten Alive* (1975), *The Hills Have Eyes* (1977) and *Tourist Trap* (1979), among innumerable others, upped the body count in the horror film by a factor which would have put most real-life serial killers to shame. But its protagonists were invariably crazed cannibal retards, taking murderous revenge on innocent passers-by for some real or perceived slight in their twisted lives.

For a film to qualify as a splatter movie, it required a plot which facilitated wholesale slaughter. This could be effected in a tiny backwoods cabin, were it to be stumbled upon accidentally by an unsuspecting family in a wandering Winnebago, but it was usually achieved through science-fictional scenarios, where hordes of ravenous zombies could be made to run amok on far-flung islands or cruise the local shopping malls. The object of the splatter movie was to disgust, and most of them attained that goal without effort.

John Carpenter's *Halloween* inaugurated the breakaway movement of the 'slasher' film in 1978, where a number of nondescript teenagers were placed in jeopardy by an unseen killer with a knife, or other equally sharp implement, in a small-town locale. In common with *The Texas Chain Saw Massacre*, *Halloween* did not feature a great deal of actual slashing, but it appeared to do so. Other films which followed in its wake were not so reticent. The *Friday the 13th* series, set in train in 1980 by Sean S Cunningham, showcased the unsavoury talents of special effects technician Tom Savini, whose wizardry with the blood-spurting prosthetic went unrivalled for a decade. The carnage in these films was most commonly visited upon a group of irreducibly stupid college co-eds, who collectively had wronged the latent maniac in their midst and who had consequently to pay the price of their misdemeanour, often in the course of a single night. Bloody this may have been, but the massacre of whole contingents of idiotic teenagers was not typical of the archetypal serial killer, who chose his victims at random and over prolonged periods of time.

As locations varied in order to avoid repetition, so concepts altered as the intervals between the requisite murders had correspondingly to lengthen. In the process, the focus of 'slasher' film killers turned increasingly myopic, and lone women became the objects of attention for knife-wielding assailants. In films like *Dressed To Kill*, *Maniac* (both 1980) and *Visiting Hours* (1981), the female-fixated psychopath replaced the single-issue mass murderer of the *Halloween* and *Friday the 13th* franchises. No lessons in late-Victorian history were needed to see where this would inevitably lead.

The first of these 'stalk-'n'-slash' thrillers to square the circle of cinematic violence and acknowledge the debt to Jack the Ripper was Lucio Fulci's *The New York Ripper* (*Lo squartatore di New York*) in 1983, although it deferred to the source of its inspiration in title only. Fulci's protagonist is a 'duck'-voiced killer who genitally mutilates sexually active women in crypto-cathartic attacks of spite because his young daughter is an amputee and will be deprived of such a 'normal' life. Fulci was a notorious practitioner of Italian *giallo* splatter-fests, like *Zombie Flesh Eaters* (1979), *The Beyond* (1980) and *The House by the Cemetery* (1981), the violent content of which led many of them to be barred from exhibition in Britain, including *The New York Ripper*.

Like most *gialli*, *The New York Ripper* is made up of a series of suspense sequences, each of them loosely connected and all leading to murder, rather than a narrative whole. The murderer's motivation is the glue that holds the film together. As *gialli* – and other stalk-and-slash thrillers – go, *The New York Ripper* is not at all bad. For Fulci, it was an opportunity to shoot on location in New York (with all the interiors filmed in his home city of Rome, which is why British actor Jack Hedley plays a badly-dubbed cop, instead of a local actor), and the director makes a cogent point in juxtaposing the hedonistic amorality of New York life with the simple needs of the young girl whose plight sets the wheels of random butchery in motion.

In this regard, Fulci's view of American life is similar to that of Antonioni's in *Zabriskie Point*, where the self-centred decadence of its inhabitants is almost reason enough in itself to justify their annihilation. It is a notion reinforced by the attitude of the Hedley character – a jaded NYPD detective and user of prostitutes – who can barely be bothered to interrogate witnesses let alone catch the killer, and who springs into action only when he is involuntarily confronted by the terrified screams of one of the Ripper's victims on the other end of a phone line. The victims in the film are representative of the moral decay that Fulci and his screen killer are wont to slash at indiscriminately; among them are a performer in live sex shows and a frustrated, nymphomaniac 'rich bitch'.

The New York Ripper is well staged and utilises its Manhattan locations to advantage; it leaves the viewer with the impression that something more has gone on to engage the attention than the series of gory murders for which so many of its ilk were conceived. But it is also extremely graphic (if not actually deserving of its notoriety as a 'video nasty'), especially in a gratuitous scene where a naked girl is tied to a bed and has her stomach, breast and left eye slit open with a razor blade while she is alive and screaming. With this single exception, Fulci's preference for violent excess does not detract

Italian poster for
The New York Ripper
(1983)

greatly from the overall efficiency of the piece, as does a similar predilection in the films of Dario Argento.

Unlike many *gialli*, *The New York Ripper* adds up to more than the sum of its parts. It started a trend, however, where the same could not so easily be said of the many Ripper rip-offs which subsequently set out to copy it.

In 1989, a protégé of Fulci's named Andrea Bianchi directed *Massacre*, in which a policeman who is possessed by the spirit of a monk kills a number of prostitutes in predictably gory fashion. The Ripper killings provided historical precedent even for this: shortly after the death of Catherine Eddowes, one J F Brewer had published a pamphlet entitled 'The Curse Upon Mitre Square', which told of a similar murder committed in the 16th century, and on the exact spot where Eddowes fell, by a monk of the Holy Trinity priory, predicating the possibility that the ghost of Brother Martin might somehow have transferred into 'Jack'. It was a sensationalist piece, put out to cash in on prurient interest, and much the same can be said of *Massacre*.

The New York Ripper (1983)

Director Abel Ferrara, notorious for his own 'video nasty', *The Driller Killer* (1979), also sent his camera down the mean streets of the real New York in *Fear City* (1984), another variant on the killer-on-the-loose scenario, with "the so-called New York Knifer" (according to a radio announcer) singling out the strippers and table-dancers of the Starlite Talent Agency owned by brooding ex-boxer Matt Rossi (Tom Berenger). The 'Knifer' is an ascetic monomaniac (Rae Dawn Chong) devoted to martial arts philosophy, who makes a memoir of his exploits in a diary titled 'Fear City'; the killer's "knowledge of anatomy" is initially used to inflict pain, rather than death, on his victims, though this aspect of the plot is dispensed with after he decapitates one of them with a Samurai sword. Rossi overcomes his reluctance to deploy the violence of his adversary with the help of some timely (but unintelligible) advice from the local Mafia boss (Rossano Brazzi), and the two confront each other in an alleyway. A ritualistic duel to the death leaves the killer with a broken neck.

Fear City is competently if lazily handled, its slasher attacks suspensefully staged, but like many other Ferrara films (*The King of New York*; 1990, *Bad Lieutenant*; 1992), it feels a deal longer than its nominal 90 minutes. It is entirely typical of the innumerable women-in-peril movies which proliferated in the 1980s and consequently would not feature here were it not for the fact that its re-release on video in the run-up to the centenary of the Whitechapel Murders saw it rehashed as *Ripper*, to cash in on the expected new wave of interest in Jack and his crimes. The erroneous advertising blurb said it all: "A psychopath believes that he is the reincarnation of Jack the Ripper, and is stalking night-club strippers." The new title did not even fully mask the old on the video print, being superimposed over a still-frame of part of it.

Changing the film's title to *Ripper* for re-release was only the beginning of the exploitation of the word on the way to the critical date of 1988. In the case of *Fear City*, it was foisted onto a well-crafted and literally hard-hitting thriller that had no need of such third-rate tactics. But waiting in the wings were others which did require some titular assistance.

Night Ripper (1986) was one such: a direct-to-video opus, also shot straight on videotape, in which a lesbian 'Ripper' targets photographic models and whose title serviced a late-entry episode of police show *T. J. Hooker* the same year (William Shatner's consolation prize for the cancellation of *Star Trek* in 1969). Another was a Jesús Franco film of 1974, called *The Black Masses of Exorcism* and originally made to capitalise on the success of *The Exorcist*. This had undergone a title-change (to *The Sadist of Notre Dame*) once already, but it had been re-cut and again reissued as *The Ripper of Notre Dame* in 1981.

Among several unassociated items was a Canadian film called *American Nightmare* (1983), another no-budget straight-to-video affair, notable only for an early appearance by Michael Ironside, himself a knife-wielding stalker in *Visiting Hours* (1982) before moving to more rewarding roles in multi-million dollar sci-fi extravaganzas *Total Recall* (1990) and *Starship Troopers* (1997). "*American Nightmare* is the story of a psychotic avenging moralist. The frantic brother is desperately trying to find his sister before she too falls victim to… the American Ripper," screamed the blurb. It had to: the potency of the R-word was all that connected these low-grade offerings to Ripper cinema.

In the heyday of the teen drive-in movie presided over by the grandiosely titled American International Pictures, scriptwriter Ralph Thornton concocted a story about a college co-ed who was turned into a blood-lusting vampire by an amulet brought back from the Carpathian mountains of Transylvania. The name of this 1957 opus was *Blood of Dracula*; it starred Sandra Harrison and was directed by Herbert L Strock.

Special effects expert Tom Savini was not alone in having been weaned on such AIP 'shockers', and a lull in his filmic fortunes after the glory days of creating blood-spurting prosthetics for video nasties in the early 1980s, from *Friday the 13th* on, inspired him to re-jig the *Blood of Dracula* story in favour of Jack the Ripper, so that his peculiar talent for evisceration might be more to the fore. *The Ripper* was cheap and, it has to be said, cheerful, with more by way of attention to detail than most of its predecessors put together. But the last thing that Jack's tarnished image needed after a decade spent in the limbo of series episodes and made-for-television films was a picture that not only went straight to video but was *shot* on video as well.

> "I do have a conscience, you know. I initially took the lives of those that society would miss the least – the waifs, the misbegotten, the misfits, the derelicts – but as time progressed, I found it increasingly difficult to make that distinction."
>
> Jack the Ripper (Tom Savini) in *The Ripper* (1985)

Professor Harwell (Tom Schreier), an Oklahoma University lecturer who specialises in 'crime cinema', happens upon a ring supposedly worn by Jack the Ripper in a Tulsa antiques shop; compelled to purchase same, he finds that he cannot prise it from his finger and, in consequence, he turns into the legendary killer by night and starts to slaughter the local inhabitants.

Shooting direct to video results in an excessively talky production, whose flat lighting and natural soundtrack undercut the few moments of suspense that director Christopher Lewis attempts to conjure from the usual female-in-peril situations. Tom Schreier, unlike the others in an amateur cast, at least exhibits a modicum of acting ability, but the pace is leaden, the result of a tyro script not having been subjected to the rigours of professional scrutiny before being put into production. Thoroughly uninspired, the piece is enlivened only by its Herschell Gordon Lewis-style gross-out gore effects.

Jack's role in *The Ripper* is that of bogeyman conjured from the ring, but he could as easily have been Dracula or any number of other monsters had opportunity demanded it. As played by effects-meister Tom Savini, when he finally makes a frontal appearance in the last reel of the film, he comes on like a Halloween ghoul. But Savini clearly relished the opportunity to play a larger-than-life villain and hammily makes the most of a few good lines. The film recreates one actual murder – that of Annie Chapman – then repeats the formula at intervals, a length of intestinal tract and a variety of internal organs being extracted from each victim in turn, and all on camera.

From Oklahoma, Jack moved due west in the direction of Los Angeles, in the hope that with the centenary of his murder-spree fast approaching, some enterprising Hollywood producer might require him to participate in a timely homage. 1988 was still three years away, however, and setting down his bag in Arizona to reminisce on his involvement in *Cimarron Strip* 17 years before, he soon found himself signed up for another made-for-television film located in the American Southwest, but in modern dress on this occasion.

Shot (and screened in the United States) as *A Bridge Across Time*, *Terror at London Bridge* was deemed a more appropriate title for the NBC telefilm's transmission in England. Jack's character in the story resembled that in the 'Ripper' episode of *Kolchak: The Night Stalker*, but here he was given some dialogue to speak, a dalliance with the ladies and a more fashionable cut to his traditional suit of clothes. The downside came when he discovered who had been contracted to star alongside him.

> "Jack the Ripper is alive. And he's right here in Havasu."
> Detective Gregory (David Hasselhoff) in *Terror at London Bridge* (1985)

'London Bridge, London, England', explains an opening title for those who are slow on the uptake. After a chase near said bridge, Jack the Ripper dies in a hail of police bullets and plunges into the icy waters of the Thames but not before his spirit has passed into a stone-block dislodged during his fall. A century later and the bridge has been transported, literally brick for brick, to Lake Havasu, Arizona (as it was for real), including the stone recovered from the bottom of the river. A prick of a lady's finger; a drop of blood on the 'cursed' stone; a cloud of fog... Hey, presto! Jack rematerialises like Dracula in *Dracula Prince of Darkness*, or any one of a number of vampire films from the Hammer stable.

A thoroughly opportunistic exercise shot in a captive theme park, *Terror at London Bridge* features handsome David Hasselhoff (in his pre-*Baywatch* days) as Detective Don Gregory, the stereotypical 'police officer with a past', surrounded by a bevy of beauties as victims, or potential victims, of a repeat Ripper killing-spree.

Essentially another monster-on-the-loose scenario, with no rhyme or reason to it beyond the need to provide a passable 90 minutes of prime-time, the tale is heavily padded with a romantic subplot which affords Hasselhoff plenty of opportunity for angst when recalling the accidental shooting that has landed him in this kiddie-corner backwater to begin with. "When they brought that thing back from the bottom of the Thames river, they brought *him* with it... Here, in our century, repeating the same murder pattern all over again," Gregory says, drawing on his long years of police experience to arrive at the most probable conclusion to the murder mystery. As the men in white coats stand eagerly by, Jack obligingly appears to prove Don right.

Not content with a phantom Ripper flailing around in the background, the film offers up *two* candidates to account for him, both of them equally weird. (This is made plain by the fact that they notionally derive from England, but speak with the kind of accent that an alien might adopt if he parked his flying saucer in Surrey and tried to mingle with the natives.) One of them is Jack in daylight guise, but the other one turns out to be 'normal' except for the Van Helsing-style crusading zeal that he exhibits when attempting to destroy the bridge and its spectral inhabitant. (How he happens to know about this is not explained.)

The vampire analogy goes further than mere staging: Jack is kitted out in a wide-brimmed fedora like Vincent Price in *House of Wax* (1953) but, apart from a lack of fangs, he is made up and photographed in vampire mould, and appears to have gained superhuman strength after his sojourn encased in a block of granite. He has acquired only transient immortality, however, for despite reappearing wraith-like in the first reel, he is easily despatched by Hasselhoff in the last with a volley from a 'Saturday-night special'.

Two years later, Hollywood *did* wake up to the relevance of the date. Jack was literally back, but his return to the film capital was short-lived. His name was on the billboards, but his presence on set was not required.

The producers of *Jack's Back* (1988) coined a glib title for their piece about a serial killer in Los Angeles, but opportunism tacked it onto a psycho-thriller in which the supposedly 'copycat' nature of the crimes was an entirely extraneous element.

> "*Some theorise that Jack the Ripper was a medical man, because of the precision of his cutting and his anatomical knowledge. I believe that would also apply in this case. The most important thing I can tell you with any certainty is unfortunately about the victim: she will be murdered in her room, some time in the next 12 hours. And she will be pregnant.*"
>
> Dr Carlos Battera (Robert Picardo) in *Jack's Back* (1988)

Jack's Back was shot under the title of 'Red Rain', accounting for the use of a song called 'Red Harvest' on the soundtrack, and its story was that of a student whose accidental involvement in a series of murders leads to his death, which is subsequently avenged by a psychic twin. Somewhere on the path to production, it was deemed appropriate to allot the killer in the film the MO of Jack the Ripper, to give the story added resonance. Inserted into the exposition were references to him choosing identical dates to his predecessor for the execution of his crimes. The last (though in a betrayal of intent, only fourth in the film) victim is pregnant, as Mary Kelly was at one time thought to have been, and the red herring of *Jack's Back* is an amateur abortionist in keeping with such speculation.

Proof that *Jack's Back* (1988)

The incorporation of the Whitechapel Murders into *Jack's Back*, in which the identity of the real killer is secreted behind an investigation into a failed abortion, was solely predicated on the fact that Mary Kelly was three months' pregnant at the time of her death. But in 1987 – coincidentally the same year that the film went into production – a number of documents relating to the Kelly murder were returned anonymously to Scotland Yard, among them the medical notes of Dr Thomas Bond. Bond had assisted Dr Phillips at the scene of the crime, as well as with the autopsy itself, and his meticulously detailed report makes it clear that Kelly was not pregnant at all. Had writer-director Rowdy Herrington been aware of this at the time, he might have had second thoughts about revamping his original for the sake of a slick title.

James Spader plays twin brothers, John and Rick – one a medical student with a social conscience, the other an embittered loner with a petty criminal past – but a neat twist introduces the latter only after the former is murdered, *Psycho*-style, at the end of the second reel, when he inadvertently stumbles upon an example of the LA Ripper's handiwork. A psychic link between the brothers, activated at the point of death, involuntarily acquaints Rick with the identity of the killer, and the remainder of the film is given over to the search.

Another twist in the tale produces the wrong man in the first instance, but the real 'Jack' is ultimately revealed to be Dr Sidney (Rod Loomis), the head of the medical centre where John Wesford was employed. His expedient nomination as a Ripper copycat begs the question of why a community doctor should choose to emulate the chronology and method of one of the most infamous killers in history, instead of being simply another run-of-the-mill psycho. No answer to this conundrum is forthcoming in Jack's Back, either in the choice of victims or in anything of relevance in the doctor's background. All of which serves to illustrate that the film's inclusion of a 'Ripper' motif was commercial in origin.

Promotional material was more blatant still: "One hundred years ago, the world was shocked by a man they called the Ripper. He was never caught..." But all of this was afterthought. When the last murder in the supposed series is quickly over and done with, Jack's Back reverts to its former storyline, with the dead twin's psychic brother determining to root out the killer and bring an end to his own recurring nightmares.

What connection there really was between Jack's Back and the Ripper murders was coincidentally to be found in the film's pivotal twist, when Rick 'sees' the killer of his twin brother in a dream. After the death of Elizabeth Stride, a Mrs Mary Malcolm of Red Lion Square in Holborn came forward to allege that the dead woman was her sister; at the time of Stride's death, she apparently experienced a presentiment: "I was lying on my bed when I felt a kind of pressure on my breast," she said. "And then I felt three kisses on my cheek. I also heard the kisses, and they were quite distinct."

Mrs Malcolm's strange story gave succour to advocates of the Spiritualist movement, forever on the lookout for evidence of life after death. Though not for long. Mary Malcolm had misidentified the body of Stride and, within days, her real sister appeared, alive and incensed, to denounce her claim.

As Jack kicked his heels in Los Angeles, the call that he had been waiting for came from England. It would have been unconscionable if the centenary of the most famous murder inquiry in British criminal history had been allowed to pass unnoticed in the mass media. Several new books (as well as several old ones) appeared to coincide, as they were always destined to do, but cinema had virtually exhausted the case through repetition by this time, and Jack's Back was transparent in its attempt to give Ripperesque resonance to a conventional psycho-thriller. It was to be left to the small screen to do justice to the occasion, and a four-hour 'special' (190 minutes, plus commercial breaks), co-financed by Euston Films and Thames Television and scheduled for transmission in the autumn of 1988, appeared ready to comply.

The show was co-written and directed by David Wickes, whose previous film credits included Sweeney! (1976) and the David Essex vehicle, Silver Dream Racer (1980). Wickes had also directed episodes four ('Panic') and six ('The Highest in the Land?' – which implicated William Gull) of Jack the Ripper in 1973, and was associated with René Dupont, one of the co-producers of Murder by Decree, so at whom the finger of suspicion was to point in Jack the Ripper was to a degree self-evident, despite a slew of advance publicity to the effect that new information from hitherto unreleased Home Office files had come to light in the meanwhile. The only information which had come to light had been incorporated into Stephen Knight's Jack the Ripper: The Final Solution, itself an outgrowth of the BBC series. New theories had

Michael Caine as
Detective Inspector
Abberline in Jack the
Ripper (1988)

surfaced – indicting, among others, Joseph Barnett – but none of these held a dramatic candle to the high romance of Knight's compulsive fantasy about two killers aboard a coach-and-pair.

Wickes further announced that he had filmed several alternative endings, and that his final solution to the identity of Jack the Ripper would not be revealed until the closing moments of the mini-series, which was planned to be shown in two two-hour segments. The structure of the drama, once seen, gave the lie to such a notion, which was more likely a publicity ploy designed to defray the guesswork that the press was inevitably bound to indulge in at the end of part one.

What *was* surprising about *Jack the Ripper* was how little Wickes and his co-writer Derek Marlowe added to the ideas advanced by Jones and Lloyd in 1973; instead, they subtracted from them to smooth the path of melodrama, for melodramatic *Jack the Ripper* most certainly was. Gone were the shenanigans involving the freemasons; gone was the royal connection (except for Eddy's nomination as one of the many red-herring suspects); gone was so much as a whisper of a government cover-up. The prime suspect remained the same, and the mechanics of murder were plundered, uncredited, from the work of the now-dead Knight. Motive was provided from an altogether more unusual source, however, which had not been tapped since the frenzied speculations of the popular press back in 1888: the work of Robert Louis Stevenson.

> "For over 100 years, the murders in Whitechapel committed by Jack the Ripper have baffled the world… What you are about to see is a dramatisation of those events. Our story is based on extensive research, including a review of official files by special permission of the Home Office and interviews with leading criminologists and Scotland Yard officials…"
>
> Opening narration from Jack the Ripper (1988)

Quite early on in *Jack the Ripper*, Inspector Fred Abberline is persuaded by psychic Robert Lees to attend a performance of *Dr Jekyll and Mr Hyde* at the Lyceum Theatre. He stands in the wings and watches aghast as Richard Mansfield stages the transformation scene: "You who have denied the virtue of transcendental medicine… You who have derided consistently your colleagues, your superiors… Behold!" The actor's features bloat and distend into a sweaty semblance of his former self, while various members of the audience faint or stare slack-jawed at the horror on display. Abberline's presence is dictated by the medium's insistence that he look for a killer with "two faces"; in the circumstances, Mansfield seems the obvious candidate. This sequence is the most striking and original aspect of *Jack the Ripper*, but it also encapsulates all that was both right and wrong about the production as a whole.

When Mansfield is subsequently questioned by Abberline on the methods that he employs to achieve such a startling effect on stage, he responds with the expected Stanislavskian explanation about borrowing from life, which in the case of Hyde involves a corpulent eunuch at a brothel which he frequents in his off-duty hours. Mansfield's television audience had not been treated to a spectacle of pure stagecraft, however (as were his stage ones in 1888), but to the cunning deceptions of the make-up department, with bladder effects and facial prosthetics applied between shots. Embellishing the facts to achieve a more desirable effect was a philosophy that was applied with equal diligence to the rest of the film.

Jack the Ripper has a surface veneer of truth and authenticity. It appears to have gone to tremendous lengths to recreate the scene of the crimes (and in the case of the crime-scenes themselves, it succeeds) but, underneath, all is trickery and sleight-of-hand: everything about

Armande Assante as Richard Mansfield in *Jack the Ripper* (1988)

the film is as histrionically overblown and distorted as the fake Richard Mansfield's latex face-mask.

The real coup for Wickes on *Jack the Ripper* was his million-dollar acquisition of Michael Caine to play Abberline, courtesy of American backers CBS. Caine had returned to permanent residence in the UK in 1987, after a long spell in the United States, and his presence not only assured the film of funding but of a quality supporting cast as well. The London settings were rendered by a makeover on a disused asylum in Virginia Water, Surrey, and through location-shooting at Greenwich Naval College (which also served on *Murder by Decree*). Over 60 sets were required for the production, most of which remained mercifully free of the excess of grime and Gothic gloom that had too often accompanied other films on the subject. The actors are also well cast, with the single exception of an uncredited Michael Gothard as

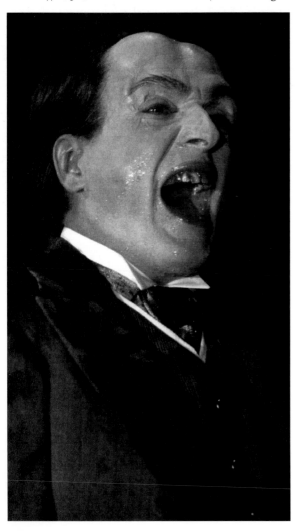

Mansfield transforms into Hyde in *Jack the Ripper* (1988)

George Lusk, who attacks his role with all the finesse of a football hooligan tanked-up on lager. But with its fight scenes and its rabble-rousing, its trilling tarts and its unrelenting air of antagonism, the whole is pitched on a puerile level and at an audience whom it assumes will switch channels if something verbally or visually strident is not seen to occur every few minutes.

Caine is at one with the others in the cast in bawling hysterically at every opportunity, epitomising all those comedic caricatures of himself as he does so and constantly recalling the moment in *The Italian Job* when he blurts out, "You were only meant to blow the bloody *doors* off!" He has the presence for Abberline and he wears his Victorian wardrobe as to the manner born, but the Inspector's investigation of the murders borders on the negligent, not to say lunatic, as the only suspects whom he appears to note in his pocket-book are those who come to see him to volunteer help. Caine is Caine, nevertheless, and he does carry the film through sheer star-power.

Where *Jack the Ripper* comes into its own is towards the end of part one. By rapid intercutting, all the chief suspects are placed in key locations on the night of 30 August, and, through a series of almost subliminal shots, the assassin's coach is seen to be made ready for excursion. The wheels of fate inexorably turn; the machinery of murder moves into action; the juggernaut that is Jack the Ripper heads towards Whitechapel. The sequence ends with the coach stationary in Mitre Square, half-hidden by fog, while Netley sits like Charon waiting to ferry the dead to Hell. Catherine

Jack the Ripper (1988)

Eddowes enters the scene and tries to make conversation with the silent driver; as she walks beside the coach, the door is thrown open and she is grappled inside. A last, low-angle shot captures the torrent of blood which comes flooding out from beneath the door of the coach and down onto the pavement. No better method of keeping the audience hooked for the concluding instalment could reasonably have been devised, as a ratings figure of 14 million viewers appeared to confirm. The sequence was copied in the later *From Hell* but, deprived of the cliff-hanger dynamic, it has little of the same impact.

The film follows to the letter the rule of thumb for whodunits: the murderer is invariably the least likely suspect. William Gull, a hitherto kindly, charming and respectable surgeon, well-bred and well-educated, with a wife, daughter and eminent son-in-law in Theodore Dyke Acland, turns Hyde-like and raving at the moment of apprehension by Abberline: "They're only whores! They're only worthless whores!" he screams, while the latter, his curiosity remarkably unmoved by so swift a transformation, opts for blowing the old man's brains out before he is talked down by Godley.

> Acland: "...For him, insanity was a disease like any other. Something to be understood before it could be cured."
> Abberline: "Understood? So he used those women as guinea pigs in some mad experiment?"
> Acland: "For God's sake, man. He'd had a stroke. He was the guinea pig!"
> **Richard Morant and Michael Caine in *Jack the Ripper* (1988)**

Lewis Collins,
Michael Caine and
Gerald Sim in *Jack
the Ripper* (1988)

The film ends with a disclaimer: "In the strange case of Jack the Ripper, there was no trial and no signed confession. In 1888, neither fingerprinting nor blood-typing was in use and no conclusive forensic, documentary or eyewitness testimony was available. Thus positive proof of the Ripper's identity is not available. We have come to our conclusions after careful study and painstaking deduction. Other researchers, criminologists and writers may take a different view. We believe our conclusions to be true."

Christopher Hudson, writing in the *Daily Mail* in May 1997, had this to say about the kind of "careful study" which led the makers of *Jack the Ripper* to their conclusion: "Some years ago I was invited to write the screenplay of a film about Jack the Ripper based on precisely such 'exclusive' Home Office files, which were said to confirm that Queen Victoria's personal physician, Sir William Gull, was the Ripper. As I inspected the photostats of these files – and what a miserably small, uninformative collection they turned out to be – it became plain that Sir William was no more likely to be Jack the Ripper than was Queen Victoria herself." But the driving force behind the show was not a search for truth; it was the dissemination of political propaganda.

At the time of *Jack the Ripper*'s production, Thatcherism was at its height; the Conservative Party was nearing the end of a second successive term in government and looking forward with certainty to a third, Britain was enjoying the fruits of a boom economy, and the 'yuppie' was alive and well and sipping champagne at the wheel of a Porsche in the City of London. The bubble had not yet burst.

If Sherlock Holmes had evinced socialist tendencies in *Murder by Decree*, the protagonists of *Jack the Ripper*, on the other hand, were true blue literally and politically. The Metropolitan

Police are Custer's 7th, standing firm in the face of a Sioux nation determined to run them down. The Vigilance (Vigilante in the film) Committee's George Lusk is depicted as a Marxist agitator, while the news reporter with whom he curries favour to foment unrest gives voice to the megalomaniac philosophies which so often are attributed to the press as a whole by the instinctively censorious in public life: "The power of the press is the *threat* of the press – even for royalty," he declares. In order to maintain this charade, Gull's Ripper is stripped of any conspiratorial connections and assigned the unrealistic role of lunatic at large. But the film's heroic portrayal of the police force went further than the fisticuffs engaged in by Godley and Abberline to quell dissent and save the country from social revolt (as the real police had saved the government of the day from the wrath of the miners only a few years before). It stretched to redressing the bad press which historians had bestowed on Charles Warren, as well.

Alone in Ripper cinema, *Jack the Ripper* depicts Warren as a tragic hero, holding the fort in the face of tribal unrest, like Gordon at Khartoum: "'Warren out?' They're shouting my name," he cries uncomprehendingly, as George Lusk's rentamob of anarchists try to batter down the doors of Scotland Yard. When informed by Abberline that the unruly mob think

Hugh Fraser as Sir Charles Warren in *Jack the Ripper* (1988)

George Sweeney as John Netley in *Jack the Ripper* (1988)

Prince Eddy might be the killer, Warren strikes a confessional pose: "If the Prince visits brothels, that's a scandal, and scandals die down. But if he's suspected of murder, we'll be facing a crisis that will rock the British Empire to its foundations..." Abberline asks for instructions. "I swore to uphold the law, Abberline, just as you did, without fear or favour. While I'm Commissioner of the Metropolitan Police, that is what I will do no matter *who* the killer is," Warren replies. An exemplary attitude, to be sure, though it fails to stretch as far as William Gull when the time comes. When Eddy is proved to have been at Balmoral on the evenings in question, the relief that writes itself across the faces of Scotland Yard's finest is a sight to behold.

With Michael Caine involved, *Jack the Ripper* catches its killer and his accomplice. There being no conspiracy to cover up, he is quietly locked away on the grounds that he will soon die and the pretext that enough grief has been inflicted on innocent parties already; in other words, the feelings of his good Lady wife and lovely daughter, as well as the interests of his family name, are held in higher regard than the interests of justice. No prosecution is brought against Gull by reason of insanity, and Netley – accessory to murder, both before and after the fact – is granted a free pardon for turning Queen's evidence. As the script has it, despite turning a trick of its own in the closing moments to uphold the honour and integrity of Abberline and Godley, the deaths of five Whitechapel prostitutes are not deemed sufficient to warrant further hurt to Lady Gull. Do me a favour, guv.

> *"You told me to bring you Jack the Ripper. You sign that piece of paper and I will... Tonight!"*
> Inspector Abberline (Michael Caine) in *Jack the Ripper* (1988)

The idea that anyone at Thames Television believed this tosh is farcical. But *Jack the Ripper* was not farce, it was travesty. Wickes reserved farce for *Jekyll and Hyde*, a straight adaptation of Stevenson's story which he directed for Euston Films – using the same stars and sets – two years later.

One of the oddities about David Wickes' *Jack the Ripper* is that none of those whom Abberline suspects to be the killer were put in the frame in life. The strictures of Victorian society in respect of the social pecking order were so deeply entrenched that it is difficult for the observer of a more egalitarian age to grasp the full impact of them. Jack could have been given unfettered access to his stamping ground of Whitechapel by the police were he to have been a member of certain esteemed professions, held a position of evident social standing, been known to them, or otherwise been considered to be going about his lawful business. Prejudice ran deep; class prejudice ran deeper.

In Warren's militarised police force, the observance of a hierarchical order was institution-alised. It exemplified a cultural preconception that extended to embrace society as a whole. The uniformed branch – those at the lowest end of the scale – were able to deal only with their own inferiors with a degree of impunity. Thomas Stowell noted, by way of illustrating the madness which he felt typified the Whitechapel murderer, that a physician of high standing was observed in the area at the time of the murders, ostensibly to section the killer were he to be apprehended at the scene of his crime. The physician whom Stowell referred to was William Gull.

One area where Wickes' *Jack the Ripper* made a significant contribution to Ripper cinema was in the murder of Mary Kelly. The Miller's Court set is a stand-out for accuracy which not even Hollywood could match in *From Hell*, where set expenditure alone cost more than a million dollars.

Plans, drawings, and photographs of the Court as it was in 1888 still exist, but they appear not to have made much impression on the consciousness of art directors prior to *Jack the Ripper*'s Tony Reading. Key to any work which attempts to unravel the mystery of Jack the Ripper is an appreciation of the topography of number 13, as well as other incidental details that relate to the Miller's Court murder. Any writers who ignore either of these but profess to have solved the crimes do so at their peril.

From Hell, the graphic novel on which the Fox film of 2001 was based, was as acquisitive of dubious detail as other books when it came to dealing with the curious circumstances relating to the night of 8 November 1888, and the supposed last of the Ripper murders. But it was at least original in proposing an alternative solution to a mystery which in the intervening years has proved to be even more tantalising than the identity of Jack the Ripper himself.

Chapter Six
Resurgence of the Ripper

"It is beginning, Netley. Only just beginning. For better or worse, the twentieth century. I have delivered it."

The words of Sir William Gull. Alan Moore, *From Hell* (Knockabout; 1996)

T he 1990s began as badly for Jack the Ripper as they did for everyone else. After the boom years of 1988-9, the recession forced him to hock his special talents to two forgettable items, *The Willies* (1991) and *Waxwork II: Lost in Time* (1992).

The first of these was a compendium of 'campfire' tales, which had undergone a period of resurgence at the turn of the decade, and in which Jack's green-faced cameo as a zombiefied Ripper in a House of Horrors was over and done with almost before the viewer had time to be aware of it. His appearance in *Waxwork II: Lost in Time* (1991) was similarly irreverent: untypically wielding a cut-throat razor (and played by Alex Butler), he is about to despatch a victim in a parody of one of his own films when a pair of time-tripping teenagers pop into his space and upset the apple cart. Explanation of this is too complex and idiotic to warrant further detailing (and most of it was only to be found in the original *Waxwork*; 1988) but to illustrate how no idea, however trite, is ever wasted in Hollywood, the sequence served as the inspiration for an entire episode of *Timecop* five years later.

In the meantime, other films were trying to keep pace with advances in the process of detecting the killer which were coming about through a host of new books published in the wake of the centenary. Having already run the gamut of likely suspects, from known murderers to drowned barristers to Royal physicians, theorists had now been forced to spread their nets so wide as to include almost anyone resident in Great Britain at the time of the Whitechapel Murders, from the supposed self-confession of Liverpool businessman James Maybrick (*The Diary of Jack the Ripper*, Smith Gryphon; 1993) to whatever secrets were still thought to be lurking in 'lost' memoranda or newly declassified police files on the case.

In August 1993, Time-Warner withdrew from the *Diary* prior to publication, but it saw print in Britain through Smith Gryphon amid much spin in favour of its authenticity but to every bit as much derision from others in the field when it was eventually examined by neutral parties. A film had been announced on the strength of the title with the cinema's best-known serial-slayer, Anthony Hopkins, proposed for the role of Maybrick, and a script by Chris de Vore, who had penned *The Elephant Man* for producer Mel Brooks. After the debacle, nothing more was heard. A documentary about the diary surfaced on television in due course, written and directed by Ripperologist Martin Howells and hosted by the irrepressible Michael Winner, but it was produced in association with the publishers of the book.

A more viable suspect than Maybrick was Albert Wicken, hairdresser. He turned up in the company of Crippen, axe-murderess Kate Webster, George Joseph Smith and an arsenic poisoner named Herbert Rowse Armstrong in a low-budget 'black' comedy of 1993 entitled *Deadly Advice*. The reason for including the character of Armstrong was the film's location: it was set in the actual Welsh border town of Hay-on-Wye where the poisoner lived.

From Hell (2001)

A young girl named Jodie Greenwood (Jane Horrocks) desires to be rid of her overbearing mother. She is visited by a quintet of imaginary friends, all of them murderers from a Chamber of Horrors that she was taken to as a child, and all of them intent on giving her advice on how to get away with the dirty deed. Jodie follows their instructions and the body-count begins to rise – first her mother, then her sister – but complications ensue. Finally she meets with Jack the Ripper who, from his unassailable position as the perfect murderer (if such can fairly be said of one who was never caught), offers her the best advice of all: "Just be the sort of person nobody suspects."

Her sister's bothersome boyfriend joins the growing list of victims with a pair of kitchen scissors embedded in his chest, and Jodie ends up married to the local doctor. The doctor knows her "little secret", though, but a knock on her bedroom door reveals that Jack is still in attendance, should the need for him arise again. "Room service?" he offers her.

Deadly Advice typified all that was wrong with the British film industry in the 1990s, and which remains so today. The germ of a good idea is undone by an underdeveloped screenplay, listless direction, a woeful lack of the expected black humour and some dreadful miscasting in key roles (one of the screen's most amiable matriarchs, Brenda Fricker, plays the tyrannical mother, a part which fits as well as a Norman Wisdom suit). A sterling cast in principle – Edward Woodward, Jonathan Pryce, Billie Whitelaw and Hywel Bennett – is reduced to amateurish inadequacy by dull dialogue and pedantic pacing, and even the five murderers, gleefully togged out in period costume, have little to say and not much more to do.

Edward Woodward, Hywel Bennett, John Mills, Jonathan Hyde, and Billie Whitelaw in *Deadly Advice* (1994)

Jack: "Nobody suspects a hairdresser, especially one my size. I even cut the hair of Inspector Abberline. That's how close he got. You don't believe me, do you, eh? Don't believe I'm a man twisted with hatred and wracked with sadistic cravings."

Jodie: "It's rather difficult."

Jack: "That's why they never caught me. That's why you never saw me in the Chamber of Horrors. But I was there. I'm in everybody's Chamber of Horrors…"

John Mills and Jane Horrocks in *Deadly Advice* (1994)

Octogenarian actor-knight Sir John Mills' cameo as Jack the Ripper, alias "Albert Wicken" as he confesses himself to be, is saved for the last act: he glides through a local dance-hall in billycock hat to the strains of Long John Baldry's 'Let the Heartaches Begin', before popping up in Jodie's kitchen to tell her what she has waited to hear all along. The film required a lightness of touch that Hollywood finds effortless and modern British filmmakers rarely find at all. A flashback to Jodie as a child sees her inadvertently causing the death of her own adulterous father, the point being that murderous impulses have been bred in her from way back. The attempt at subtext is out of place: black comedy has no moral conscience, so no need to concern itself with the sins of the fathers. The script's loss of focus must have had something to do with the gloom of the Welsh valleys.

Deadly Advice was indicative of the inability of indigenous British media to treat its murderers with anything other than due deference and a modicum of historical respect, while American television, on the other hand, continued to ply Jack like some cartoon creation, endlessly regenerating him in whatever guise might fit the latest bill. Meanwhile, American films went back to basics and checked the history books in case something had been missed. It had, and it was swiftly pressed into action for Mike Norris.

As to how the producers of the 1994 part-mystery, part-martial arts thriller *Ripper Man* thought they might utilise their new find, they evidently read the synopsis of *Ripper*, the video re-release of Abel Ferrara's *Fear City*, realised that the film it described bore no relation to what was actually in the box, and so decided to make *that* film themselves.

> "When you told me Walken thought he was a reincarnated killer called George, I checked out some library books. Tonight he tells me his name is George Chapman. Do you know who George Chapman is? They never solved the case, but George Chapman is the guy most experts agree was Jack the Ripper. It's Jack the Ripper, man. Walken thinks he's the reincarnation of Jack the Ripper!"
>
> Tony (Carey Scott) in *Ripper Man* (1996)

A killer who disembowels his victims and removes internal organs is on the loose in San Diego. Mike Lazo (Mike Norris), a disgraced ex-cop turned nightclub hypnotist, is asked by a sinister stranger named Walken (Timothy Bottoms) to hypnotise him in private session; Walken thinks himself possessed by the spirit of someone called 'George' and is desirous to know precisely who. Lazo at first co-operates, but Walken's increasingly erratic behaviour gives him pause for thought.

All the while, the bodies continue to pile up. When Lazo refuses to aid him further, Walken seeks out his more mercenary assistant, who establishes that Walken's alter ego is George Chapman (alias Severin Klosowski), the 'Borough poisoner' who was hanged for the murder of his common-law wife, Maude Marsh, in 1903, and of whom no less an authority on the Whitechapel Murders than Inspector Abberline himself was supposed to have said at the time of his arrest, "You've got Jack the Ripper at last." Irked by Lazo's hostile stance, Walken frames him for the killings and then kidnaps his son and new girlfriend. All ends in hand-to-hand combat inside Walken's self-constructed shrine of crime, when Walken/Chapman disembowels himself and Lazo is redeemed in the eyes of the local police.

After an interesting and original opening, stylishly directed by Phil Sears and inventively played by the principals, the film soon descends into formula: Walken's motivation changes to that of vendetta against Lazo for alerting the police, and his son and lover become subject to his murderous attentions. The podgy Norris comes off better as the amateur hypnotist trying to conquer stage-fright by listening to tapes of his own hypnotherapy sessions than he does when dispensing with his Clark Kent persona to engage in the martial arts action set-pieces of his better-known and more Superman-like brother, Chuck.

Timothy Bottoms in
Ripper Man (1994)

The killer, despite an intense portrayal by Timothy Bottoms (whose career also descended into formula after an early success in *The Last Picture Show*; 1971), is required to assume a similar Jekyll-and-Hyde posture, one minute indulging his sadistic fantasies, the next desiring to be rid of them. A neat plot twist sees Walken hypnotised by Lazo and then, when the latter refuses, turning to his less scrupulous assistant, who obliges him in the manner of the Sorcerer's Apprentice; at length, Walken hypnotises *himself*. The concept of hypnotic regression releasing dormant rage goes all the way back to *I Was a Teenage Werewolf*, but here it is made to seem novel and fresh.

The climax goes wildly out of control, as Walken/Chapman is revealed to be a religious maniac who worships at a 'shrine of knives' in the abandoned psychiatric hospital from which he had originally escaped. In the best Norris tradition, brother Mike manages to high-kick the killer into near-submission despite a crippled left hand, a knife to the back and a battery of bear-felling blows. Deflected from an inexplicably low-key attempt to kill Lazo's lover with a mere gun, Walken commits full-frontal *hara-kiri* and departs the scene with a cliché on his lips: "You won this battle but not the war, because... I never die. I am evil; evil never dies."

Ten years previously, *Ripper Man* would have been direct-to-video trash, but it benefits enormously from the high production values which had filtered through

Ripper Man (1994)

to films of all budgets by the 1990s, and there is much to commend it, both in the writing and staging: one particularly effective scene has Walken stalk a victim in cat-and-mouse fashion, prowling the rooftops above while she scurries vainly along the streets below. Its deployment of Ripper lore is also above average for a film whose target audience is best indicated by a scene in which the upper and lower halves of a woman's torso are shown protruding from adjacent dustbins: a note pinned to a door advises, 'From hell... signed Catch-me-when-you-can', and its naming of George Chapman as the Ripper is a bold stroke of original thinking, when more prestigious productions have rarely managed to advance beyond Gull, a fictitious Royal, or the ubiquitous unknown doctor.

Abberline gave a fuller account of his own suspicions against Chapman to the *Pall Mall Gazette* on 24 March 1903, nine months after he retired from the Met: "As I say, there are a score of things which make one believe that Chapman is the man; and you must understand that we have never believed all those stories about Jack the Ripper being dead, or that he was a lunatic, or anything of that kind. For instance, the date of [his] arrival in England coincides with the beginning of the series of murders in Whitechapel; there is a coincidence also in the fact that the murders ceased in London when Chapman went to America, while similar murders began to be perpetrated in America after he landed there. The fact that he studied medicine and surgery in Russia before he came over here is well established, and it is curious to note that the first series of murders was the work of an expert surgeon, while the recent poisoning cases were proved to be done by a man with more than an elementary knowledge of medicine. There are many other things extremely remarkable. The fact that Klosowski when he came to reside in this country occupied a lodging in George Yard, Whitechapel Road, where the first murder was committed, is very curious, and the height of the man and the peaked cap he is said to have worn quite tallies with the descriptions I got of him. All agree too that he was a foreign-looking man, but that of course helped us little in a district so full of foreigners. The story told by Chapman's wife of the attempt to murder her with a long knife while in America is not to be ignored."

In instancing the murder of Annie Chapman, the Inspector pointed up the fact that a deal of circumstantial evidence was in play to connect the crime to her namesake, George. Apart from what Abberline himself had to say on the subject, press reports at the time told of a trail of blood leading from Hanbury Street to the rear entrance of George Yard buildings. These have since been dismissed as fanciful, yet there was not enough blood in the area around the body to testify to murder at the scene. None of the residents of the building heard anything unusual. A market porter in the yard next door spoke of a 'thump' against the fence, as though a weight had struck, rather than fallen, against it. There were discrepancies about the exact time of death. But George Chapman was neither a strangler nor a knifeman; he was a poisoner by trade. Nevertheless, it is possible that in the case of Dark Annie at least one of the victims was not in fact killed where the body was found, and that *her* killer might already have been practised in the black art of homicide.

Untimely ripp'd

From his pseudo-factual deployment in *Ripper Man*, Jack the Ripper went about as far as fiction could send him in 1995, when he arrived by shuttle on *Babylon 5*, a multiracial space platform presided over by firm but fair Captain Sheridan (Bruce Boxleitner), for an episode entitled 'Comes the Inquisitor'.

For reasons mainly to do with the strategic interests of the various warring factions who colonise the periphery of the show, a proxy inquisitor is sent by the Vorlan to test the mettle of Ambassador Delenn (Mira Furlan), a potential ally. He introduces himself as 'Sebastian' before inflicting 40 minutes of psycho-babble on both the ambassador and the steely-jawed Sheridan. The two survive the mental and physical tortures which are visited upon them through a display of humility and self-sacrifice, and their interrogator is released from his 400-year quest to find the 'chosen one', a penance imposed on him by the Vorlan for the Lucifer-like pride which he apparently displayed during his own 'mission' back on Earth in the year 1888.

> *"Good luck to you in your holy quest, Captain Sheridan; may your choices have better results than mine... Remembered not as a messenger. Remembered not as a reformer. Not as a prophet. Not as a hero. Not even as Sebastian. Remembered only... as Jack."*
> Sebastian (Wayne Alexander) in *Babylon 5*: 'Comes the Inquisitor' (1995)

Babylon 5 was another self-righteous sci-fi soap enriched by creative input from Harlan Ellison. The Babylon station is a metaphor for Planet Earth, with all its problems, political intrigues and social injustices, while overall control of the complex is exercised by a paternalistic military governor who appears to subscribe to the moral philosophies of Dr Seuss. 'Comes the Inquisitor' is heavy-handed and pretentious in execution, with every gesture writ large and every line of dialogue delivered with the funereal gravity of the Angel Gabriel sounding the last trump.

Wayne Alexander as Jack the Ripper in 'Comes the Inquisitor' (1995)

Sebastian, aka the Ripper, is played (by Wayne Alexander) as a posturing stage-Englishman of a kind that vanished from the theatrical scene with Tod Slaughter – sneering and sadistic, each inflection mannered to the point of caricature and beyond. His plight in the episode is derived from that of the title character in Charles Maturin's Gothic masterpiece of 1820, *Melmoth the Wanderer*, in which the Faustus-like Melmoth sells his soul to the Devil and is then forced to roam the globe in search of someone who is prepared to lift the burden of eternal life from his shoulders. When disgraced Irish author Oscar Wilde (a descendent of Maturin's) went into exile in Paris in 1897 after two years spent in Reading Gaol, he adopted the name *Sebastian* Melmoth. Thus, Sebastian for Jack in 'Comes the Inquisitor'.

The show may have been up on its Gothic allusions, but its knowledge of the Whitechapel Murders was no better than *Fantasy Island*'s: at the fade-out, Sheridan makes reference to 11 November, "the morning after a string of murders in the East End." Aside from the error in the dating, he can clearly be seen to mouth the word 'West' instead of East, the mistake being spotted in post-production and corrected by judicious overdubbing.

More stage-Englishmen were to be found in *Sliders*, though these at least were intentional. The protagonists of this Universal teleseries are a quartet of scientists in the demographic mould of peak-time – one white, one black, one female, one egg-head – who have stumbled upon a space-warp which allows them to travel inter-dimensionally. Unable to extricate themselves from the 'slide' once it has begun, they are trapped into travelling through an infinite number of parallel worlds in the hope of one day being returned to their own. In terms of television fantasy, the parallel world scenario is almost as trusty a science fiction staple as that of time travel, in that a series can be enabled by the use of standing sets and hackneyed plot themes, but without the need for historical verisimilitude. The 'sliders' of the title remain in their own time, but they emerge as different personae in the various alternative worlds into which they are deposited.

'Murder Most Foul', a 1996 Season Three episode, landed the show's original team of Maximillian Arturo (John Rhys-Davies), Wade Wells (Sabrina Lloyd), Quinn Mallory (Jerry O'Connell) and Rembrandt Brown (Cleavant Derricks) in a Kafkaesque world where anything unconventional is considered aberrant and met with state intervention in the form of Dr Bolivar (David Purdham) and his peculiar line in psychotherapy. Our sliders are nothing if not aberrant, and the bumptious Professor Arturo is promptly whisked off to Bolivar's funny farm for protesting in a loud shirt. At this point, the real plot cuts in: Bolivar's radical therapy for dealing with 'fractures' consists of an elaborate charade in which patients are required to role-play their way through a pre-ordained task and thus regain some sense of their place in the scheme of things. There is a convoluted logic in here somewhere, but Arturo is sadly not programmed to discover it. Instead, he is hypnotically implanted with the personality of one 'Reginald Doyle' ("He's like Sherlock Holmes on our world," Mallory explains, for any on whom the allusion might be lost) and placed in a theme park filled with 'actors' in costume, all of whom are engaged in an orchestrated hunt for 'Jolly Jack' the Ripper.

> "Gentlemen, I would advise you strongly to redouble your patrols in the Whitehall area tonight. 'Jolly Jack' is not one to make idle threats."
>
> Reginald Doyle (John Rhys-Davies) in *Sliders*: 'Murder Most Foul' (1996)

His fellow travellers follow Arturo into the charade, in order to rescue him from the clutches of Bolivar before the next slide comes due, but matters are further complicated when a real murder occurs in Jolly Jack's name in place of the Cluedo variety that have featured hitherto. To cut to the chase of a fatuous and tediously plotted exercise in eye-candy, Bolivar is revealed to be the guilty party through a simple comparison of handwriting (and his size 11 shoes), having fallen under the spell of his own manufactured fantasies and consequently become a fracture himself. Mad, in other words.

Being more astute than Bolivar has given him credit for, Arturo begins to sense along the way that all is not as it appears to be in his Doylesque world, but as he is not privy to the distinction between a play-acted murder and a real one, he arrives at another explanation for the anomaly: "*Two* different killers," he exclaims. His surmise turned out to be right with respect to *Sliders* – albeit for the wrong reason – but his logical solution to an illogical situation touched upon an element of the historical crimes which came to feature more strongly in Ripper research *and* Ripper cinema as the millennium came to its close.

The one posturing stage-Englishman to become a Ripper suspect for real was His Royal Highness, Prince Albert Victor Christian Edward – 'Eddy' – who first surfaced as a candidate for the killer as far back as 1962, in *Edouard VII* by Phillippe Julien. The hints in that book were followed by the Stowell article of 1970, which was also thought to implicate Eddy on the strength of papers belonging to Sir William Gull, which purported to show that he was treating the prince for syphilis, thus providing the royal Ripper with motive.

Next up was Frank Spiering, whose idea of non-fiction in *Prince Jack* was to quote few sources for his alleged facts and to invent as much as possible as he went along. Here is the heir apparent to the throne of England after he has notionally murdered Catherine Eddowes: "Eddy ran across Houndsditch right into the series of connecting alleys from Harrow Place to Middlesex Street. He stopped a second to catch his breath. There was blood all over his hands and the front of his coat. He managed to conceal the knife in the section of the woman's dress he had cut from the body. He had to rid himself of the blood, to wash it off somehow. He crouched in the darkness for a long moment, and then raced across Middlesex into another alley between two rows of buildings. He hated the blood all over him. He had to get it off before it began to dry. At the end of the alley, just off Goulston Street, was a passageway leading to a staircase..."

Spiering's mastery of factual accuracy was matched only by his talent for clairvoyance, it seems, and a right royal row erupted when he challenged the Palace to prove him wrong. This it eventually did, to everyone's satisfaction but Frank's. Not that Spiering's assault was confined to Victoria's grandson: Eddy's Cambridge tutor, James Kenneth Stephen (himself a suspect in other eyes), was roped into the plot to pen the Ripper letters, Sir William Gull was trundled around the East End in a vain attempt to prevent the murders, and both the Metropolitan Police and the government of the day were party to the subsequent cover-up. To be affronted by Spiering's sanctimonious humbug about the supposed activities of the British Establishment is to live in a world where the CIA does not exist.

Spiering's book went unpublished in the UK, while the Universal telefilm which eventually took its outlandish theory on board was consigned to cable and satellite.

"I'm not Jack the Ripper; he's a madman! But I understand his madness... These women he's killing are part of an invasion: they carry a disease that is just as much a threat to this country as the Armada was."

Prince Eddy/Jack the Ripper (Samuel West) in *The Ripper* (1997)

Samuel West as
Prince Eddy in
The Ripper (1997)

Despite its superficial sheen, *The Ripper* occupies a place on that mystical movie-making plateau that is Hollywood never-never land, where half facts are sprinkled over a dubious narrative to give it a semblance of veracity:

Prince Eddy is murdering tarts in Whitechapel. Something has to be done, and Inspector James Hanson (Patrick Bergin) is the man for the job. Hanson is a detective on the make, under the wing of the snobbish and ineffectual police commissioner Sir Charles Warren and consequently able to fraternise with royalty, in the shape of said Eddy. A trap is eventually laid and the Royal Ripper is brought to book. Hanson's silence is bought with promotion, but he realises that he is a man out of Victorian time and opts, instead, for a new life overseas.

Originally a two-hour telefilm, Universal's *The Ripper* is a dog's breakfast of hackneyed plot themes, with disparate scraps of associated detail tossed into the mix to no particular purpose. The characters of Sir William Gull (only mildly complicit, in this instance) and Metropolitan Police Commissioner Sir Charles Warren were now almost a regulatory requirement, and as played by Michael York, Warren is the archetypal pompous English prig, whose only concern is networking with royalty. These two and Prince Eddy apart, no other factual references to people, place or period intrude on the narrative to disturb its propensity for self-delusion: Eddy comes and goes in a mythical East End that is bereft of police, save for the dashing hero, while the streets through which he passes are populated entirely by Irish or Irish-Americans, speaking in a variety of strangled accents. (If foreign-made films dealing with the Whitechapel Murders have one thing in common, it is their abuse of the cockney tongue; *The Ripper* is no exception.) He kills the tarts by the 'novel' means of a sword-stick, and his motive is revenge for his having contracted syphilis from one of their number.

Hanson is an 'East End boy' made good, but his attitude and philosophy are that of the token Yank, in the manner of Sangster's Sam Lowry in *Jack the Ripper* – bemused and angered by turns to find himself in the midst of a society which is more concerned with the correct way to knot a tie, or which spoon to use at table, than it is with the slaughter of the poor on the streets of the capital city. A sharper script might have made something pertinent out of this, but *The Ripper* is rabid in its anti-British sentiment, caricaturing all the players in the piece except the trusty police hero and his 'tart with a heart' or, as the film has it, the true love that he finds in the slums.

Unlike Euston's mini-series of nine years before, the intention behind *The Ripper* is not to identify the killer or even to treat the Whitechapel Murders as viable drama, but to launch an assault against the institutions and values of Victorian Britain. In the process, it becomes a slanderous catch-penny piece which gloats over scenes of a potential British monarch slitting the throat of a woman whom he feigns to enter from behind. It may have nothing to do with history, but it has much to do with how sections of the American media view Britain and British society. The film's most grotesque sequence has nothing to do with the murders in Whitechapel either. In a fit of pique, Prince Eddy torches his horse because the animal has had the audacity to throw him at a jump; the sequence would be farcical if it were not so horrifying. To suggest that he might murder peasants is one thing, but the very idea that a member of the British aristocracy would so much as ruffle the mane of a pure-bred stallion is something else.

The Ripper is as devoid of moral, factual or logical considerations as was the book from which it was precipitously drawn. Even with a murder taking place every several minutes, it is also curiously undramatic and uninvolving; having played its hand as to the Ripper's identity in the opening sequence, the remainder becomes a matter of how and when he is to be caught, rather than who he is. Robert Rodat's rag-bag script even manages to pinch a line of Lord Henry Wotton's from Wilde's *The Picture of Dorian Gray* (which was published three years after the events depicted in the film): "That depends on whether I embrace your principles or your mistress," Hanson says in reply to a jocular aside that his behaviour will lead him to the gallows. Bergin might have profited from watching George Sanders deliver the same line, properly, in Albert Lewin's 1945 adaptation of Wilde's novel.

Awash with historical and constitutional inaccuracies, the film divests itself of any pretence at reality during the climax, when Hanson breaks into a royal palace and engages in hand-to-hand combat with an heir presumptive to the throne who wields ball-and-chain against him. This arrant nonsense, like so much contemporary Hollywood product, not only does great disservice to the cause of factual accuracy but also to the canon of films that merely claim to deal with the theme as entertainment. No surprise, then, that *The Ripper* did not see release in Britain; Universal could hardly have expected even the most cynical of modern-day British audiences to swallow such guff wholesale and root, instead, for the American Way.

A measure of the film's political outlook can be gauged from the following exchange. "I'm going to America," Florry declares. "America? Why?" Hanson asks. Florry continues, "It's not like England. Here, only a few people matter and everybody else is dirt... In America, everybody's equal." "Well, maybe they're all dirt," Hanson counters. "At least they're equal," Florry replies.

Finding this fatuous argument deeply inspirational, Hanson rebels against the strictures placed on him by Warren and sets about bringing the Ripper to book on his own. The predictable cover-up follows, with Hanson bought off by a promise of promotion. Having been informed that he's now "one of us" by Sir Charles, the unimpeachable Inspector turns his back on the grace and favour of the British Establishment and sets sail for the land of the free with Florry. Had he raised his eyes to the sky, he might have seen a flight of pigs accompanying him on the journey.

The fact that *The Ripper* was directed by a woman, Janet Meyers, makes the ugliness of its prejudices all the more unpalatable. But neither its facile premise nor its palpable distortions of the truth were enough to stop Bergin, an actor of Irish extraction, from pronouncing in time-honoured fashion about how daring he thought the film was in exposing the licentious practices of the ruling class: "The extremes of evil are there. The extremes of corruption are there. The implications that corrupt aristocracy, the implications that corrupt society, the implications where people are wealthy – prostitutes, poverty, used and abused by royalty."

Filming on *The Ripper* was out-sourced to studios in Melbourne, Australia, but no matter where it sets its stall, Hollywood is a hall without mirrors.

The Ripper's blatant disregard for history, credibility and the sensibilities of those native to the nation against which it chose to launch its intemperate assault is a crude example of cultural imperialism in action. Since the sixties, the American popular media has attempted to hijack the Ripper and make him its own, in the way that it did with Frankenstein, Dracula, Dr Jekyll and more. Brainwashed and bound to the cause, he is seen as inseparable from the many home-grown monsters whose activities in the field of exploitation are interchangeable. But Jack is not Jason Voorhees, a bogus bogeyman conjured up to the call of the dollar, nor is he Dracula or even Dr Jekyll. Literature may be internationalist in principle, but Jack the Ripper was real, and he cannot be separated from his roots on the streets of London's Whitechapel in quite the way that modern myth-makers would like. Jack's origins require repeated explanation, unlike other mythic monsters for whom explanation resides in the subconscious of an audience; he cannot be purloined or permutated so easily. He is an irreducible part of British history, not British fantasy, but with Universal clearly determined to launch a hostile take-over, the inaugural episode of a 1997 teleseries called *Timecop* tried its best to sever even that umbilical link.

> *"The Ripper is a time traveller. This watch is his passport back to the future. I've been sent to stop him."*
> Jack Logan (T W King) in *Timecop*: 'A Rip in Time' (1997)

Based on a 1994 sci-fi thriller starring Jean Claude Van Damme, *Timecop* the series features one of those androgynous hi-tech agencies set in train by a future world government to monitor the space-time continuum in defiance of Einstein's Theory of Relativity. When the temporal co-ordinates of history are disturbed, a Timecop named Logan is catapulted through a wormhole to investigate the breach.

'A Rip in Time' opens on a brazen pre-credits sequence in which the 'real' Jack the Ripper (in the predictable form of William Gull) is cursorily disposed of by a time-travelling psychotic with a ray-gun, who plans to continue Jack's killing-spree by proxy. Logan follows suit and lands in 'Dorset Mews', scene of the Kelly murder and a thoroughfare that lies, according to the film, "in the shadow of Big Ben", which must be a lot taller than anyone previously thought. With the kind of precision targeting that is exhibited by *Timecop*, one is left to wonder if history might not be better served were Logan to stay at home.

Of all the film treatments which have dealt with the Whitechapel Murders, 'A Rip in Time' is the most efficient at mangling the facts: dates, places and personnel are as strewn with errors as though no pen had ever been put to paper in connection with the period in question. If this was an example of the Time Enforcement Commission in action, the collateral damage that resulted from its activities must have been incalculable. "You're going to have to trust me on this one: the Ripper just wants to be famous," Logan assures, with all the insight of a bar-room psychologist.

The surrogate Ripper is the oddly named Ian Pascoe (Tom O'Brien), who blasts his way into the plot halfway through – in a scene which is a direct steal from Harlan Ellison's 'Soldier' episode in the original *The Outer Limits* – and who refers to his role-model as a "side-show freak," which is precisely what series like *Timecop* seemed intent on turning him into. Pascoe, TEC-enemy number one, popped up again in episode four but, by then, *Timecop*'s audience was dwindling fast. After his second outing, no further shows were screened, despite 13 having been filmed.

A more creditable attempt to re-engage with history was made the following year by *Love Lies Bleeding*, an American-financed production that was shot in the Czech Republic; the film featured Emily Raymond, daughter of Gary (best remembered by fantasy fans for his role as Acastus in *Jason and the Argonauts*; 1964), as a young journalist on the trail of the infamous killer. This low-budget opus offered an eclectic mix in terms of its cast – Malcolm McDowell (making his second entry in the canon) and Paul Rhys, alongside Wayne Rogers from television's M*A*S*H (as Inspector Abberline) and sixties diva Faye Dunaway. It also offered a new take on the familiar tale by having the crimes investigated by a reporter, instead of glamourised by one. The suffrage (or feminist) angle is better integrated into the plot than it was in 1997's *The Ripper*, and the nomenclature of veracity is much in evidence – John Pizer, W T Stead, James Monro – but the Ripper's surgeonly credentials are a mundane echo of the solution forwarded by Jimmy Sangster back in 1959, in keeping with Jack's subordinate role to the film as a whole. Both nominal lead (Rhys) and real-life location were to feature more prominently in *From Hell*, the production of which might have contributed to the fact that *Love Lies Bleeding* has thus far been confined in release to mainland Europe and territories in the southern hemisphere.

> *"Has Mister York told you that the Ripper is actually some kind of creature? That this... thing leaps from woman to woman, killing them, then the women spew green bile...?"*
> Inspector Langford (David Warner) in *The Outer Limits*: 'Ripper' (1999)

As well as making him a conveyance for all kinds of improbable suspects, the anonymity of Jack the Ripper had made him into a conduit for all manner of cinematic conceits. The Whitechapel killer was now an amorphous entity, adaptable either as man or monster, as well as everything in between. The nebulous threat that hovers in the fog at the very edge of vision was realised as precisely that in an episode of *The Outer Limits* in 1999, a venerated and more enlightened series in every respect, and one for which such intangibles had always provided the very wellspring of drama.

"Even in the darkest corners of despair, there are glimmers of a light we call truth. But what if it is a light to which the rest of the world is blind?"

The question was posed in typically ominous style as the curtain-raiser to a Season Five episode in the new series of *The Outer Limits*, the cult sixties sci-fi show which was revived by Canada-based Trilogy Entertainment in 1996. In the long saga of trying to twist Jack's cinematic tail, 'Ripper' was by far the most original, as well as the most outlandish, variant: it not only twisted the tail, it turned the beast inside out.

In the London of 1888, disillusioned medico John York (Cary Elwes) takes it upon himself to hunt down and kill a number of women after he stumbles upon the fact that they are playing host to an alien creature that indulges in 'body-hopping'. As his executions of those possessed by the 'Ripper' mount, he himself comes under suspicion; when he is eventually caught in the act, he is strait-jacketed into a lunatic asylum, consigned to history and those in the know as 'Jack'... the Ripper.

The idea stretches back to *Dracula's Daughter* (1936), where Van Helsing is arrested in the prologue for hammering a stake through the chest of the hapless tenant of Carfax Abbey. It has cropped up in several vampire films since. The concept itself is a simple but effective one, whereby what is taken for granted in respect of the actions of a protagonist within the framework of a fantasy film would render him liable to prosecution, or incarceration under the Mental Health Act, were they to be carried out in life. The converse is the case in the average horror thriller, where Yorkshire Ripper Peter Sutcliffe, for example, would be depicted as a loner on a one-man mission to wipe out a scourge afflicting the streets of Bradford, aided by psychic ability, in the manner of *Buffy the Vampire Slayer* (as he thought he was doing for real). It is not so much role reversal, as a reversal of perception.

On this basis, the film's creature is little more than a digital revision of the 'ageless pathological monster' of Bloch's 'Yours Truly, Jack the Ripper'. But no explanation for its existence is offered, beyond the fact that it appears to be extraterrestrial in origin – "Did Robinson Crusoe choose his island?" it asks rhetorically, by way of enlightening York on its presence in Whitechapel – and rather than flee from its swordstick-wielding pursuer, it lies oddly in wait. Its curious behaviour provides for the requisite historical body-count (six, in the film's estimation), but inferred is the notion that it somehow feels the need to supply a scapegoat for its activities. "Why me?" York asks number four in its roster of host bodies.

"You're the perfect lightning-rod," she replies, with the vocal rasp of Mercedes McCambridge. "They already have enough clues to suspect you of the murders. I'll just keep entertaining myself until they finally have enough clues to convict you." By the time Mary Kelly is despatched in a welter of gore as police burst into the room, York has indeed been 'fitted up'. Or has he?

The Outer Limits (1999)

On the face of it, the alien 'Ripper' is a literal treatment of the infection that Judge Lomax sought to stamp out in *Night After Night After Night* – a sexual parasite like those in David Cronenberg's *Shivers* (1974). But turn it around, and the two have a greater affinity. York, like Lomax, is a sexually frustrated, self-loathing fantasist, who prior to his first sighting of the creature has spent the evening in a laudanum-induced stupor, reading Jules Verne's *From the Earth to the Moon*; the following morning, he cannot recall a thing. "Haven't you heard?" his fiancée asks him. "He struck again last night. The Ripper... In Whitechapel."

The key scene comes near the end. "I'm a nightmare, Jack," Cathy Eddowes (singularly credited among the victims only as the 'Woman in Cream Dress') tellingly informs York as she walks off with his watch, ready to place it at the scene of her own murder. Moments later, she is found dead on the very spot where he first encountered her, giving the lie to the previous exchange. It is a piece of staging reminiscent of Alan Parker's *Angel Heart* (1987), where dream and reality were similarly confused, and where the hero also turned out in the end to have committed the murders that he nominally set out to investigate. The creature is not literal at all; it is metaphor, and it exists only in York's fevered imaginings. As an attempt to depict the demons which can drive a man to murder, 'Ripper' is cleverer than most.

The purpose of the original series of *The Outer Limits* was to invite fresh thinking about extant preconceptions. The postmodern, post-1996 version of the show does not embrace the same spirit of uplift as did its more innocent forerunner, preferring shock tactics and downbeat endings to moral allegory. 'Jack' is banged up at the climax, while the creature sidles off to conduct its business in the new world of America. (As it spews green bile, it could be concluded that it ends up in *The Exorcist*'s Regan MacNeill). The killer turns out to be the deluded Doctor York after all, but as an in-joke for film buffs, it is David Warner who ostensibly embodies the 'Ripper' at the close as he did for director Nicholas Meyer in *Time After Time*, 20 years earlier.

For much of 'Ripper', the supposed victims are themselves complicit in the crimes, proactively seeking out the next of their number, and the Woman in the Cream Dress, in particular, stalks her prey on the streets of Whitechapel in the manner of the Martian *femme fatale* who slinks into the White House in search of the President in Tim Burton's *Mars Attacks* (1996). Though nonsensical on the face of it, more than a little of this possibility exists for real in at least the last of the Ripper murders, that of Mary Jane Kelly.

What shouts from the pages of all inquiry into Kelly's behaviour is that she was self-evidently the centre of a group of like-minded females to whom men were outsiders, regarded either as prospect or meal-ticket. As most of those who write on the subject are male, this side-bar to the Kelly affair seems to pass them by yet it remains one of its most salient features: Kelly was wont to share her room (and therefore her bed) with *women*, not men, on a casual basis, which was the reason her lover, Joseph Barnett, gave to the police for leaving her. Sapphic activity among such women was widespread, and not illegal, unlike its male counterpart. A 1975 novel by John Brooks Barry called *The Michaelmas Girls* postulated just such a scenario in a fictional treatment of the Whitechapel Murders, wherein Kelly herself is co-author of the crimes. Ripperologists like Richard Whittington-Egan found much to commend in the novel, freed as it was in fiction terms from having to account for all the 'facts' which are pored over endlessly by more dedicated pursuants. This aspect of the case was also picked up on by Alan Moore, who employed it in *From Hell* to enable the possibility of Kelly's escape from the knife.

There are too many imponderables in play with regard to Kelly herself for researchers to reach a sustainable conclusion about what exactly happened in Miller's Court on the night of 8 November, but time and again, writers have returned to the notion that Mary Kelly was somehow complicit in at least one of the Ripper murders: her *own*. If the murder *was* an attempt at subterfuge – and if so, it was one which succeeded – then the crime scene befits it. Body and room were both left in such a way as to indicate that a concerted attempt was made to dispose of evidence and allow the killer time to escape, neither of which considerations had seemed to concern Jack the Ripper before. Only Thomas Bowyer's unplanned intervention, and his chance decision to peer in the window, pre-empted the plot from working itself through exactly as might have been intended.

Committing an unrelated murder to take advantage of the fact that a killer is on the loose, and thereby transfer the blame for same onto someone else, was uniquely the plot of a 1970 Spanish-Italian thriller called *The Next Victim* (*Lo Strano Vizio della Signora Wardh* in its original, but released on video in the US as the more opportunistically titled *Blade of the Ripper*).

A razor-killer at large provides perfect cover for a debt-ridden husband and mercenary lovers old and new to plot the demise of wife Julie Ward (Cristina Airoldi), under the pretext that she, too, is being stalked by the maniac. All is revealed at the climax in the manner of a 1960s Sangster psycho-thriller or the more intricate obfuscations of French writers Boileau and Narcejac (*Les Diaboliques*; 1955, *Vertigo*; 1958). A dire and ham-fisted production in other respects, *The Next Victim* nevertheless benefited from a more interesting plot device than most films with the word 'Ripper' incorporated into their titles for export, notionally or otherwise. For one thing, its storyline (by Edwardo Manzanos Brochero) is plausible; for another, its climax comes as a genuine surprise.

A more sophisticated and straightforward reading of Ripper murder came in *Jill the Ripper* (2000), a hard-nosed sex thriller starring Dolph Lundgren and based on a novel by Fredrick Lindsay. A headline in a local paper justifies the film's claim for inclusion in the canon: "JILL RIPS AGAIN – Female "Jack the Ripper" responsible for latest grisly murders in Boston."

Lundgren is suitably taciturn (and a better actor than his 'beefcake' image had intimated hitherto) as Matt Thorensen, a private detective investigating the brutal murder of his own brother, and others, at the hands of a psychotic dominatrix. The killer is eventually revealed to be the brother's wife, and the homicides a direct result of long years of male domination and abuse. Much is made of the paraphernalia of bondage and the sadomasochistic practices of 'specialist' sex slaves, and the pervading sense of alienation is compounded by the well-chosen location of Boston in the middle of a freezing winter.

The film has little to do with Jack the Ripper beyond the superficial, but its affinity to Pabst's *Pandora's Box* is striking: 'Jill the Ripper' is a post-feminist Lulu, however, and her degradation at the whims of a variety of deviant male suitors is not to be taken lying down. On the contrary, she trusses them up in bondage ropes, before hanging them ceiling high and castrating them with a kitchen knife. *Jill the Ripper* was appropriately graphic, justifying its R-rating in the States, but Jack himself had been every bit as graphic for the the previous ten years – though in a different medium altogether.

Graphic gore

The idea that Mary Kelly might have initiated the murder in Miller's Court, rather than been victim to it, has been the source of some debate in Ripper circles since an article was published in the *Criminologist* in 1988 called 'Did Mary Kelly Die?', which took as its starting point the unequivocal testimony of Caroline Maxwell to the effect that she spoke to Kelly, and saw her on two separate occasions, hours after the murder had theoretically taken place. A leap of logic is required to extend this idea and have Kelly become Jack the Ripper herself – though not much of one – and author John Brooks Barry had already made it.

The possible complicity of Kelly, if not her actual name, was also used as the basis of a 1997 novel by thriller-writer Douglas Clegg, called *Bad Karma* (published under his pseudonym of Andrew Harper), which was filmed by American World Pictures in 2001. As well as side-stepping Jack in favour of a female accomplice, the tale borrowed heavily from the reincarnation theme which was used so effectively in *Ripper Man*, but elaborated on it by deploying flashbacks to the supposed former existence of the lady killer who harbours the delusion.

> "She thinks you're Jack the Ripper... ?"
>
> Carly Campbell (Amy Locane) in *Bad Karma* (2001)

Caged psychopath Maureen Hatcher (Patsy Kensit) believes herself to be the reincarnation of Agnes, the erstwhile lover and murderous accomplice of Jack the Ripper. To complicate matters, she also believes that her personal shrink at the Darden State medical facility on Rhode Island, to which she has been confined, is himself the reincarnation of the Ripper, whom she originally roasted to death in an oven in a fit of pique during their joint escape from the scene of one of his crimes. (This is a potboiler, remember.)

When said shrink, Trey Campbell (Patrick Muldoon), takes his family on vacation, Maureen/Agnes escapes from the asylum intent on hunting him down and reuniting with him in death – a circumstance denied her previously by her impulsive action over the furnace – in order that they can continue to reincarnate as a pair of butchering lovers for all eternity. Or something of that sort.

The film was directed by John Hough, of *Twins of Evil* (1971), *The Legend of Hell House* (1972), and *Incubus* (1982) fame, and it was shot in unsuitably inclement weather in and around Roger Corman's Kinvara studio complex in Galway, Southern Ireland, for economy's sake. The Irish locations work well for the flashbacks to the streets of Whitechapel but not for the sun-bleached, post-colonial facades of Rhode Island. Clegg's plot is essentially *Cape Fear*, with the Lecter-like psychotic Maureen/Agnes substituting for the brutal Max Cady, and once the expositional encumbrance of its reincarnation theme has been disposed of, the action devolves to that of a conventional chase-thriller, with bodies stacking up along the way.

> "Some say that he committed suicide, or went crazy and got locked up in a mental institution without anyone ever knowing who he was. But Hatcher says she knows what happened to him because... she thinks she killed him."
>
> Trey Campbell (Patrick Muldoon) in *Bad Karma* (2001)

Patrick Muldoon, Patsy Kensit and Fiona Reynard in *Bad Karma* (2001)

Whether the leading characters are, in fact, a reincarnated Ripper and his mistress is left to the audience to decide, though the fact that both versions of each are played by the same actors leaves no more room for doubt than a screenplay that spins a supernatural rebirth fantasy of its own making: "Both of these people had to die at precisely the same time if they were going to remember who each other was in their next lives," Campbell informs his wife Carly, "but that didn't happen; their souls got separated." Carly takes this news on the chin. "And now she's trying to *reunite* them?" she asks, having employed the only logic that one can in this kind of pulp horror fare.

To try to defer judgment on the matter for as long as practicable, Hough holds back on Jack till the last reel of the film, where his presence is integral to a prolonged flashback depicting the murder of a prostitute, his flight from the police and his death in a baker's oven (a thoroughly nasty demise, and typical of the sort of source material from which *Bad Karma* was drawn). The murder of the tart is equally savage: Agnes cuts her throat from behind while Jack attacks her from the front, both of them experiencing shared pleasure in their act of murder, in the manner of Myra Hindley and Ian Brady, or Fred and Rosemary West. The removal of victims' organs is instrumental to the ritual of reincarnation, in this instance.

These scenes are among the most effective in *Bad Karma*, partly due to their brevity and their extreme nature; they carry a convincing sense of charnel horror, above and beyond that found in more overt slasher films and despite some obvious deficiencies in the special effects department in terms of mustering up the required degree of realism. Of all John Hough's excursions into screen horror, they are most reminiscent of *Incubus* in the speed and ferocity with which the violence is executed. He had originally thought to design his Ripper along the lines of reported eyewitness sightings, complete with coat and peaked cap. Muldoon looked foolish in this get-up, however, and Jack was reverted to stereotype.

A clever touch retained from the novel (which was set on Catalina Island, off the Californian coast) was to have the climax take place in an abandoned monastery called Capello Blanco, literally 'White Chapel', although the final few minutes, in which Maureen has her manacled hand lopped off by an axe before she tumbles into a roaring fire, smack a little too much of the gorefest which closed the director's own *Twins of Evil*.

Hough's direction is professional and engaging and makes no attempt to ape the cartoon quality of the fog-shrouded cityscape that he was required to create for *The Avengers*, but it is undercut at every turn by a lack of budget in all departments, including Patsy Kensit's wardrobe. He does what he can to make up the deficit, increasing the tempo of his cutting to compensate for a slack script and indifferent production values, but *Bad Karma* went straight to cable regardless, whereas another million or two would have seen it play theatres as a perfectly respectable popcorn B-feature.

In September 1888, a notice in the *Times* advertised a work of theological fiction which had originated in Denmark in 1868 but had just been translated into English by Dr George McDonald. The book was called *Letters from Hell* and it purported to be exactly that, as a damned soul named Philip reported on the view from Purgatory in an admixture of social pleading and *Inferno*.

The writer of the following letter, received by George Lusk of the Mile End Vigilance Committee on the evening of 16 October in company with a half-eaten portion of human kidney, ostensibly culled from the body of Catherine Eddowes, may have partaken of that other, more illustrious organ, as well:

"From hell
Mr Lusk Sor I send you half the Kidne I took from one women prasarved it for you tother piece I fried and ate it was very nise I may send you the bloody knif that took it out if you only wate a whil longer
signed Catch me when you can Mishter Lusk"

Of all those who have stood accused of the Whitechapel Murders in the kangaroo court of Ripperology, none have featured so persistently as Sir William Withey Gull, Physician-in-Ordinary to Queen Victoria, knight of the realm, fellow of the Royal College of Surgeons, and septuagenarian stroke victim during the period in question. Gull has held pride of place as Jack the Ripper since Stephen Knight honoured him with that distinction in *Jack the Ripper: The Final Solution*, only for his crown to slip a tad in recent years in favour of Liverpudlian James Maybrick, nominal 'author' of *The Diary of Jack the Ripper*. While the two opposing camps squabbled over their respective client's right to the title, Gull found a new champion in Alan Moore, the graphic novelist responsible for *Watchmen*. In all real worlds, a less likely candidate for the role of Ripper than the eminent and physically-impaired Gull would be hard to come by, but Ripperologists operate on a level that is unattainable to anyone not subject to the seductive charms of collective fantasy. Moore took as his starting point the return 'address' on the Lusk letter and wove an even more elaborate fantasy than Knight had around the proposition that Jack the Ripper was poor, benighted William Gull.

The original 'From hell' letter

I am concerned with cutting into and examining the still-warm corpse of history itself.
Alan Moore, writing in Volume One of From Hell
(1992)

To anyone unfamiliar with the concept of the 'graphic novel', it is in effect a comic-book sty listically occupying a halfway house between novel and film. Graphic novels are the product of artists raised on the moving image, rather than the static tableaux of conventional illustration. Multiple panels are utilised to provide a more fluid break-down of action, often depicting the same scene with only minor changes, in the manner of a frame-by-frame sequence from a film; the overall approach has much in common with the 'storyboards' that film directors employ to dictate set-ups.

The effect upon the reader is one of increased visual continuity, as graphic novels often decry the convention that succeeding illustrations should embody a proportionate advance in narrative action. This consciously cinematic representation

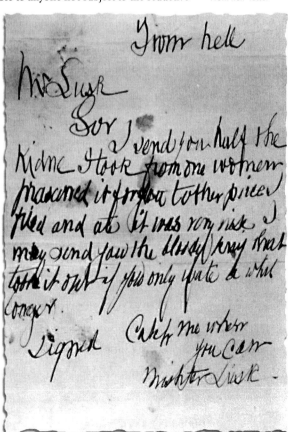

Knockabout edition
of *From Hell* (2000)

is amplified by the deployment of a panoply of effects culled from the grammar of film: panels are arranged out of sequence to simulate flash-frames or cutaways. Narrative structure is also that of film, with its elliptical use of flashes backwards or forwards, and admixtures of dream and reality. In line with its modernist take on the old-style comic book, the graphic novel is often more adult in its choice of subject matter, as well.

Since their commercial arrival in the 1970s as a cross between the work of innovative comic artists in the underground press and the *manga* tradition of Japan, graphic novels have become increasingly sophisticated both in style and content, and their influence has conversely re-engaged other media: if the visual style of such novels was informed by film, so film has equally been influenced by the penmanship and artistic conceptions of the graphic artists: Francis Coppola's *Bram Stoker's Dracula* (1992) was a particular example of this, the storyboard for which could have found favour in either medium.

From Hell, written by British-born Alan Moore and studiously illustrated by Eddie Campbell, began life as one component of a now-defunct comic called *Taboo*. When that title folded, it took on a life of its own as a self-contained part-work whose first volume (it eventually ran to 16) was issued by Mad Love Publishing in February 1992.

Drawing heavily on the theory concocted from Joseph Sickert's story by Stephen Knight in *Jack the Ripper: The Final Solution*, *From Hell* focuses on the life of Sir William Gull and attempts to document the influences, experiences and circumstances which, in Moore's opinion, turned him from prodigious student into delusional schizophrenic and notional Whitechapel murderer. No mean undertaking. It is to Moore and Campbell's credit that they achieve this goal with unequivocal success. In a cleverly wrought climactic sleight-of-hand, the tale leaves Mary Kelly alive and back in her native Ireland at its close, though this may not be obvious at first reading; Eddie Campbell's artwork is at pains to disguise the fact by depicting the witness to her survival, Caroline Maxwell, as a drunken harridan.

There is much brilliance in the novel, and Campbell's visual inventiveness is occasionally stunning, often striking, and almost always up to the complex task of capturing the intricate nuances of the narrative. Only in the Miller's Court murder does Campbell's evocative style fail him. In spite of opting for a welter of bloody detail over two dozen pages, he nevertheless fails to capture the sheer horror which can still be experienced from a brief glance at the real result of Jack's handiwork in the scene-of-crime photographs of the body.

If there is a brittle bone of contention in relation to *From Hell* – and there is a whole skeleton, in fact – it lies in the *content* of the book, not the manner of its execution, and in Moore's reliance for his inspiration on a palpably flawed source and a myriad of unsupported ghost stories.

"I am escaped from space into the sphere of mind and myth and angels. I am Jack. I rise up hungry through the human night towards a naked moon."

The words of Sir William Gull. Alan Moore, *From Hell* (Knockabout, 1996)

Moore's prose strives for – and sometimes attains – the heights of literacy: "Our story's written, Netley. Inked in blood long dry... engraved in stone," Gull says, in a passage that echoes the words of Captain Ahab in Melville's *Moby Dick*: "This whole act's immutably decreed. 'Twas rehearsed by thee and me a billion years before this ocean rolled." However, his omnipresent tendency to reduce the story to a metaphysical meander through the 'fourth dimension' reads at times like the navel-gazing didacticism of an unreconstructed hippie. Writing in an epilogue on the glut of theories which have since supplanted his own, he employs "the fractal shape known as Koch's snowflake" to literally illustrate his point that the field of Ripper study has become saturated.

The graphic novel is a visual medium and such tactics serve a dual purpose, but *From Hell* too often seems like a criminological case history viewed through the eyes of Lobsang Rampa. In one notation, Moore ponders his reaction to the destruction visited upon Kelly and remarks that the killer's work appears to him to exhibit "evidence of a childlike, mystical absorption in the world of the organic." Defence lawyers please note.

In the bound version, Moore adds an appendix where he brings the Ripper story up to date and even incorporates his own contribution to it. In this, he goes some way towards washing his hands of much of what has passed in the pages of his novel, as Joseph Sickert did after the publication of Knight's book: "The idea of a solution, any solution, is inane." Earlier, amid more than 4,000 words of notes on the text, he echoes a sentiment mouthed by the Abberline of his own creation, and comments that the character's cynical remark could equally sum up *his* position as "one currently making part of his living wrapping up miserable little killings in supernatural twaddle." But such is the extent of the research in *From Hell*, such is the painstaking detail in its artwork, that it is hard to resist the impression that Alan Moore was not genuinely enthralled by Knight's hypothesis when he initiated the project. His apologia is more like a bet-hedge than a disclaimer; he dismisses *The Diary of Jack the Ripper* (published in 1993) as "profoundly silly", when it is, on the face of it, no sillier than anything here. And a revealing touch of petulance is in play as reluctantly he acknowledges the fact that his version of events had been subject to the same "brute Darwinian mechanics" as everyone else's, even before the epic undertaking had run its course.

For all that, *From Hell* is a well-intentioned pictorial primer on the nature of the debates which have informed the uncertain science of Ripperology, even if it does not, of itself, offer up as worthy a contribution to that argument as it appears to imagine.

Taken as a work of speculative fiction, Moore and Campbell's *From Hell* is a remarkable achievement, in which seemingly disassociated detail is woven seamlessly into a cohesive tale of political intrigue by a narrative strategy of epic proportion, and even its extensive appendix of footnotes can be seen as merely discursive of further reading for anyone interested in the wide range of sources consulted by Moore in support of his thesis. If it were to be taken as fact, though, the tapestry of uncorroborated assertion that forms the basis of *From Hell*'s plot adds little to and subtracts much from the

Teaser poster for
From Hell (2001)

Johnny Depp
as Abberline in
From Hell (2001)

present state of knowledge about events surrounding the Whitechapel Murders.

The influence of this particular graphic novel – spawned as it was from the creators of the revered *Watchmen* series, and leading as it has to a feature film – is in peril of eroding in the most susceptible reader the comprehensive deconstruction of Knight's theory which has painstakingly been undertaken by dedicated researchers. In the closing pages of the novel, Moore himself can occasionally be seen to be afflicted with the same desire as Knight had to propagate his vision at the expense of any opposing facts unearthed to discredit it. To this more unsavoury end, he was aided in 2001 by the myth-making might of Twentieth Century-Fox.

In December 1887, Inspector Fred Abberline attended a dinner held in his honour at the Unicorn Tavern, Shoreditch. The previous month, he had been transferred to a new post at Central Office, Scotland Yard, after having spent the best part of that year in Whitehall's 'A' Division. Abberline was presented with a gold watch and sum of money as a token of "esteem and regard" and as a thank you for 14 years' service to the people of Whitechapel. Little did he know that, in eight months' time, those same people would need him to serve them again as they had never needed him before.

This historic recall to duty was, in essence, the starting point for Euston's *Jack the Ripper* in 1988. The self-same situation sets the 2001 Fox film *From Hell* in motion also. The only real difference between the two is in the type of drug that the maliciously maligned Inspector Abberline is alleged to be in the process of imbibing when the call comes.

"He's not doing this for fun. This is ritual."

Inspector Abberline (Johnny Depp) in *From Hell* (2001)

From Hell is the Whitechapel killings as they never were but as they might have been were they to have been researched by Charles Berlitz or Whitley Streiber and turned into a screenplay by Oliver Stone. As it is, *From Hell* was turned into a film by the Hughes Brothers, whose previous escapades of note were *Menace II Society* (1993) and *Dead Presidents* (1995). Add the word 'Victorian' to the former title and some measure is gained of the film's overall style. Given their pedigree, Albert and Allen Hughes are mercifully less concerned about the metaphysical aspects of Moore's plot than they are about depicting the social conditions in the London equivalent of a Los Angeles ghetto, circa 1888. Notwithstanding this, the narrative of the film derives from Alan Moore out of Stephen Knight; *From Hell* is not a pseudo-factual docudrama based on real events, it is a fantasy spun around them as was the graphic novel on which it is based.

Nowhere is this more apparent than in the murder of Mary Kelly (or Kelly substitute, as the film has it). Campbell's outrageously extravagant treatment of this in the comic has the killer at work by the light of a blazing fire, which shoots laser-like beams of light into the Whitechapel night through cracks in the door and gaps in the curtain at the window. The film version does not go quite that far, preferring shadow-play to greet the Ripper's entry to the room, but neither novel nor film can manage the correct placement of Kelly's bed in spite of the fact that two scene-of-crime photographs of 13 Miller's Court have been widely disseminated in recent years. A minor point, perhaps, but if room layout can be abandoned in the cause of dramatic expedience, what price the novel's supposedly supportive footnotes?

The film version of *From Hell* is equipped with the requisite tricks of the modern blockbuster: it looks like a million dollars (literally, in this instance, as that was the cost of the Whitechapel sets which were constructed on a 20-acre site near the Barrandov studios in Prague, Czechoslovakia), it stars Johnny Depp (*Sleepy Hollow*, *The Ninth Gate*; both 1999) as Abberline, and it draws on a legendary killer *and* a cult novel for its inspiration. For all that, *From Hell* is anodyne at its core, lacking the courage of its publicised convictions that it was to be the last cinematic word on Jack the Ripper. Even the graphic violence comes in short measure, like Jack himself.

The story is imbued with violence, but it is violence of the Hollywood kind: physical threats and macho posturing, strong-arm tactics and general bad attitudes all round. *From Hell* is Whitechapel by way of *Escape from New York*. Violence in London's East End of the 1880s was of the 'Saturday night' variety: sudden, inconsequential and alcohol-fuelled. Jack the Ripper has gone down in history because his were *extreme* acts, different from anything that local police officers might have expected to encounter after a street brawl or domestic dust-up; the way the film has it, the Ripper's murders are only marginally more brutal than the penalty which one is given to imagine might be extracted for crossing the ghetto thugs of the 'Old Nicholls Gang'. Playing up the danger inherent in such minor characters has a negative effect on the impact which Jack makes subsequently and, in point of fact, he is alarmingly absent from the first half of the film, despite three murders to his credit by then. Only when it comes time for the double event, with Liz Stride's throat slashed open in close-up, does Jack's presence finally begin to be felt. (Curiously, the most graphic murder in *From Hell* – that of Stride – is the one to which the least violence attached in life.)

> "*Below the skin of history are London's veins. These symbols: the mitre, the pentacle star... Even someone as ignorant and degenerate as you can sense they course with energy... and meaning. I am that meaning. I am that energy.*"
>
> Sir William Gull (Ian Holm) in *From Hell* (2001)

From Hell is scripted and dramatised in the formulaic manner of the typical Hollywood serial-killer thriller, with the whole then transplanted to a far-off land and peopled by characters with funny 'foreign' accents. It has neither the tone nor the pace of the place it purports to depict. The Hughes brothers have extracted the essence of their source, but the overall impression is identical to one that an American audience might gain if a British production tried to recreate New York from reading a *Superman* comic. (A simple map of London would have made it clear that there is no need to cross the Thames to get from the West End of the city [Mayfair] to the East, as Gull does at the climax.)

Victorian London was a dramatically divided society of 'haves' and 'have nots', as was evidenced in an article that George Bernard Shaw penned for the *Star* after the murder of

Annie Chapman, and in response to the fact that a recent riot had resulted in the princely sum of £78,000 being allocated to the area: "If the habits of duchesses only admitted of their being decoyed into Whitechapel backyards, a single experiment in slaughterhouse anatomy on one aristocratic victim might fetch in around half a million and save the necessity of sacrificing four women of the people." But From Hell features no such contrasts; it is unrelentingly downbeat – dark, dismal and depressing – and places all of its emphasis on the seamier side of East End street life and none at all on the commerce, camaraderie and cheeriness of spirit for which Eastenders themselves were justly famous.

Most of the great Hollywood films set in this period, as well as many of the films about Jack the Ripper, have seen fit to include a music-hall sequence to illustrate the lighter side of Victorian life. The 'halls' were everywhere: one of the most famous of them, the Eagle Tavern in City Road, Shoreditch, was less than two miles from Whitechapel High Street, while the equally popular Pavilion Theatre was in Whitechapel Road itself – the 'Drury Lane of the East End' and very epicentre of the Ripper murders. Yet none of this luminance is allowed to intrude on the studied gloom of From Hell.

Nor is there any evidence of industry, only indolence, even though Eastenders barely slept, and not because of tarts or criminal gangs roaming the streets, but because of 18-hour day market traders pursuing their professions. Britain was still a 'workshop of the world' at this point in time, and its workers required feeding. Life in the East End was hard beyond endurance for many – parts of it were not dissimilar to a Delhi slum, and night on Ratcliffe Highway could present as many dangers to the unaccustomed stranger as that on the Hong Kong waterfront – but much of the area also teemed with commerce.

The Vigilance Committees were set up, not to capture Jack the Ripper per se, but to reassure local residents and buttress trade. It is easy to be carried away on the horns of hyperbole when describing conditions among the poor of London in 1888, and modern filmmakers incline to dwell on the sordid, in any event. However, Victorian London was the very pinnacle of civilisation at this juncture and a more accurate representation of its quality, as well as its opposing cultures, can be found in William Logsdail's exquisite painting 'The Ninth of November', which illustrates the street-scene in the City of London during Lord Mayor Sir James Whitehead's inaugural procession at the very moment that Mary Kelly's body was discovered inside Miller's Court, and at less than three quarters of a mile from the site of the murder. Logsdail's unwitting memento mori provides the perfect counterpoint to all the Gothic trappings which tend to accompany the Ripper scare in popular culture.

Chapter five of Moore's novel is titled 'The Nemesis of Neglect', after Alice illustrator John Tenniel's famous Punch cartoon, and it contrasts the lifestyle of William Gull with that of the drabs in the doss-houses of Whitechapel, with particular emphasis paid to Polly Nichols. Moore leaves much of this chapter dialogue-free, relying on Campbell's draughtsmanship to make his point for him by exchanging his regular pen-and-ink for a watercolour wash in the panels which portray Gull's featherbedded existence. The visual effect on the printed page is startling, and says more than any number of polemical pamphlets ever could about the disparity between rich and poor in Victoria's Britain. No such allusions find their way into From Hell 'the movie' (as Moore refers to it in his own epilogue).

Apart from a scene where Abberline and Kelly saunter through Hampton Court Gardens, with their famous Maze created by William of Orange, From Hell offers no relief from the squalor and dark-age superstition which it sees as epitomising the period: a prefrontal

'The Ninth of November' by William Logsdail (1890)

lobotomy is performed with hammer and spike, while the professional classes as a whole are only shown congregating in shadowy enclaves of the Guildhall, participating in esoteric Masonic ritual.

None of this is helped by the screenplay's decision to have the historically respectable Detective Inspector Fred Abberline while away his leisure hours in an opium den, where he expires in an anticlimactic finale while his real-life counterpart went on to crown a career in the Metropolitan Police by working for the Pinkerton agency in Monte Carlo, before retiring to Bournemouth and the less stressful pleasures of the garden. As if to underscore the Gothic evocation, Abberline himself is a 'seer' afflicted by precognitive glimpses of the murders as they are occurring, and subject to insights in their connection when he is in contact with the bodies. This neatly circumvents a good deal of exposition, although Abberline's psychic abilities seem to desert him when he comes into contact with the actual *murderer*.

Given that the film had two hands on the directorial tiller, in the brotherly shape of Albert and Allen Hughes, it is very conventionally handled. Endless crane-shots and a surplus of lap-dissolves work against the scripted action, which seeks to compress the (unspecified) chronology of the murders out of dramatic necessity. One sequence employs time-lapse photography to show the gathering of a crowd around the body of Polly Nichols in Bucks Row, but this is a gimmick used in isolation and reminiscent of the 'glass-ceiling' shot in Hitchock's *The Lodger*. It is virtuoso filmmaking, but it adds nothing to the dynamic of the piece and only distracts the eye from the matter in hand.

> "So… Jack the Ripper isn't just merely killing whores. He's executing traitors. He's a mason fulfilling a duty."
>
> Inspector Abberline (Johnny Depp) in From Hell (2001)

Unlike the novel, the film adds the police complicity of 1997's *The Ripper* and the government cover-up of *Murder by Decree* to its already extravagant rendering of Stephen Knight. The result is conspiracy on a scale beyond Watergate, in which Sir William Gull is the mere instrument to be disposed of when his bloody work is done. Britain is ruled by a medieval clique of master Masons whose disdain for the proletariat would put Stalin to shame. A quintet of whores have stood witness at the marriage of one of their own to the heir apparent to the throne of England; as they also know the whereabouts of the royal bastard who has resulted from this union, they have to be silenced. Gull is hired by dint of fraternal association to perform the deed, which he does in accordance with his own peculiar reading of Masonic lore, even going so far as to choose specific locations for the murders which in combination will form a sacred pentacle on a map of the East End.

(Several authors, Knight and Aleister Crowley included, have tried to read symbolic significance in the topography of the murder sites; this was best exemplified in *The Hour of 13*, where the killer nicknamed the Terror spelled the letter 'T' on a map of London through the choice of sites in which he committed his murders of policemen.)

The screenplay appends a new character in the form of Ben Kidney (Terence Harvey), a sinister 'Special Branch' Inspector and agent of the Crown, whose foot-soldiers facilitate Gull's state-sponsored campaign of assassination. The reason for his inclusion is the decision to back-pedal on Knight and Moore's blackmail plot and have all the victims executed merely for standing witness to the marriage of Eddy and Annie Crook. This makes nonsense of Knight's already nonsensical hypothesis, as Kidney's list of those 'in the know' does not seem to extend to the priest who officiated at the ceremony, the Special Branch officers who assist him (not all of whom can be masons, surely?), and sundry others drawn into the plot who appear to be somehow immune from 'spilling the beans' in a way that the whores are not. The same lack of focus afflicts the script's treatment of Abberline, who alone is singled out for threats while his sidekick Godley is ignored. This kind of anomaly is the fly in the ointment of conspiracy theory in general: dozens of individuals have to be drawn into a scheme to eliminate a mere handful, all of whom become privy to the same supposedly 'secret' knowledge in the process.

In films like this, *everyone* is either plotting or plotted against, with the rest of humanity represented by a handful of bystanders in between the two. Chief among these is Peter – as opposed to the real *George* – Godley, Abberline's trusty sergeant-at-arms, in the reassuring form of Robbie Coltrane. Godley's predilection for Platoesque asides rewards him with most of the best lines in the film (aside from those reserved for Jack), and his nomination as 'Chorus' (commenting on, if not directly participating in, the unfolding events), as well as Abberline's untimely death, give *From Hell* an overtone of Greek tragedy. His quote from *Hamlet* – "Goodnight, sweet prince" – as he bids a fond farewell to his erstwhile boss only adds to the impression, and as flights of symphonic angels sing the Inspector to his rest, the sergeant places a penny-piece on each of Abberline's eyes, to prevent him from having "to wander forever, lost between two worlds," as the inspector had himself explained when paying a similar compliment to Annie Chapman. All that is missing to complete the allusion is a voice-over from Godley in the style of *Sunset Boulevard* (1950), the reason for which would have become clear at the climax with the surprise demise of the film's main player.

Abberline's death is a direct consequence of his promotion to protagonist in the film, whereas Gull holds that position in Moore's novel; it is Gull who experiences a death-vision of

From Hell (2001)

Kelly before his own ignominious expiration in an insane asylum. In retaining this precognitive glimpse, Abberline is thus required to expire in similar fashion, though in the opium den. There is no accounting for the thought processes of studio executives.

To retain an element of mystery about who, of the only possible suspect, Jack the Ripper actually is, Ian Holm is required to play Gull as a beneficent confidant of Abberline's throughout much of his inquiry. Only when it comes time for Kelly's murder does the mask fall and the Hyde-like persona emerge but, by then, Abberline has the measure of him anyway. (The part of Gull was originally to have been played by Nigel Hawthorne, who had to relinquish the role because of illness; he died on Boxing Day 2001.) All kinds of technical tweaks are used to disguise the fact that Gull is the killer, from electronically altering Holm's voice to swapping him for a stand-in (a la Mid-Century's *Jack the Ripper*) for much of the murderous action, but to no avail. No sooner does the name William Gull crop up in a Ripper film, than the die is cast from that point on. Holm does give *From Hell* its most chilling moments, however, from the expression on his face when he finally realises that his subterfuge has been uncovered by Abberline, to his pep-talk to an unravelling Netley as he ushers him verbally into his own private *Inferno*.

> Netley: "I'm just a simple chap, sir. I'm not a great man like you. I just don't know where I am anymore."
> Gull: "There, there, Netley. I shall tell you where we are. We are in the most extreme and utter region of the human mind, a radiant abyss, where men meet themselves."
> Netley: "I don't understand. I don't understand, sir."
> Gull: "Hell, Netley... We are in hell."
>
> Jason Flemyng and Ian Holm in *From Hell* (2001)

With an obligatory 'happy ending' required to justify the film's budget (at least one where the two lead players were not seen to perish), history played conveniently into the hands of separate-draft screenwriters Terry Hayes and Rafael Yglesias. Moore had hinted at Kelly's escape in the novel, aided and abetted by ambiguous panels from Campbell, and this scenario was adopted for the film: before the hour of the murder, Kelly has fled London and sought the sanctuary of her native Ireland (all of which is vouchsafed to Abberline in a vision at the moment of his death; in the novel, it was revealed to Gull), her place in the bed in 13 Miller's Court having been gratefully taken by a French ingénue of fortuitously similar build and appearance.

For once, Hollywood cannot be accused of bending history to suit its own commercial needs. This scenario is as valid as any other, and is supported by as many 'facts' after the event as is the popularly held belief that it was Kelly who died at the hands of the Ripper. Only the stately arrival of William Gull's funereal carriage intercedes to spoil the one innovative touch in a film which decries original thinking at every turn.

At the climax of *From Hell*, Jack the Ripper enters Miller's Court to murder Mary Kelly. He puts down his bag and sits, contemplatively, on the edge of the bed, before suddenly wielding the first, savage blow against the sleeping girl. This strange interlude, with the Ripper seated at the foot of the bed while the girl sleeps upon it, her face turned away from her killer, is a nod to one of a series of pictures by Walter Sickert, collectively entitled 'The Camden Town Murder'. The painting in question ostensibly depicts a real-life murder, similar to that of Kelly, which occurred near Sickert's Camden Town studio in 1907. The man tried and acquitted of the crime was named Robert Wood, who was a friend of Sickert's and whose counsel for the defence was hired by the artist himself.

In December 2001, the world of Ripperology was astonished and the art world outraged by the actions of American multimillionaire author Patricia Cornwell, whose criminological investigations had previously been confined to the fictional adventures of forensic psychologist Kay Scarpetta in novels like *Body of Evidence*. Bitten by the Ripper bug, Cornwell had bought Sickert's writing desk as well as 31 of his great impressionist works – though not, fortunately, 'The Camden Town Murder' – at a total cost of $3 million of her own money, for the purposes of procuring a DNA sample which could be matched against the Ripper letters and prove her theory that Walter Sickert *was* Jack the Ripper.

> Roarke: *"Miss Peters has evolved a theory which she believes solves the identity of the infamous Whitechapel murderer."*
> Tattoo: *"You mean Jack the Ripper?"*
> Roarke: *"Precisely."*
> Ricardo Montalban and Hervé Villechaize in *Fantasy Island*: 'With Affection, Jack the Ripper' (1980)

Cornwell, like many others before her, seems to have been swayed by the reasoning of Stephen Knight in relation to Sickert's supposed 'coding' of his paintings. To the horror of art lovers the world over, she then proceeded to rip one of the canvases to shreds in her search for Sickert DNA and, finding nothing, settled for the similarity between a watermark on Sickert's personal stationery and that on the paper used in one of the letters as proof of Walter the Ripper. (Given that none of the letters was proved to have come from the Whitechapel murderer, the whole exercise appears to have been misguided from the start.) Despite Cornwell's self-proclaimed "100 per cent" certainty about the Hollywood-style solution of a killer who "painted by day, murdered by night", it is likely that her theory will turn out to be another in a line of Ripper red herrings brought about through a combination of naïveté and over-enthusiasm.

The idea of using DNA profiling to buckle Jack is as sound as they come, provided that one can be sure of the killer's DNA in the first place. The dealers who sold Cornwell her paintings took comfort from the fact that she paid above market value, but the only thing that Patricia Cornwell has managed to show for her efforts thus far is that there seems to be no limit to the philistinism of the super-rich.

In the eyes of those to whom Walter Sickert represents their best guess at the identity of Jack the Ripper, 'The Camden Town Murder' is the murder in Miller's Court viewed through a filter of artistic licence. The strange death of Mary Kelly continues to intrigue writers and artists alike, more than any other element of the Ripper killings. So redolent with mystery is this most heinous of crimes that it now crops up in films with remorseless regularity, as though the horror of it can only be expunged through constant repetition. The latest example of such cultural catharsis came in a Dreamworks teleseries of 2000, which retold the event with textbook veracity and, unusual in popular drama, without extraneous comment.

> *"It's about Mary Jane. You're right; she's real; I found out who she is… She has to be Mary Jane Kelly, of the East End of London. On November 9th 1888, she was Jack the Ripper's final victim."*
> Miles Ballard (John Billingsley) in *The Others*: 'Don't Dream It's Over' (2000)

NBC's *The Others*, which debuted on 5 February 2000, chose to venture along the Whitechapel Road in an episode called 'Don't Dream It's Over', a title borrowed from a Crowded House chart-topper of 1986. The premise of the show is similar to that of 1972's *The Sixth Sense*. A disparate group have one thing in common: they share a facility for extrasensory perception which is beyond their individual ken but which they collectively attempt to come to terms with through mutual association. The series as a whole has more than a little stylistic affinity with *The Outer Limits*.

A young medico named Mark Gabriel (Gabriel Macht) becomes subject to a recurring dream in which he sees a mysterious girl (Tushka Bergen), seated lonely and tearful in a small room. To the dismay of his associates, he begins to fall in love with her. Aware that she might be a real person who is appearing to Mark through psychokinesis, the Others attempt to discover her identity before he can become too involved. All Mark can tell them about her is her name, her age and the fact that she is given to singing a peculiarly plaintive ballad: "…while life does remain to cheer me, I'll retain this small violet I plucked from mother's grave." In-putting this data to a computer turns up a profile of Mary Jane Kelly, last known victim of Jack the Ripper. The group decide to hold a seance to see if there is any way in which they can warn her of her impending fate. Instead, they find themselves witnesses to it.

To those familiar with the territory, the twist in the tail of 'Don't Dream It's Over' is telegraphed when the dream-woman reveals that her name is Mary – more so when she elaborates it to Mary Jane – but to the casual viewer, the element of surprise is sustained remarkably well, right up to the point of the seance: "She's with a man. He's carrying some sort of a bag... Oh God, it's *him*..." Ultimately the episode has nowhere to go; true to history, Kelly is killed and Mark is left to look for another woman of his dreams.

As with tales of time travel, there is a central flaw in any story which tries to postulate parallel worlds, breachable by psychic link. Either the protagonist is forced to re-enact his or her own death in perpetuity, like the phantom in the castle keep, or they are required to meet up with some very strange characters on the way to it. Neither is ever entirely satisfactory. Nevertheless, *The Others* is better than most of its kind. At least writer and director Mick Garris took the trouble to read a book, and 'Don't Dream It's Over' tries to recreate Kelly's last hours on earth with some sense of accuracy. Kelly trills 'Sweet Violets' throughout, which a witness reported her singing on the night of her death. There is also something unerringly authentic in feel about the tale's depiction of Jack the Ripper (John Vickery, late of *Babylon 5* and *Star Trek: Deep Space 9*). He looks right; he picks Kelly up in a bar, on the pretext that he is a doctor and can prescribe something for a hacking cough; he peers warily over his shoulder as he accompanies her back to her room; he puts her at her ease before suddenly slaying her on the bed. Only the set design of Miller's Court falters slightly in the face of an otherwise well-crafted vignette of Ripper murder.

The film has another surprise in store. In the year that brought U-571 onto international screens, in which Hollywood credited American naval personnel with the capture of the German Enigma machine in World War II (as a result of which a disclaimer was attached to the film on its British run, after protests from war veterans), Jack the Ripper, for the first time on screen, is portrayed as an *American*: "I've a friend with that accent; you an American?" Kelly asks him. "That's very perceptive of you," Jack replies. If the change of nationality was intentional, then the book that the makers consulted was Evans and Gainey's *The Lodger: The Arrest and Escape of Jack the Ripper* (*The First American Serial Killer* as it was re-titled for publication in the US), and the doctor in the film is therefore Francis Tumblety.

Tumblety was a Canadian-born quack who hailed from Rochester, New York, against whom the evidence seems to be that he might, at one time, have rented rooms near to where the murders took place. As the co-authors of *The Lodger* are both British ex-policemen, it would be fair to say that *The Others* did not so much lay claim to Jack in the name of the stars-and-stripes as nominate him for American citizenship by default.

The Others is an artistic outpouring of post-millennial angst, the product of a culture that has returned to the dark, where people live in perpetual twilight and the only meaningful relationships are those with the long dead. In 'Don't Dream It's Over', the characters all function in a half-world of post-Christian, postmodern, nihilistic non-existence. Man has moved back into the realm of spirit-reading, table-rapping and ectoplasmic evacuation. The episode – and the series – sings the lost song of a society at the end of history, desperate to reconnect with its past but ultimately unable to bridge the divide. As Marie Belloc Lowndes' contemporary G K Chesterton wrote (in the paraphrasing of his biographer, Emile Cammaerts): "The first effect of not believing in God is to believe in anything." *The Others* is a perfect example of an adage which is as true of today as it was of the period to which Chesterton was referring, around the turn of the 19th century, when Spiritualism was widely viewed as a new religion. Arthur Conan Doyle was himself a convert, as were many of his peers. A hundred years on and little has changed: the New Age mystic of the modern world is still a Rosicrucian by any other name.

It is, above all, the murder of Mary Jane Kelly which haunts the history of the Ripper killings, and something of its enduring horror can still be felt when it tragically is echoed for real. On 25 November 2001, a 90-year-old woman named Mabel Leyshon was murdered in her home on the Isle of Anglesey, on the North Wales coast. She was ferociously stabbed to death, after which her killer cut out her heart and removed it to another room of the house. Two fireside pokers were arranged to form a cross on the floor. The Welsh police consulted occult experts to ascertain if there were any significance to this but reached no conclusion. A local teenager was later arrested and charged.

More than that of any other of the alleged victims of Jack the Ripper, it is the death of Mary Kelly which most represents unfinished business. Like the grieving mother of a murdered child, who feels she cannot rest until the killer of her offspring is found, popular culture continues to replay the murder in Miller's Court to serve as a focus for collective responsibility and communal guilt, and to remind us all that the dream – the nightmare – is not yet over, the monstrousness of Jack the Ripper not yet come to terms with.

Concurrent with American World's *Bad Karma*, Prophecy Entertainment released *Ripper: Letter from Hell*, which also went direct-to-video at the end of 2001, with *Letter from Hell* dropped from the title in response to the Hughes brothers film. Taking account of the various teleseries episodes, this was the fifth film to rely entirely on the emotive word 'Ripper' to supply it with a marketable hook. *Ripper (Letter from Hell)*, to distinguish it from the rest of the pack, was a throwback to the good old days of stalk-and-slash thrillers like *Friday the 13th*, but the whole was also cloaked in the knowing reflexes of the post-*Scream* era.

The plot is straightforward enough when disentangled from the psychedelic whirl of images and constant flash-frame editing that passes for direction in *Ripper (Letter from Hell)*: another Ripper copycat is out to decimate the students of a class exploring the psychology of serial murder and presided over by the twitchy Marshall Kane (a remarkably subdued Bruce Payne). Much trashy, flashy mayhem follows, and those who are still standing by the halfway point establish that the killer is taking copycat murder to new comparatives by not only aping

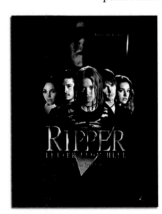

the modus of Jack but singling out victims with the same initials as the originals. This lets both Marshall Kane and Molly Keller (the survivor of a previous teen massacre five years before) off the hook, as their initials appear to prime at least one of them for final victimhood. Not so, of course, and Kane takes the fall for the killings while Keller (A J Cook) is revealed to have been the murderer on both of the relevant occasions.

The murders borrow much from Italian *gialli* and are often so elaborately staged that the notion that these are somehow 'Ripper' copycat killings soon becomes laughable, as does the unremitting gloom, which seems to imply that this is a campus where electricity grids have not yet penetrated. On top of that, the story appears to be taking place on a planet of incessant thunder and lightning, especially at times of collective tension.

In quiet periods, which are few and far between, there is much discussion as to the identity of the Ripper. Kane favours Montague Druitt, while others in the class prefer Joseph Barnett. All this is a blind to mask the surprise that awaits in the last frames of the film. The tragedy of *Ripper*'s tired but still acceptable plot – and undoubtedly part of the reason why it was denied a theatrical release – is its self-consciously pretentious directorial design. When it becomes possible to spot the influences at work behind the

stroboscopic style, they are all here: Argento, Alan Parker, Sam Raimi even. A thoroughly eclectic mix. But in practice, much of the action and most of the dialogue is unintelligible, if not impenetrable, to the extent that *Ripper (Letter from Hell)* is proof positive that there are some filmmakers who should never be allowed anywhere near a steadicam or computer editing suite.

> *"I mean... this is 1888, isn't it?"*
>
> Molly Keller (A J Cook) in *Ripper: Letter from Hell* (2001)

Ripper (Letter from Hell) does, however, have a strikingly impressive final scene, which is almost worth sitting out the preceding two hours of eyestrain for. If the film itself plays like the mind of a madman – dark, confused, full of disconnected images – then the last shot takes us inside that mind. As Kane goes to his execution in the electric chair for a series of murders which he did not commit, Keller closes the door on her flat and walks downstairs to the street below. On the wall of the flat is a painting of a horse and carriage and as the camera comes to rest on it, we see her exit the building that forms the backdrop to the *painting*. The camera then pulls back to show her entering a Whitechapel street scene, circa 1888. She strides into frame in slow motion, reprising the famous declamatory speech of Jack Gurney's from *The Ruling Class* which begins, "This is 1888, isn't it?" The implication is clear: Jack the Ripper was Mary Jane Kelly.

Inquest

There are ideal series of events which run parallel with the real ones. They rarely coincide.
Men and circumstances generally modify the ideal train of events, so that it seems imperfect, and its
consequences are equally imperfect.

Edgar Allan Poe, *The Mystery of Marie Roget* (1842)

"Jack the Ripper's not finished," says Johnny Depp's Inspector Abberline in *From Hell*, and if works of fact and fiction, films, series episodes, 'fan' journals, web-sites, cults and conventions are anything to go by, he might never be. Every passing year produces new theories about the murders in Whitechapel in 1888, and new suspects too, author Patricia's Cornwell's being but the latest in a long line.

The *Jack the Ripper A-Z* (Headline, 1991) lists over a hundred separate suspects. But the word 'suspect' is a misnomer in this context; most of those named are not (and nor were they ever) genuinely suspected of the crimes but have found themselves promoted to the role by indiscriminate theorists over the years, regardless. No case has yet been advanced against any named suspect that ties them to all *five* of the canonical victims. From this it may be concluded that the real Jack the Ripper has not yet been unmasked, but it may also be supportive of the contention that there was *no* 'Jack' the Ripper to begin with.

> *"See... ? Nobody ever gives you any credit. Commit the perfect series of murders and who gets the blame? Harley Street surgeons. Russian anarchists. Queen Victoria's private physician. Prince Albert..."*
>
> Jack the Ripper (John Mills) in *Deadly Advice* (1993)

Just as notional strangler 'Bible John', who was supposed to have murdered three women in the Barrowland area of Glasgow during 1968-9, is now thought to have been a conflation of different killers, so the search for the identity of Jack the Ripper has not only exacerbated confusions which already were apparent in the evidence to hand, but also diminished the possibility that the Whitechapel murderer ever truly existed in the form which is commonly attributed to him.

The world of Ripperology has arrived at the point where a single unearthed document is deemed sufficient to warrant another dip into the murky waters of amateur detection, and another theory cobbled together on the strength of it. Any interpretation of the facts is possible, with each new slant on the case made to seem as likely or unlikely as the one before. The myth of the phantom killer is feeding on itself, and comparisons with crop circles, the search for alien life, even the Loch Ness Monster have become unavoidable. As Alan Moore wryly observed at the close of *From Hell*, "Soon, somebody will notice the disturbing similarities between the Ripper crimes and recent cattle mutilations, from which they will draw the only sensible conclusion."

The situation was neatly encapsulated by a sketch in Universal's *Amazon Women on the Moon* (1987), a pastiche of popular culture and the culture of television in particular, with its bent for sensationalism and its self-perceived need to summarise everything in easily digestible

Previous page:
Murder in Miller's
Court. *From Hell*
(2001)

sound-bites. In a parody of 'stranger-than-fiction' series like *Ripley's Believe It or Not*, host
Henry Silva postulated the logical extension of the Ripperologists' dream for a show that was
appropriately entitled 'Bullshit or Not?'

Deadly Advice (1994)

> "Jack the Ripper... Was he a prosperous London surgeon? Perhaps a member of British royalty? Well,
> our Bullshit team has unearthed spectacular new evidence that Jack the Ripper was, in fact... the Loch
> Ness Monster!"

Henry Silva in *Amazon Women on the Moon* (1987)

The Bullshit reconstruction shows 'Nessie', clad in outsize plaid cloak and billycock hat,
enticing an oblivious streetwalker up a dark alleyway, smirking as he goes. There is a scream,
and Silva reappears to deliver his summary: "Is this the way it happened? Was Jack the
Ripper, in fact, a 60-foot sea serpent from Scotland? Did I take this job for a quick buck?
We may never know the answers to these questions. Next week – " At this point, he is cut off
mid-sentence by an invisible channel-surfer.

Amazon Women on the
Moon (1987)

Amazon Women on the Moon was a spoof, but mention of the Loch Ness Monster in connection with Jack the Ripper can no longer be adjudged extreme in the wake of a sci-fi teleseries of 2001, financed, in part, by the people who brought *Sliders* to the small screen. *Sir Arthur Conan Doyle's The Lost World* was a Commonwealth co-production between Canada, New Zealand and Australia, filmed in Queensland, New South Wales, and spun-off from a 1998 telefilm of the same name, starring Patrick Bergin.

In a third season episode called 'The Knife', Professor Challenger (Peter McCauley) and his band of Club 18-30 explorers come across 'Jack' holed up on their prehistoric plateau, in the twin forms of Inspector Robert Anderson and William Gull. With no obvious tarts in the locality, the two have taken to disembowelling dinosaurs instead. A painful encounter with the post-feminist Amazons who pass for the show's female interest does little to deflect the deadly duo from their evil ways and after the regulatory skirmishes, Anderson falls to his death from a tree-house and Gull is eaten by velociraptors. One simply could not make it up.

> Roxton: "Now, what's an inspector from Scotland Yard doing in the jungles of South America?"
> Anderson: "I'm tracking a criminal, perhaps the most notorious criminal the world has ever known. I've been on his tail for 30 years."
> Marguerite: "Thirty years...? Who is this criminal?"
> Anderson: "Jack the Ripper."
>
> Will Snow, John Noble and Rachel Blakely in *Sir Arthur Conan Doyle's The Lost World*: 'The Knife' (2001)

The premise of the tale is again lifted from Knight, without anyone having bothered to read his book to its end. 'The Knife' posits the notion that Gull, Netley and Anderson were the original murderers, whereas Knight swapped Anderson for Sickert in his closing argument. With the episode set in 1918 (going by the fictional Anderson's remark that he has chased the Ripper for 30 years), *Assistant Commissioner* Anderson would have been 77 at the time, with Gull clocking in at 101. "He's the right age," Challenger declares, when considering the suspect's credentials. The professor's sojourn in exotic exile has clearly eroded his mental faculties; he exhibits a similar debilitation of memory when confirming the fourth Ripper victim as Cathy *Beddowes*.

Sir Arthur Conan
Doyle's The Lost World
(2001)

This cavalier lack of any attention to detail is all too typical of what passes for light entertainment in the multi-channel maw of modern television, an antediluvian attitude compounded by the fact that these are not fictional characters which writer and co-producer Greg Mullally is throwing to the beasts to devour, but *real* people. Sir Robert Anderson was a devout and dutiful servant of the Crown, who died at home in his bed in the very year that this slapdash slice of digitised dross has him supposedly trudging around a lost world in search of fair-haired game; his biography was written by his son in 1947. William Gull died in 1890.

If *Sir Arthur Conan Doyle's The Lost World* reduced screen characterisation of Jack the Ripper to the point of exhaustion, a sense of tiredness can now be discerned to be creeping over the pages of the latest outpourings from the hitherto tireless Ripperologists, as well a sense that the game is no longer afoot, that it is nearing its end. A sense of *ennui*, to borrow from Sickert.

Sir Arthur Conan Doyle's The Lost World (2001)

Jack to the future

From Hell took $11.6 million at the US box-office on its opening weekend of 19 October 2001 – five million less than predicted, and just under $19 million less than that of Johnny Depp's last big-budget excursion into period horror, Tim Burton's *Sleepy Hollow*. On a film that cost a 'mere' $35 million to make, it was nevertheless a respectable start, especially at a time when the minds of its American audiences were on atrocities committed closer to home than those carried out in Whitechapel over a century before.

Facts have again been replaced by the most attractive of the available fictions and *From Hell* is not only the new *Lodger*, it is the new *Mystery of Jack the Ripper* as well. The fanciful vision of the man in black, stalking the midnight streets around Whitechapel, will always be preferable to the probable reality: sudden and sordid death at the hands of a dysfunctional nobody. So it is likely to remain, until and unless some new evidence is produced which will lay the mystery down, once and for all. *From Hell* has demarcated Jack's cultural persona for a generation, if for no reason other than the scale of the project and reach of the potential audience, as *Bram Stoker's Dracula* did for the Count in 1992.

> "My name is William Withey Gull and I am dying. I am Catch-Me-If-You-Can and I am Leather Apron. I am Jack the Ripper on my way to heaven."
>
> The words of Sir William Gull. Alan Moore, *From Hell* (Knockabout; 1996)

The first hundred years of Jack the Ripper have been the first hundred years of the cinema as well. He has played his part. It remains to be seen whether the deadly allure of Jack's knife will continue to attract the unwary over the next hundred, or if the best of him is now behind us.

It would be true to say that the better screen treatments of Jack the Ripper, as well as that in Marie Belloc Lowndes' story *The Lodger*, are likely to be as close to the truth in their depiction of the anonymous killer who slew one or more women in the East End of London in 1888 as any; it is certainly true of films which were made before the 'pop' culture of the 1960s turned him into a mythic caricature of himself, and before the all-too-knowing postmodern reflexes of the 1980s and beyond attempted to make him 'real' again by blackening the names and reputations of historical personages no longer able to defend themselves against slanderous assault.

The nonentity of Pabst's *Pandora's Box*, in particular, strikes a chord, as does the deviant Sergeant Ottermole. But the casual pickup in the episode of *The Others* also has a convincing feel to it, as does the denial exhibited by the protagonist in *The Outer Limits*; even the indoor murder scene in *Dr Jekyll & Sister Hyde* resonates authentically. Combine elements of each of these and a reasonable approximation of Jack the Ripper might be obtained. As to the glut of grandiose theories relating to characters who already were large in life to the degree that their names are to be found in the historical record – Gull, Maybrick, Eddy, Chapman, Sickert,

Dr Jekyll & Sister Hyde
(1971)

Tumblety, not to mention a raft of lesser mortals, including Barnett, Druitt, William Bury and more – these are unwarrantably charged on the strength of existing evidence. Put simply, there is no case to answer for any single one of them having been Jack the Ripper, certainly none which a contemporary prosecuting authority like the CPS would have enough confidence in to bring before a court.

The mass media's representation of Jack as an omniscient antichrist fulfils the need of an increasingly desperate Western culture to be forever creating devils in its midst, as did the scribes of medieval times. It is a preoccupation of the fundamentalist Right, whose influence on popular taste is widespread. Truth is merely an impediment to large numbers of cultural spin-meisters, and as fact fades and prejudicial fantasy triumphs, the epitome of political and social failure is remoulded to become just another allegorical expression of the eternal Enemy of mankind.

The killer known to history as Jack the Ripper was none of this. He was, most probably, a disenfranchised sociopath who found an outlet for his warped world view in the protests which could be made with the point of a knife. If Jack is to be found in the modern world, he is in the secret stalkings of the mass media and the populist press, whose congenital lack of moral constraint, callous butchery of the truth, and enthusiasm for reducing every argument to the irrational cut-and-thrust of a witch-trial, turns men into monsters with Luciferian efficiency.

In these days of received wisdom, half-truth, spin, and the fancy dressed as fact that is disseminated by authors with a vested interest in advancing myths of their own, Jack the Ripper is likely to remain every bit as real as the creature that was created by the fictional Baron Frankenstein; he has gone too far to be brought to book. He will stalk the streets of Whitechapel for all time, as Dracula strides the battlements of his Transylvanian pile, undead and undying. He is now an elder statesman of crime and cinema, but even after he is finally laid to rest, he will always be the shadow that dances on the flickering Victorian stage, scalpel at the ready.

Those who harbour dreams of solving the age-old mystery in the future from the comfort of their own living rooms, and without the benefit of new and incontrovertible evidence to support them in their quest, might be wise to reflect on a similar exercise in armchair detection which was conducted by one of the intellectual heavyweights of his day: Edgar Allan Poe. In *The Mystery of Marie Roget*, Poe employed a fictional construct to postulate a solution that he deemed probable in a real-life murder case, that of Mary Cecilia Rogers in a suburb of New York in 1842. Poe was a logical thinker, as might be expected of the writer who created C Auguste Dupin, one of the forerunners of Sherlock Holmes.

Mary Rogers was brutally raped and garrotted, and as another incident of gang-rape (but without the fatality) had been perpetrated in the same area beforehand, it was commonly assumed that the 'gang of ruffians' who had carried out the first crime were responsible for both. Poe set out to prove this notion erroneous and to show that blame for the deed rested with one man alone, who was previously involved with the dead girl. This he did in his fictional context, drawing only on newspaper reports of the real murder to support his arguments, and to the unquestioning satisfaction of all who subsequently read the tale.

As Poe annotated in his introductory footnote to *The Mystery of Marie Roget*: "All argument founded upon the fiction is applicable to the truth; and the investigation of the truth was the object." But to keep things in perspective, it must be pointed out that the theory expounded by Poe to solve the murder of Mary Rogers was ultimately proved to be *wrong*.

Overleaf:
Ian Holm as Sir
William Gull in
From Hell (2001)

From Hell (2001)

Appendix

CASTS & CREDITS

The following films, in whole or in part, have derived their inspiration from the Whitechapel Murders. Not all of them feature a characterisation of Jack the Ripper as such, but most do. Some films which *have* featured the Ripper but whose link to the actual crimes is tenuous at best – *Amazon Women on the Moon* (1987) and *The Willies* (1991) for example – are covered in the text but not included in detail here. The same applies to exploitation films whose connection to the subject matter of this book extends only as far as the use of the word *Ripper* in their titles. In most instances, these credits are as they appear on the title-cards of the original films, with the addition of data from other sources to make them as complete as possible.

1915
Farmer Spudd Takes His Missus to Town

1923
Erdgeist
(aka Earth Spirit)

1924
Waxworks
(Das Wachsfigurenkabinett)

Waxworks (1924)

• SELECTED CAST & CREDITS
Emil Jannings/Conrad Veidt/Werner Krauss (Spring-heeled Jack)/Wilhelm [William] Dieterle/Olga von Belajeff/Ernst Legal/John Gottowt/Georg John
Director: Leo Birinsky, Paul Leni/Screenplay: Henrik Galeen/ Cinematography: Helmar Lerski/Art Directors: Paul Leni, Ernst Stern, Alfred Junge
Neptun-film 63 minutes Black-and-white Silent

1927
The Lodger: A Story of the London Fog
(American Title: The Strange Case of Jonathan Drew)

• CAST
The Landlady..Marie Ault
Her Husband.................................Arthur Chesney
Daisy, their daughter..June
Joe, a police detective............................Malcolm Keen
The Lodger/Jonathan Drew......................Ivor Novello
Extra in arrest scene...........................Alfred Hitchcock
Anne Rowley...Helena Pick
• CREDITS
Directed by...............................Alfred Hitchcock
Produced by......Michael Balcon/Carlyle Blackwell
Screenplay by..............................Eliot Stannard
from the novel The Lodger *by Marie Belloc Lowndes*
Music Composed by............................Paul Zaza
Cinematography.......Baron Giovanni Ventimiglia
Art Directors......C Wilfred Arnold/Bertram Evans
Editor..Ivor Montagu
Assistant Director..........................Alma Reville
Title Designer..E McKnight Kauffer/Ivor Montagu
Gainsborough 71 minutes Black-and-white Silent

1928
Pandora's Box
(Die Büchse der Pandora)
• CAST
Lulu...Louise Brooks
Dr Ludwig Schoen...............................Fritz Kortner
Alwa Schoen..........................Franz [Francis] Lederer
Schigolch...Carl Goetz
Rodrigo Quast....................................Carl Raschig
Countess Geschwitz.............................. Alice Roberts
Jack the Ripper....................................Gustav Diesel
Charlotte M A von Zanik.........................Daisy D'Ora
Instructor..Sig Arno
Marquis Casti-Piani................Michael von Newlinsky
• CREDITS
Directed by.......................Georg Wilhelm Pabst

Produced by...........................Seymour Nebenzal
Screenplay by............................Ladislaus Vajda/
...................Joseph Fleisler/Georg Wilhelm Pabst
from the plays Erdgeist and Die Büchse der
Pandora by Frank Wedekind
Cinematography........................Günther Krampf
Art Director........Andrej Andrejew/Gottlieb Hesch
Nero-film 132 minutes Black-and-white Silent

1932

The Lodger
(Re-release title: The Phantom Fiend)
• CAST
The Lodger/Michel Angeloff.....................Ivor Novello
Daisy Bunting.................................Elizabeth Allen
Mr Bunting......................................A W Baskcomb
Mrs Bunting.....................................Barbara Everest
Joe Martin...Jack Hawkins
Detective Snell..................................Shayle Gardner
Lord Southcliffe..............................Peter Gawthrone
Bob Mitchell...............................P Kynaston Reeves
Silvano..Anthony Holles
Rabinovitch............................Andrea Malandrinas
Commissioner...................................George Merritt
Gladys...Molly Fisher
Mrs Coles..Drusilla Wills
with Iris Ashley
• CREDITS
Directed by.....................................Maurice Elvey
Produced by.......................................Julius Hagen
Screenplay by...............Miles Mander/Paul Rotha
from the novel The Lodger by Marie Belloc Lowndes
Adaptation by..............................H Fowler Mear
Musical director..................................W L Trytel
Cinematography.........Basil Emmott/William Luff
Art Director....................................James Carter
Editor..Jack Harris
Olympic 85 [67] minutes Black-and-white

1944

The Lodger
• CAST
Slade [Jack the Ripper]............................Laird Cregar
John Warwick...................................George Sanders
Kitty Langley.......................................Merle Oberon
Robert Burton...........................Sir Cedric Hardwicke
Ellen...Sara Allgood
Superintendant Sutherland..................Aubrey Mather
Daisy..Queenie Leonard
Jennie...Doris Lloyd
Detective Sergeant Bates..........................David Clyde
Annie Rowley...................................Helena Pickard

The Lodger (1927)

Charlie...Harold De Becker
Wiggy.......................................Anita Sharp-Bolster
Man with cart...................................Skelton Knaggs
Bartender..Billy Bevan
Doctor Sheridan................................Lumsden Hare
Harris...Olaf Hytten
Sir Edward Willoughby...................Frederick Worlock
Conductor...Harry Allen
Cab driver...Jimmy Aubrey
Vigilante...Wilson Benge
Manager..Edmund Breon
Harold...Colin Campbell
Hairdresser..Ruth Clifford
Conductor..Herbert Clifton
Stagehand..Cyril Delevanti
Aide..Frank Elliott
Constable..Herbert Evans
Porter...Douglas Gerrard
Comedian..Charlie Hall
Milkman..Gerald Hamer

The Lodger (1944)

Curse of the Wraydons
(1946)

Conductor	Alec Harford
Cobbler	Forrester Harvey
King Edward	Stuart Holmes
Policeman	Colin Hunter
Mounted Inspector	Kenneth Hunter
Policeman	Boyd Irwin
Plainclothesman	Colin Kenny
Aide	Crauford Kent
Vigilante	Charles Knight
Woman	Connie Leon
Plainclothesman	Clive Morgan
Mounted policeman	John Rice
Down and outer	John Rogers
Boy	Raymond Severn
Stage Manager	C Montague Shaw
Policeman	Yorke Sherwood
Plainclothesman	Leslie Sketchley
Newsboy	Will Stanton
Plainclothesman	Bob Stevenson
Concertina Player	Donald Stuart
Call Boy	Walter Tetley
Sergeant	David Thursby
Girl	Heather Wilde

• CREDITS

Directed by	John Brahm
Produced by	Robert Bassler
Screenplay by	Barré Lyndon

from the novel The Lodger *by Marie Belloc Lowndes*

Associate	Walter M Scott
Music	Hugo W Friedhofer
Musical Director	Emil Newman
Director of Photography	Lucien Ballard
Art Director	James Basevi/John Ewing
Set Decorator	Thomas Little
Film Editor	J Watson Webb Jr
Sound	E Clayton Ward/Roger Heman
Make-up Artist	Guy Pearce
Costumes	Rene Hubert

Dance Director	Kenny Williams
Special Photographic Effects	Fred Sersen

20th Century-Fox 84 minutes
Black-and-white

1946
Curse of the Wraydons

• SELECTED CAST & CREDITS

*Tod Slaughter/Bruce Seton (Spring-heeled Jack)/
Andrew Laurence/Alan Lawrance/Pearl Cameron/
Loraine Clewes/Ben Williams/John E Coyle/Henry
Caine/Gabriel Toyne/Daphne Arthur/Barry O'Neill/
Herbert Appleby/Joe Cunningham/Lionel Gadsden/
Patricia Grant*

Director: Victor M Gover/Producers: Gilbert
Church, J C Jones/Screenplay: Owen George
from the play *Spring-Heeled Jack; or, the Terror of
London* by Maurice Sandoz/Cinematography:
S D Onions/Editor: Victor M Gover/Music: De
Wolfe/Art Director: Victor Hembrow/Make-up:
Peggy Carly, H Wright/Production Manager: John
Rayner/Sound: K Wiles/Cutter: John F House/
Continuity: Doris Martin/Camera Operator:
W Noakes

Ambassador 96 minutes Black-and-white

1950
Room to Let

• CAST

Curly Minter	Jimmy Hanley
James 'JJ' Jasper	J A La Penna
Harding	Aubrey Dexter
Sergeant	Reginald Dyson
PC Smith	Charles Mander
Mansfield	Cyril Conway
Dr Fell [Jack the Ripper]	Valentine Dyall
Alice	Merle Tottenham
Molly	Constance Smith
Mrs Musgrave	Christine Silver
Editor	Lawrence Naismith
Michael	Charles Hawtrey
Atkinson	John Clifford
Porter	Stuart Saunders
Tom	Charles Houston
Matron	Harriet Peterworth
Butler	F A Williams

• CREDITS

Directed by	Godfrey Grayson
Produced by	Anthony Hinds
Screenplay by	John Gilling/Godfrey Grayson

from the BBC feature by Margery Allingham

Music composed/conducted by	Frank Spencer

Director of Photography............Cedric Williams
Camera Operator............................Peter Bryan
Art Director.................................Denis Wreford
Editor..James Needs
Recordist.......................................Edgar Vetter
Cutter...Alfred Cox
Production Manager....................Arthur Barnes
Assistant Director.....................Jimmy Sangster
Makeup..Phil Leakey
Hairst...Monica Hustler
Dress Design.............................Myra Cullimore
Continuity...................................Renée Glynne
Casting......................................Prudence Sykes
Hammer 68 minutes Black-and-white

1954

Man in the Attic

• CAST

Slade [Jack the Ripper]..........................Jack Palance
Lily Bonner...................................Constance Smith
Inspector Paul Warwick.......................Byron Palmer
Helen Harley...................................Frances Bavier
William Harley.................................Rhys Williams
First constable.................................Sean McClory
Second constable.............................Leslie Bradley
Daisy...Tita Phillips
Chief Inspector Melville.....................Lester Mathews
Sergeant Bates.................................Harry Cording
Mary Lenihan....................................Lisa Daniels
Annie Rowley.....................................Lilian Bond
Katy..Isabel Jewell
Men in audience................Stuart Holmes/Jeffrey Sayre

• CREDITS

Directed by...............................Hugo Fregonese
Produced by.................................Robert L Jacks
Screenplay by.......Robert Presnell Jr/Barré Lyndon
from the novel The Lodger by Marie Belloc Lowndes
Musical Director.........................Lionel Newman
Original Music.........................Hugo Friedhofer
Director of Photography.......................Leo Tover
Art Director...............Lyle Wheeler/Leland Fuller
Set Decorations.............................Eli Benneche
Film Editor.............................Marjorie Fowler
Sound...Arthur Kirbach
Asst Director............................Buddy Erickson
Makeup artist...................................Lou Hippe
Wardrobe Direction..................Charles Le Maire
Costume Design...................................Travilla
Choreography.............................Willetta Smith
Executive Producer................Leonard Goldstein
Panoramic/20th Century-Fox 85 minutes
Black-and-white

1957

Alfred Hitchcock Presents: The Hands of Mr
Ottermole

• CAST

Sergeant Ottermole/London Strangler.......Theodore Bikel
Mr Summers, the reporter...................Rhys Williams
Mr Whybrow..............................A E Gould-Porter
Constable...Torin Thatcher
Whybrow's Nephew.............................Barry Harvey
Policeman..John Trayne
Publican...Charles Davis
with Nora O'Mahony/Nelson Welch/Mollie Roden/James
McCallion/Hilda Plowright/Gerald Hamer

• CREDITS

Directed by.................................Robert Stevens
Produced by..........................Alfred Hitchcock
Teleplay by................................Francis Cockrell
Associate Producer......................Joan Harrison
Music Supervisor.........................Stanley Wilson
Director of Photography...............John E Warren
Art Director......................................John Lloyd
Set Decorator...............................James S Redd
Editorial Supervisor....................Richard G Wray
Film Editor.........................Edward W Williams
Sound...Richard Tyler
Assistant Director.........................Hilton Green
Make-up...Jack Barron
Hair stylist...................................Florence Bush
Costume Supervisor.........................Vincent Dee
Shamley/Revue 26 minutes Black-and-white

1958

The Veil: Jack the Ripper

• CAST

Walter Durst...................................Niall MacGinnis
Judith Durst.....................................Dorothy Alison
Constable...Robert Brown
Fat woman...Mai Bacon
Inspector McWilliam.........................Clifford Evans
Warden.......................................Robert Brooks Turner
Mrs Willowden...............................Nora Swinburne
Dr Hatherley.....................................Charles Carson
Host..Boris Karloff

• CREDITS

Directed by.............................David MacDonald
Screenplay by................................Michael Plant
Music composed by........................Edwin Astley
Cinematography...............................Stephen Dade
Art Director......................................Denys Pavitt
Film Editor.............................Ann Chegwidden
Recording supervisor......................Harold King
Production Manager.........................Victor Peck

The Veil (1958)

Series created by.............................Frank P Bebis
Casting Director.........................Robert Lennard
Executive Producer.........................Hal Roach Jr
Hal Roach/Medallion 26 minutes Black-and-white

Grip of the Strangler

(American title: The Haunted Strangler)

• CAST

James Rankin/The Haymarket Strangler.....Boris Karloff
Cora Seth.....................................Jean Kent
Mrs Barbara Rankin...........................Elizabeth Allen
Superintendent Burk........................Anthony Dawson
Pearl...Vera Day
Dr Kenneth McColl................................Tim Turner
Lily Rankin.......................................Diane Aubrey
Turnkey...Max Brimmell
Prison Governor..................................Leslie Perrins
Asylum maid......................................Jessica Cairns
Hannah..Dorothy Gordon
Dr Johnson.....................................Desmond Roberts
Medical Superintendent..........................Roy Russell
Hospital Superintendent..........................Derek Birch
Kate..Peggy Ann Clifford
Young Blood......................................John Fabian
Can-Can girl......................................Joan Elvin
Edward Styles.............................Michael Atkinson
Male nurse..John G Heller
Lost Property man...............................George Hirste
Male nurse......................................Arthur Mullard
Hangman..George Spence

• CREDITS

Directed by......................................Robert Day
Produced by......................................John Croydon
Screenplay.....................Jan Read/John C Cooper
Original story......................................Jan Read
Music composed by.........................Buxton Orr
Conducted by............................Frederic Lewis

Cinematography..............................Lionel Banes
Camera Operator..............................Leo Rogers
Set Designer...................................John Elphick
Film Editor....................................Peter Mayhew
Sound Recordist..............................H C Pearson
Dubbing Editor.............................Terry Poulton
Assistant Director.....................Douglas Hickox
Make up...Jim Hydes
Hairdresser.............................Barbara Barnard
Dress Supervisor...............................Anna Duse
Continuity..Hazel Swift
Special Effects...................................Les Bowie
Executive Producer [uncredited]...Richard Gordon
Producers Associates/Eros 79 minutes
Black-and-white

1959

Jack the Ripper

• CAST

Sam Lowry...Lee Patterson
Inspector O'Neill...................................Eddie Byrne
Anne Ford......................................Betty McDowall
Sir David Rogers [Jack the Ripper]...............Ewen Solon
Dr Tranter......................................John Le Mesurier
Clarke...George Rose
Music Hall manager...........................Philip Leaver
Kitty Knowles/Mary Clarke...................Barbara Burke
Helen..Anne Sharp
Simes...Denis Shaw
Louis Benz...Endre Muller
Nelly..Esma Cannon
Blake.......................................George Woodbridge
Lord Sopw...Bill Shine
Drunken woman...........................Marianne Stone
Dr Urquhart.......................................Garard Green
Asst Commissioner...................................Jack Allen
Hazel...Jane Taylor
Margaret..Dorinda Stevens
Pickpocket..Hal Osmonde
Station Sergeant...................................George Street
Lady Almoner......................................Olwen Brooks
Stage Door Keeper.............................Charles Lamb
Beth.......................................Jennifer White Hospital
porter..Cameron Hall
Coroner..Alan Robinson
Drunk...Anthony Sagar
Singer...John Mott
Salvation Army woman.......................Lucy Griffiths
1st victim.......................................Helena Digby
with The Ballet Montparnasse

• CREDITS

Directed/Produced/Photographed by..................

..........................Robert S Baker/Monty Berman
Screenplay by...........................Jimmy Sangster
Original story.........Peter Hammond/Colin Craig
Music written and conducted by.......Stanley Black
Camera Operator..........................Dudley Lovell
Art Directo...............................William Kellner
Film Editor............................Peter Bezencenet
Sound Recordist..........................Buster Ambler
Dubbing Editor.....................Jeanne Henderson
Production Manager...................Jack Swinburne
Assistant Director.........................Peter Manley
Make-up..................................Jimmy Evans
Hairdressing..............................Bill Griffiths
Wardrobe.................................Jack Verity
Continuity..............................Yvonne Richards
Mid-Century/Paramount 84 minutes
Black-and-white

1961

Thriller: Yours Truly, Jack the Ripper
• CAST
Host...Boris Karloff
Sir Guy Hollis.................................John Williams
John Carmody [Jack the Ripper]...........Donald Woods
Captain Pete Jago.................................Edmon Ryan
Hymie Kralek.......................................Adam Williams
Arlene...Nancy Valentine
Lester Baston.............................Ransom Sherman
Police Official...................................Sam Gilman
Street singer................................J Pat O'Malley
Maggie Rattivic..............................Gloria Blondell
Miss Beverly Hills...............................herself
with Pamela Curran/Jill Livesey/Johnny Melfi/Ralph
Clanton/Ottola Nesmith/ Art Lewis
• SELECTED CREDITS
Directed by.....................................Ray Milland
Produced by...................................William Frye
Teleplay by...................................Barré Lyndon
from the short story by Robert Bloch
Original Music..........................Jerry Goldsmith
Musical Supervision....................Stanley Wilson
Director of Photography...........Kenneth D Peach
Art Director...................................Loyd S Papez
Set Decorators..........John McCarthy/Joseph Kish
Graphic Arts...............................Jerome Gould
Editorial Supervisor.................David J O'Connell
Film Editor............................Danny B Landres
Sound..Robert Bertrand
Assistant Director.........................James Hogan
Makeup..Jack Barron
Hairstylist.....................................Florence Bush
Costume Supervisor..........................Vincent Dee

Hubbell Robinson/NBC 50 minutes
Black-and-white

1962

Lulu
(aka No Orchids for Lulu)
• SELECTED CAST & CREDITS
Nadja Tiller/O E Hasse/Hildegard Knef/Mario Adorf/
Rudolf Forster/Leon Askin/Sieghardt Rupp/Klaus
Hoering/Fritz Friedl/Charles Régnier (Jack the Ripper)
Director: Rolf Thiele/Producer: Otto Dürer/
Screenplay by Rolf Thiele from the plays Erdgeist
and Die Büchse der Pandora by Frank Wedekind/
Music: Carl de Groof/Cinematography: Michel
Kelber/Production Design: Fritz Moegle, Heinz
Ockermüller/Editor: Eleonore Künze/Costume
Designer: Gerdago
Vienna Filmproduktion 100 minutes
Black-and-white

1963

Twilight Zone: The New Exhibit
• CAST
Martin Lombard Senescu....................Martin Balsam
Mr Ferguson..Will Kuluva
Emma Senescu..............................Maggie Mahoney
Dave..William Mims
Gas man..Phil Chambers
Van man..Lenny Bremen
Sailors.....................................Ed Barth/Craig Curtis
The Guide..Marcel Hillaire
Host...Rod Serling
Wax Figures:
Henri Desiré Landru..........................Milton Parsons
Jack the Ripper...................................David Bond
Albert W Hicks..................................Bob Mitchell
Burke..Robert L McCord
Hare..Billy Beck
• CREDITS
Directed by.....................................John Brahm
Produced by....................................Bert Granet
Written by............................Charles Beaumont
Director of Photography.........George T Clemens
Art Director...........George W Davis/Paul Groesse
Set Decoration.......Henry Grace/Frank R McKelvy
Film Editor...................................Everett Dodd
Sound..............Franklin Milton/Joe Edmondson
Production Manager...................Ralph W Nelson
Assistant Director............................John Bloss
Assistant to producer...................John Conwell
Series created by.............................Rod Serling
Cayuga/MGM 50 minutes Black-and-white

The Monster of London City (1964)

1964

The Monster of London City

(Das Ungeheuer von London City)

• CAST

Richard Sand.................................Hansjörg Felmy
Ann Morley....................................Marianne Koch
Dr Michael Greely.........................Dietmar Schönherr
Inspector Dorne.............................Hans Nielsen
Sir George Edwards........................Fritz Tillman
Horrlick..Walter Pfeil
Betty Ball.....................................Chariklia Baxevanos
Teddy Flynn..................................Peer Schmidt
Maylor...Kurd Pieritz
Housekeeper..................................Elsa Wagner
Assistant......................................Gerda Blisse
Helen Capstick..............................Kai Fischer
Detective......................................Manfred Grothe
Maid..Adelheid Hinz
Evelyn Nichols..............................Gudrun Schmidt

• SELECTED CREDITS

Directed by...................................Edwin Zbonek
Produced by..................................Artur Brauner
Screenplay by................................Robert A Stemmle
from the novel by Bryan Edgar Wallace
Music..Martin Böttcher
Director of Photography.................Siegfried Hold
Set Decoration..............................Hans Jürgen Kiebach/
....Ernst Schomer
Editor...Walter Wischniewsky
Production Manager.......................Heinz Willeg
Assistant Director..........................Lucie Berndsen
Executive Producer........................Artur Brauner
CCC/Omnia 90 minutes Black-and-white

1966

A Study in Terror

• CAST

Sherlock Holmes............................John Neville
Dr John Watson.............................Donald Houston
Edward Osbourne, Lord Carfax [Jack the Ripper]..........
....John Fraser
Dr Murray....................................Anthony Quayle
Max Steiner...................................Peter Carsten
Joseph Beck...................................Charles Régnier
Mycroft Holmes.............................Robert Morley
Annie Chapman.............................Barbara Windsor
Angela Osbourne............................Adrienne Corri
Michael Osbourne...........................John Cairney
Inspector Lestrade..........................Frank Finlay
Prime Minister...............................Cecil Parker
Home Secretary..............................Dudley Foster
The Duke of Shires..........................Barry Jones
Landlady.......................................Avis Bunnage
Singer..Georgia Brown
P C Benson....................................Patrick Newell
Sally..Judi Dench
Cathy Eddowes...............................Kay Walsh
Polly Nichols.................................Christiane Maybach
Mary Kelly....................................Edina Ronay
Chunky..Terry Downes
Elizabeth Stride.............................Norma Foster
Mrs Hudson..................................Barbara Leake
Rupert...Jeremy Lloyd
Rupert's friend...............................Corin Redgrave
Emma Smith..................................Donna White

• CREDITS

Directed by...................................James Hill
Produced by..................................Henry E Lester
Original Story and Screenplay by......Donald Ford/
....Derek Ford
based on the characters created by Sir Arthur Conan Doyle
Music composed and conducted by.......John Scott
Director of Photography.......Desmond Dickinson
Camera Operator.........................Norman Jones
Production Design.....................Alex Vetchinsky
Set Dresser................................Helen Thomas
Film Editor............................Henry Richardson
Sound Editor..............................Jim Roddan
Sound Mixer..............................H L Bird
Sound Supervisor...............John Cox Production
Manager....................................Robert Sterne
Assistant Director.......................Harry Langley
Make-up....................................Tom Smith
Hairdresser...............................Gladys Leakey
Costume Design...........................Motley
Wardrobe.................Laura Staffell/Larry Stewart
Continuity..............................Gladys Goldsmith
Casting.....................................Maude Spector
Special Effects...........................Wally Veevers
Executive producers.................Michael Klinger/
.................................Tony Tenser/Herman Cohen
Compton/Sir Nigel 98 minutes
Eastmancolor

1967

Star Trek: Wolf in the Fold

• CAST

Captain James T Kirk.........................William Shatner
Mister Spock.....................................Leonard Nimoy
Doctor McCoy..................................DeForest Kelley
Hengist [Jack the Ripper]........................John Fiedler
Jaris..Charles Macauley
Sybo..Pilar Seurat
Scott..James Doohan
Sulu...George Takei
Morla...Charles Dierkop
Tark..Joseph Bernard
Kara...Tania Lemani
Transporter Chief................................John Winston
Karen Tracy....................................Virginia Aldridge
Yeoman Tankris............................Judy McConnell
Nurse...Judi Sherven

• SELECTED CREDITS

Directed by.....................................Joseph Pevney
Produced by.....................................Gene L Coon
Written by..Robert Bloch
Associate Producer.................Robert H Justman
Theme Music by.....................Alexander Courage
Additional Music composed and conducted by......
....Gerald Fried
Director of Photography.............Jerry Finnerman
Art Director.........................Walter M Jefferies
Film Editor............................Bruce Shoengarth
Unit Production Manager.................Gregg Peters
Assistant Director...........................Rusty Meek
Make Up Artist...........................Fred B Phillips
Hair Styles...................................Pat Westmore
Costumes created by............William Ware Theiss
Castin....................................Joseph Dagosta
Special Effects.....................................Jim Rugg
Executive Producers...............Gene Roddenberry/
....Herbert F Solow

Desilu/Norway 50 minutes Colour

1968

Cimarron Strip: Knife in the Darkness

• CAST

Marshall Jim Crown.........................Stuart Whitman
Francis Wilde.....................................Randy Boone
MacGregor.......................................Percy Herbert
Dulcey Coopersmith............................Jill Townsend
Josie...Jennifer Billingsley
Tal St. James.....................................David Canary
Kallman..Philip Carey
Pony Jane..Jeanne Cooper
Tipton..Patrick Horgan

Bladgey...George Murdock
Maddie Lennart..................................Victoria Shaw
Enoch Shelton [Jack the Ripper]................Tom Skerritt
Shadow Feller.......................................Ron Soble
Doc Kihlgren...................................Karl Swenson
Peddigrew...Don Hanmer
Katie...Grace Lee Whitney
Gomer..Joey Tata
Odell...William Phipps
1st Indian....................................Richard Angarola
Trapper..Cal Bolder

• CREDITS

Directed by............................Charles R Ronde
Produced by.........................Douglas Benton
Written by..............................Harlan Ellison
Story Consultant............................Albert Aley
Supervising Producer.............Christopher Knopf
Theme by...............................Maurice Jarre
Music composed and conducted by....................
....Bernard Herrmann
Director of Photography...........Harry Stradling Jr
Art Director..................................Gibson Holley
Set Decorator.............................Buck Henshaw
Film Editor.............................Danny B Landres
Unit Production Manager...........Lloyd Anderson
Assistant Director..................Christopher Seiter
Assistant to the producers...............James Heinz
Make Up Artist..........................Richard Cobos
Costumes............Richard Egan/Dorothy Rodgers
Casting......................................Pam Polifroni
Executive Producer.....................Philip Leacock
Stuart Whitman/CBS 75 minutes Colour

1969

Night After Night After Night

• CAST

Judge Charles Lomax...............................Jack May
Helena Lomax.....................................Justine Lord
Inspector Bill Rowan..........................Gilbert Wynne
Pete Laver....................................Donald Sumpter
Jenny Rowan....................................Linda Marlowe
Chief Inspector.............................Jack Smethurst
Carter..Terry Scully
Powell.......................................Peter Forbes-Robertson
Josie Leach....................................Jacqueline Clerk
Solicitor..................................Michael Nightingale
Marion Brown...............................Elisabeth Murray
Doctor......................................Walter Horsbrugh
Witness..Bernard G High
Counsels..............Simon Lack/Gary Hope/Roy Skelton/
....John Gabriel
1st prostitute.....................................Carol Haddon

2nd prostitute..................................Yvonne Paul
1st stripper.....................................April Harlow
2nd stripper..................................Shirley Easton
• CREDITS
Directed by........Lewis J. Force [Lindsay Shonteff]
Produced by..................................James Mellor
Story and Script.............................Dail Ambler
Music and 'Helena's Theme' composed and
conducted by............................Douglas Gamley
Director of Photography...................Douglas Hill
Camera Operator.............................John Shann
Art Director................................Wilfred Arnold
Film Editor..................................John Rushton
Sound Recordist...............................Robert Cox
Sound Editor................................Peter Compton
Production Manager.....................Walter James
Assistant Director............................Ernie Lewis
Make-up.....................................Eleanor Jones
Wardrobe..Pat Fisher
Butcher's 87 minutes Colour

The Avengers: Fog
• CAST
John Steed....................................Patrick Macnee
Tara King....................................Linda Thorson
Sir Geoffrey Armstrong..........................Nigel Green
Mark Travers/The Gaslight Ghoul...............Guy Rolfe
Mother...Patrick Newell
Carstairs..Terence Brady
Sanders.................................Paul Whitsun-Jones
Maskell..David Lodge
Fowler...Norman Chappell
with David Bird/Patsy Smart/John Garrie/Frederick
Peisley/Arnold Diamond/ John Barrard/Frank Sieman/
Virginia Clay/Bernard Severn/Stan Jay/William Lyon
Brown
• SELECTED CREDITS
Directed by.....................................John Hough
Produced by..........Albert Fennell/Brian Clemens
Teleplay by..............................Jeremy Burnham
Music...Laurie Johnson
Director of Photography................David Holmes
Camera Operator.......Geoff Seaholme Production
Designer..Robert Jones
Associate Art Directors...................Kenneth Tait/
....Richard Harrison
Editor...................................Manuel del Campo
Sound Recordist.....................Claude Hitchcock
Sound Editor..............................Peter Lennard
Production Manager...........................Ron Fry
Assistant Director............................Ron Purdie
Make-up..Jim Hydes

Hairdressing..............................Mary Sturgess
Costume Supervisor............................Ivy Baker
Continuity......................................Kay Perkins
Casting Director.............................G B Walker
Executive Producer..................Gordon L T Scott
ABC 52 minutes Colour

1970
Blade of the Ripper
(aka Lo strano visio delle Signora Ward; The Next
Victim)

1971
Jack the Mangler of London
(aka Jack, el Destripador de Londres; Sette
cadaveri per Scotland Yard)
• CAST
Peter Dockerman.................................Paul Naschy
Kathy..Patricia Loran
Winston Damery-Christi.................Renzo Marignano
Sandy......................................Orchídea de Santis
Commissioner Campbell......................Franco Borelli
with Miguel Minuesa/Teresita Castizir/Isibbro Novella/
Carmen Roger/Victor Iregua/Paloma Moreno/Alfonso
Castiz/Irene Mir/Antonio Ramis/Victor Bilanova/Enrique
Beltra/Maika/Andres Resino
• CREDITS
Directed/Produced by............... José Luis Madrid
Screenplay by........Tito Carpi/Sandro Continenza/
....José Luis Madrid
Original Story by........Tito Carpi/José Luis Madrid
Music..Piero Piccioni
Director of Photography..................Diego Úbeda
Production Designer...............Francisco Castillo
Art Director...........Juan Alberto Sol/Bruno Cesari
Editor...Luis Puigvert
Production Managers....................Sandro Amati/
....Jose Maria Tellez
Special Effects..........................Antonio Molina
Cinefilms/International Apollo 86 minutes
Technicolor

Dr Jekyll & Sister Hyde
• CAST
Dr Jekyll [Jack the Ripper].......................Ralph Bates
Sister Hyde [Jack the Ripper]..............Martine Beswick
Professor Robertson..................................Gerald Sim
Howard...Lewis Fiander
Mrs Spencer.......................................Dorothy Alison
Older policeman......................................Neil Wilson
Burke..Ivor Dean Sergeant
Danvers.....................................Paul Whitsun-Jones

Byker...Philip Madoc
Hare...Tony Calvin
Susan..Susan Brodrick
Town Crier.....................................Dan Meaden
Betsy.......................................Virginia Wetherell
1st policeman.................................Geoffrey Kenion
Yvonne.......................................Irene Bradshaw
Julie...Anna Brett
Jackie..Margie Poole
Marie..Rosemary Lord
Petra...Petula Portell
Helen..Pat Brackenbury
Emma..Liz Romanoff
Mein Host.......................................Will Stampe
Knife grinder....................................Roy Evans
1st sailor..Derek Steen
2nd sailor...John Lyons
Jill...Jannette Wilde
Young apprentice.................................Bobby Parr
Street singer......................................Julia Wright

• CREDITS

Directed by...............................Roy Ward Baker
Produced by..........Albert Fennell/Brian Clemens
Screenplay by..............................Brian Clemens
from the story by Robert Louis Stevenson
Music composed by....................David Whitaker
Musical Supervisor.......................Philip Martell
Song 'He'll Be There', words and music by Brian Clemens
Director of Photography.....Norman Warwick BSC
Camera Operator.........................Godfrey Godar
Production Designer.........................Robert Jone
Assistant Art Director..................Len Townsend
Editor....................................James Needs GBFE
Recording Director........................A.W. Lumkin
Sound..Bill Rowe
Sound Editor...................Charles Crafford GBFE
Production Manager.........................Don Weeks
Assistant Director...............................Bert Batt
Make-up...............................Trevor Crole-Rees
Hairdressing.............................Bernie Ibbetson
Wardrobe Supervisor.............Rosemary Burrows
Wardrobe Mistress.....................Kathleen Moore
Continuity..Sally Ball
Casting Director............................Jimmy Liggat
Construction Manager......................Bill Greene
Production Supervisor.......................Roy Skeggs
Hammer 97 minutes Technicolor

Hands of the Ripper

• CAST

Dr John Pritchard....................................Eric Porter
Anna...Angharad Rees
Laura.....................................Jane Merrow Michael
Pritchard...Keith Bell
Dysart..Derek Godfrey
Mrs Golding.......................................Dora Bryan
Mrs Bryant....................................Marjorie Rhodes
Long Liz..Lynda Baron
Dolly...Marjie Lawrence
Police Inspector.................................Norman Bird
Madame Bullard......................Margaret Rawlings
Mrs Wilson....................................Elizabeth Maclennan
Mr Wilson.......................................Barry Lowe
Rev Anderson.......................................A J Brown
Catherine...April Wilding
First cell whore...................................Anne Clune
Second cell whore...............................Vicki Woolf
First pub whore..................................Katya Wyeth
Second pub whore............................Beulah Hughes
Third pub whore...............................Tallulah Miller
Pleasants...Peter Munt
Seamstress..Ann Way
Police Constable...............................Philip Ryan
Maid...Molly Weir
Guard...Charles Lamb

• CREDITS

Directed by.......................................Peter Sasdy
Produced by.......................................Aida Young
Screenplay by..............................L W Davidson
Original story....................Edward Spencer Shew
Music composed by............Christopher Gunning
Musical Supervisor.......................Philip Martell
Director of Photography........Kenneth Talbot BSC
Camera Operator.......................Robert Kindred
Art Director....................................Roy Stannard
Editor...Chris Barnes
Sound Recordist............................Kevin Sutton
Dubbing Mixer.................................Ken Barker
Production Manager.............Christopher Sutton
Assistant Director...............................Ariel Levy
Make-up Supervisor......................Bunty Phillips
Hairdressing Supervisor...............Pat McDermott
Wardrobe Supervisor.............Rosemary Burrows
Wardrobe Mistress.......................Eileen Sullivan
Continuity..............................Gladys Goldsmith
Special Effects.....................................Cliff Culley
Construction Manager...................Arthur Banks
Hammer 85 minutes Technicolor

1972

The Ruling Class

• SELECTED CAST & CREDITS

Peter O'Toole/Alastair Sim/Arthur Lowe/Harry Andrews/

Coral Browne/ Michael Bryant/Nigel Green/William Mervyn/Carolyn Seymour/James Villiers/ Kay Walsh/ Patsy Byrne/Graham Crowden/Hugh Burden/James Grout/James Hazeldine/Joan Cooper

Director: Peter Medak/Producer: Jules Buck, Jack Hawkins/Screenplay: Peter Barnes from his play *The Ruling Class*/Associate Producer: David Korda/ Musical Direction and Original Music: John Cameron/Director of Photography:Ken Hodges/ Camera Operator: Herbie Smith/Production Designer: Peter Murton/Set Dresser: Peter Young/Editor: Ray Lovejoy/Sound Mixer: Robin Gregory/Production Manager: Tim Hampton/ Assistant Director: Bert Batt/Make-up created by: Charles Parker/Choreographer: Eleanor Fazan

Avco Embassy 155 [147] minutes

De Luxe colour

The Sixth Sense: With Affection, Jack the Ripper

• CAST

Dr Michael Rhodes	Gary Collins
Elizabeth	Patty Duke
Adam	Robert Foxworth
Lieutenant Woods	Percy Rodrigues
2nd girl	Jannis Durkin
Policeman	Mitch Carter
1st girl	Heather Lowe
Secretary	Marilyn Nix

• SELECTED CREDITS

Directed by	Robert Day
Produced by	Stan Shpetner
Writer/Executive Story Consultant	Don Ingalls
Associate Producer	Robert F O'Neill
Music Score	Bob Prince
Theme	Billy Goldenberg
Director of Photography	Enzo A Martinelli
Key Decorations	Leonard Mazzola
Art Director	William Tuntke

The Sixth Sense (1972)

Editorial Supervision	Richard Belding
Film Editor	John Elias
Sound	John Carter
Unit Manager	Frank Losee
Assistant Director	Robert Saunders
Costumes by	Grady Hunt

ABC/Universal 24 minutes Technicolor

1973

Terror in the Wax Museum

• CAST

Harry Plexner	Ray Milland
Julia Hawthorn	Elsa Lanchester
Inspector Daniels	Maurice Evans
Claude Duprée	John Carradine
Sgt Michael Hawks	Mark W Edwards
Tim Fowley	Louis Hayward
Mr Southcott	Patric Knowles
Madame Yang	Lisa Lu
Karkov	Steven Marlo
Margaret Collins	Nicole Shelby
Laurie Mell	Shani Wallis
Amos Burns	Broderick Crawford
1st constable	Ben Wright
1st charwoman	Matilda Calnan
2nd charwoman	Peggy Stewart
Constable Parker	Leslie Thompson

Wax Figures:

Jack the Ripper	Don Herbert
Lizzie Borden	Judy Wetmore
Mrs Borden	Jo Williamson
Bluebeard	George Farina
Girl in bed	Diane Wahrman
Lucretia Borgia	Rosa Huerta
Attila the Hun	Ben Brown
Marie Antoinette	Rickie Weir
Ivan the Terrible	Paul Wilson
Willie Crossman	Ralph Cunningham
Constable Henry Bolt	Don Williamson
Flower woman	Evelyn Reynolds

• SELECTED CREDITS

Directed by	George Fenady
Produced by	Andrew J Fenady
Screenplay by	Jameson Brewer
Story by	Andrew J Fenady
Music	George Duning
Music Editor	Else Blangsted
Director of Photography	William Jergensen
Production Designer	Stan Jolley
Set Decorator	Carl Biddiscombe
Film Editor	Melvin Shapiro
Sound Editor	James J Klinger

Unit Production Manager/Assistant Director........
....Floyd Joyer
2nd Assistant Director.......................Lee Rafner
Make-up created by........................Jack H Young
Hair Stylist..................................Virginia Jones
Costumes........Oscar Rodriguez/You Lee Ciokaris
Casting...Irving Lande
Executive Producer......................Charles A Pratt
Bing Crosby/Fenady 93 minutes
De Luxe colour

1974

Knife For the Ladies
(aka Jack the Ripper goes West; Silent Sentence)
• SELECTED CAST & CREDITS
Jack Elam/Ruth Roman/Jeff Cooper/John Kellogg/Gene
Evans/Richard Schaal/Diana Ewing/Jon Spangler/Derek
Sanderson/Fred Biletnikoff/Peter Athas
Director: Larry G Spangler/Producers: Larry G
Spangler, Stan Jolley/ Screenplay: George Arthur
Bloom, Seton I Miller/Original Story: Robert
Shelton, Seton I Miller/Associate Producers:
Robert Shelton, Ron Janoff/Director of
Photography: Irving Lippman/Production
Design: Stan Jolley/Editor: Anthony Carras/Unit
Production Manager: Ann Kindberg/Assistant
Director: Ray Marsh/Executive Producer: Lou
Peraino
Bryanston 54 minutes Colour

Kolchak: The Night Stalker: The Ripper
• CAST

Carl Kolchak	Darren McGavin
Tony Vincenzo	Simon Oakland
Jane Plum	Beatrice Colen
Emily Cowles	Ruth McDevitt
Ron Updyke	Jack Grinnage
Capt Warren	Ken Lynch
Masseuse	Marya Small
Policeman	Donald Mantooth
Mail Boy	Robert Bryan Berger
Det Cortazzo	Roberta Collins
Driver	Clint Young
Jack the Ripper	Mickey Gilbert

• CREDITS

Directed by	Allen Baron
Produced by	Paul Playdon
Written by	Rudolph Borchert
Created by	Jeff Rice
Story Consultant	David Chase
Music	Gil Mellé
Music Supervision	Hal Mooney

Director of Photography	Donald Peterman
Art Director	Raymond Beal
Set Decorations	Robert Freer
Film Editor	Robert Leeds
Editorial Supervision	Richard Belding
Sound	John Kean
Unit Manager	Ralph Sariego
Assistant Director	John Gaudioso
Main Title Design	Jack Cole

MCA/Universal 53 minutes Technicolor

1975

What the Swedish Butler Saw
(aka Champagne pa Sengekanten;
Champagnegalopp; The Groove Room)
• SELECTED CAST & CREDITS
Ole Søltoft /Sue Longhurst/Charlie Elvegard/Malou
Cartwright/Martin Young (Jack the Ripper)/Diana Dors/
Joe Grey/Steven Lund/Larry Leonard/Peter Rose/Julie
Bernby/Barry Melvin/Neal Lund/Barbara Hart/Gil
Holmes/Tina Monell
Director, Producer: Vernon P Becker/Screenplay
by: Vernon P Becker, Barry E Downs/Music:
H C Lundbye/Director of Cinematography: Tony
Forsberg/Production Designer: Ralph Larson/
Editor: Ingemar Ejve/Production Manager: Tom
Younger
Constellation/Unicorn 93 minutes Colour

1976

Jack the Ripper
(Der Dirnenmorder von London)
• CAST

The Doctor [Jack the Ripper]	Klaus Kinski
Cynthia	Josephine Chaplin
Inspector Selby	Herbert Fux
Charlie	Hans Gaugler

with Lina Romay/Nikola Weisse/Ursula von Wiese/
Francine Custer/Olga Gebhard/Angelika Arndts/Lorli
Bucher/Otto Dornbierer/Regine Elsener/Mike Lederer/Peter
Nüsch/Friedrich Schönfelder/Esther Studer/Andreas
Mannkopff
• CREDITS

Directed by	Jesús Franco
Produced by	Erwin C Dietrich
Screenplay by	Jesús Franco
Music	Walter Baumgartner
Cinematography	Peter Baumgartner
Editor	Marie-Luise Buschke
1st Assistant Director	Mark M Rissi
2nd Assistant Director	Alfi Sinniger

Cinemec/Ascot 95 minutes Eastmancolor

1979

Murder By Decree

• CAST

Sherlock Holmes	Christopher Plummer
Dr Watson	James Mason
Inspector Foxborough	David Hemmings
Mary Kelly	Susan Clark
Sir Charles Warren	Anthony Quayle
Prime Minister	John Gielgud
Inspector Lestrade	Frank Finlay
Robert Lees	Donald Sutherland
Annie Crook	Genevieve Bujold
Doctor Hardy	Chris Wiggins
Mrs Lees	Teddi Moore
William Slade	Peter Jonfield
Sir Thomas Spivey [Jack the Ripper]	Roy Lansford
Carrie	Catherine Kessler
Makins	Ron Pember
Annie Chapman	June Brown
Dock guard	Ken Jones
Danny	Terry Duggan
Catherine Eddowes	Hilary Sesta
Lance	Anthony May
Mrs Dobson	Betty Woolfe
Elizabeth Stride	Iris Fry
Home Secretary Henry Mathews	Geoffrey Russell
Lees' housekeeper	Peggy Ann Clifford
Jane	Ann Marie Mitchell
Molly	Katherine Stark
Ellen	Elaine Ives Cameron
Betty	Stella Courtney
Emily	Judy Wilson
Carroll	Roy Pattison
Prince of Wales	Victor Langley
Princess Alexandra	Pamela Abbott
Duke of Clarence 'Eddy'	Robin Marshall
Doctor	Richard Dedmon
Nurse	Pat Brackenbury
Constable Long	Dan Long
Constable Watkins	Michael Cashman
Police Constable	Peter Dean

• SELECTED CREDITS

Directed by	Bob Clark
Produced by	René Dupont/Bob Clark/ Robert A Goldston
Original Screenplay by	John Hopkins
Music Composed by	Carl Zittrer/Paul Zaza
Director of Photography	Reginald H Morris
Camera Operator	James Turrell
Production Designer	Harry Pottle
Art Director	Peter Childs
Editor	Stan Cole
Sound Recordist	John Mitchell
Supervising Sound Editor	Ken Heeley-Ray
Production Manager	John Davis
1st Assistant Director	Ariel Levy
Chief Make-up Artist	Peter Robb-King
Chief Hairdresser	Colin Jamison
Wardrobe Supervisor	Ron Beck
Continuity	Marjorie Lavelly
Casting Director	Irene Lamb
Special Effects	Michael Albrechtson
Executive Producer	Len Herberman

Avco-Embassy 127 minutes Colour

Time After Time

• CAST

Herbert George Wells	Malcolm McDowell
Dr John Leslie Stevenson [Jack the Ripper]	David Warner
Amy Robbins	Mary Steenburgen
Lt Mitchell	Charles Cioffi
Assistant	Ken Williams
Mrs Turner	Andonia Katsaros
Shirley	Patti D'Arbanville
Edwards	James Garratt
Harding	Keith McConnell
Richardson	Leo Lewis
McKay	Byron Webster
Jenny	Karin Mary Shea
Carol	Geraldine Baron
Inspector Gregson	Laurie Main
Adams	Joseph Maher
Sergeant	Michael Evans
Jeweler	Ray Reinhardt
Bank officer	Bob Shaw
Clergyman	Stu Klitsler
Diner	Nicholas Shields
Cab driver	Gene Hartline
Bobby	Clement St George
Dolores	Shirley Marchant
Guard	Larry J Blake
Nurse	Antonie Becker
2nd nurse	Hilda Haynes
Booking cop	Read Morgan
London bobby	Mike Gainey
1st cop	Jim Haynie
2nd cop	Wayne Storm
3rd cop	John Colton
Boy at museum	Corey Feldman
Man	James Cranna
4th cop	Earl Nichols
Pawnbroker	Bill Bradley
Newscaster	Clete Roberts
Maid	Rita Conde

Woman cop..*Gail Hyatt*
Docent...*Shelley Hack*
Man on street....................................*Daniel Leegant*
Women......................*Regina V Waldron/Liz Roberson*
Men..........*Anthony Gordon/Lou Felder/Doug Morrisson*
5th cop..*Glenn Carlson*
Stunts................*Everett Greach/Brad Eide/Gadie David/*
....*Larry Duran*

• SELECTED CREDITS
Directed by.................................Nicholas Meyer
Produced by.......................................Herb Jaffe
Screenplay by............................Nicholas Meyer
Story by.....................Karl Alexander/Steve Hayes
Associate Producer..............Steven-Charles Jaffe
Music..Miklos Rozsa
Director of Photography...............Paul Lohmann
Camera Operator...............................Tim Wade
Production Designer.............Edward C Carfagno
Set Decorator............................Barbara Krieger
Editor.......................................Donn Cambern
Sound...Jerry Jost
Supervising Sound Editor............Michael Colgan
Unit Production Manager...............Austen Jewell
Assistant Director.........................Michael Daves
2nd Assistant Director.................Paul Magwood
Make-up Artist............................Lynn Reynolds
Hairstylist......................................Dione Taylor
Men's Costumer.............................Sal Anthony
Women's Costumer......................Yvonne Kubis
Casting....................................Diane Crittenden
Special Effects..............Larry Fuentes/Jim Blount
Orion/Warners 112 minutes Metrocolor

1980

Fantasy Island: With Affection, Jack the Ripper
• CAST
Mr Roarke................................Ricardo Montalban
Tattoo...Hervé Villechaize
Dr Albert Z Fell [Jack the Ripper]...............Victor Buono
Lorraine Peters.............................Lynda Day George
Robert West..Alex Cord
Old woman......................................Kathryn Fuller
Bobby..John Brandon
First girl..Philece Sampler
Second girl..Rosemary Lord
• SELECTED CREDITS
Directed by...Mike Vejar
Produced by.......................................Don Ingalls
Written by..Don Ingalls
Associate Producer..............Christopher Chulack
Music.....................................Charles Albertine
Director of Photography..........Emmett Bergholz

Fantasy Island (1980)

Camera Operator...............................Cliff Ralke
Art Directors.............Ross Bellah/David Marshall
Film Editor...............................Steven C Brown
Unit Production Manager...........Robert M Beche
Assistant Director................Wallace van Allen III
Second Assistant Director.................Bob Rolsky
Make-up Artist...........................Nora de la Torre
Hairstylist......................................Lee Crawford
Wardrobe..Grady Hunt
Casting..Claire Newell
Special Effects.....................................Bill Clove
Executive Producers.....................Aaron Spelling/
....Leonard Goldberg
Spelling/Goldberg/ABC 47 minutes Colour

Lulu
• SELECTED CAST & CREDITS
Anne Bennent/Michele Placido/Jean-Jacques Delbo/
Hans-Jürgen Schatz/Bruno Hübner/Beate Kopp/Carlo
Enrici/Pierre Saintons/Udo Kier (Jack the Ripper)/Heinz
Bennent

Lulu (1980)

Director: Walerian Borowczyk/Producers: Robert
Kuperberg, Jean-Pierre Labrande/Written by
Walerian Borowczyk from the plays *Erdgeist* and
Die Büchse der Pandora by Frank Wedekind/Music:
Giancarlo Chiaramello/Cameraman: Ulli Meier/
Production Designer: Roland Mabille/Art
Director: Walerian Borowczyk/Editor: Alex Pront/
Production Supervisor: Ralph Baum/ Make-up:
Susanne Schroder/Costumes: Elisabeth Schewe/
Executive Producer: Kadicha Bariha
Parafrance Film 85 minutes Fujicolor

1981
New York Ripper
(Lo squartatore di New York)
• Selected Cast & Credits
Jack Hedley/Almanta Keller/Howard Ross/Andrew
Painter/Alessandra Delli Colli/Paolo Malco
Director: Lucio Fulci/Producer: Fabrizio De
Angelis/Written by: Lucio Fulci/ Music composed
and directed by Francesco De Masi/Director of

Fear City (1984)

Photography: Luigi Kuveiller/Production Design
and Costumes: Massimo Lentini/Editor:
Vincenzo Tomassi
Fulvia Film 97 minutes Colour

1983
American Ripper

1984
Fear City
(aka Ripper)
• Selected Cast & Credits
Tom Berenger/Billy Dee Williams/Jack Scalia/Melanie
Griffith/Rossano Brazzi/Rae Dawn Chong/Joe
Santos/Michael V Gazzo/Jan Murray/ anet Julian/Daniel
Faraldo/Maria Conchita/Ola Ray/John Foster
Director: Abel Ferrara/Producer: Bruce Cohn
Curtis/Written by Nicholas St. John/Music: Dick
Halligan/Director of Photography: James
Lemmo/Editor: Jack Holmes, Anthony Redman/
Executive Producers: Stanley R Zupnik, Tom
Curtis
Zupnik-Curtis/Rebecca 99 minutes Colour

1985
The Ripper
• Cast
Prof Harwell..Tom Schreier
Carol..Mona Van Pernis
Steve..Wade Tower
Jack the Ripper.......................................Tom Savini
Cindy..Andrea Adams
Fred..Randall White
Clark...Bennie Lee McGowan
Brian..Jeffrey Fontana
Mrs Pratt...Wilma Cummins
Harlot..............................Karen Morgan Williams
Waitress..Patti Beth Abbott
Judy..Alicia Todd
Officer..Vic Seals
Amy..................................Vicki Pemberton-Thomson
Policemen....................Edward Compos/Eddie Majors/
........Dennis MacDonnell/ Robert McCall/C Scott Walton
Students......Rusty Cook/Clayton Farmer/GeorgiaKnight/
..............Mark Massey/ToddNeice/Raymond Woodson
Carriage driver...Steve Rush
Dancers........Kimberly Banks/Nicholson Billey/Elizabeth
................Govaerts/ Monica Jackson/Marilyn Marloff/
.............DerrickMinter/Kim Stephens/Pamela Williams
Children.......Shawn Johnson/Teddy Johnson/Betsy Stice/
....Amy Stice
Brian's friend...Samantha

The Ripper (1985)

• SELECTED CREDITS
Directed by............................Christopher Lewis
Produced by....................................Linda Lewis
Written by...Bill Groves
Associate Producer................................Jill Clark
Music...Rod Slane
Director of Photography.............Paul MacFarlane
Editor...Jim Lenertz
Sound...Victor Thomas
Assistant Director................................Jill Clark
Make-up.....................Jerry Martin/Shawn Owen
Hair Design.......................................Bradley's
Fashions..Renberg's
Special Effects..............................DFX Studios
Executive Producer...........................Bill F Blair
United Entertainment 102 minutes Colour

Terror at London Bridge
(aka The Bridge Across Time; Arizona Ripper)
• CAST
Detective Don Gregory.......................David Hasselhoff
Angie...Stepfanie Kramer
Joe Nez....................................Randolph Mantooth
Lynn Chandler...............................Adrienne Barbeau
Chief Pete Dawson................................Clu Gulager
Elaine Gardner.................................Lindsay Bloom
Ed Nebel...Ken Swofford
Alma Bellock..Rose Marie
Anson Whitfield.....................................Lane Smith
Mr Latting..................................David Fox-Brenton
Dave Williamson................................Michael Boyle
Alice Williamson...........................Barbara Bingham
Jack the Ripper.....................................Paul Rossilli
Lab technician................................Cameron Milzer
Mr Daly...Charles Benton
Amy Phelps...Nancy Skillen
Waiter...Ray Favero
Mayor McCoy...Jim Hodge
Lord Mayor of London...........................Peter Vernon
Guard #1...Mike Wilkins
Tom Hale...Steve Archer
Child......................................Stephanie Ann Stone
• SELECTED CREDITS
Directed by..............................E W Swackhamer
Produced by.........Jack Michon/Richard Maynard
Written by................................William F Nolan
Music..Lalo Schifrin
Music Supervisor.............................John Fresco
Director of Photography.....................Gil Hubbs
Camera Operator........................Ray De La Motte
Art Director...........................William McAllister
Editor...........................Tom Fries/Leslie Dennis

Sound Mixer.................................James La Rue
Production Manager.................Claude Binyon Jr
First Assistant Director...................Gerald Walsh
Second Assistant Director...............John Whittle
Make-up Artist.....................Pamela S Westmore
Hairstylist...............................Frankie Campbell
Costumer..Kathy Dover
Casting....................Jaki Brown/Toni Livingston
Special Effects Coordinator.........John C Hartigan
Executive Producers........Charles Fries/Irv Wilson
Charles Fries/NBC 100 minutes Colour

1986
Night Ripper

1987
Amazon Women on the Moon

1988
Jack's Back
• SELECTED CAST & CREDITS
James Spader/Cynthia Gibb/Jim Haynie/Robert
Picardo/Rod Loomis/Rex Ryon/Chris Mulkey/Wendell
Wright/John Wesley/Bobby Hosea/Danitza Kingsley/
Anne Betancourt/John Sutherland/Diane Erikson
Director: Rowdy Herrington/Producers: Tim
Moore, Cassian Elwes/Written by Rowdy
Herrington/Music: Danny Di Paola/Director of
Photography: Shelly Johnson/Production
Designer:Piers Plowden/Editor: Harry B Miller III
Casting: Kimba Hills
Palisades/Paramount 101 minutes Colour

Jack the Ripper
• CAST
Chief Inspector Frederick Abberline...........Michael Caine
Sergeant George Godley.........................Lewis Collins
Richard Mansfield...........................Armand Assante
Sir William Gull [Jack the Ripper]..........Ray McAnally

Edge of Sanity (1989)

Robert James Lees	Ken Bones
Catherine 'Kate' Eddowes	Susan George
Emma Prentiss	Jane Seymour
Coroner Wynne E Baxter	Harry Andrews
Mary Jane Kelly	Lysette Anthony
Rodman	Roger Ashton-Griffiths
Sergeant Kerby	Peter Armitage
Copy boy	Desmond Askew
Lanyon	Trevor Baxter
Lady Gull	Ann Castle
Annie Chapman	Deirdre Costello
Mr Thackeray	Jon Croft
Liz Stride	Angela Crow
Annette	Kelly Cryer
Prince Albert Victor, Duke of Clarence	Marc Culwick
Isenschmid	John Dair
Doorkeeper	Roy Evans
PC Watkins	John Fletcher
Millie	Sheridan Forbes
Sir Charles Warren	Hugh Fraser
Newsvendors	Martin Friend/Mike Carnell
Sergeant Brent/Beggar	Christopher Fulford
Pizer	Bruce Green
Pickpocket	Rikki Harnet
Henry Matthews...Ronald Hines Assistant Commissioner	
Anderson	Denys Hawthorne
Dr Rees Llewellyn	Michael Hughes
Mr Paulson	Peter Hughes
1st passerby	Frank Jarvis
DCS of Police Arnold	Edward Judd
Louis Diemschutz	Gertan Klauber
Inspector John T Spratling	Jon Laurimore
Duty guard	Mike Lewin
Mortician	Rod Lewis
Derek	Gary Love

Old man	George Malpas
Publican	Eric Mason
Woman in doorway	Bernadette Milne
Benjamin Bates	Jonathan Moore
Dr Theodore Acland	Richard Morant
O'Connor	T P McKenna
Dresser	John Normington
Davis	Ronald Nunnery
Mrs Acland	Sandra Payne
Cabinet Secretary	Neville Phillips
Tough policeman	Iain Rattray
Thomas Bowyer	David Ryall
Billy White	Gary Shail
Dr George Baxter Phillips	Gerald Sim
John Netley	George Sweeney
Lord Salisbury	David Swift
Richardson	Norman Warwick
Porter	Brian Weske
George Lusk	Michael Gothard

• SELECTED CREDITS

Directed/Produced by	David Wickes
Screenplay by	Derek Marlowe/David Wickes
Associate Producer	Al Burgess
Music	John Cameron
Director of Photography	Alan Hume
Camera Operator	Martin Hume
Production Designer	John Blezard
Editor	Keith Palmer
Production Controller	Bill Launder
Costume Designer	Raymond Hughes
Wardrobe Master	Paul Vachon
Executive Producers	Lloyd Shirley/Robert O'Connor/Leonard Hill

Euston/Thames 190 minutes Colour

1989
Edge of Sanity

• CAST

Dr Henry Jekyll/Jack Hyde	Anthony Perkins
Elisabeth Jekyll	Glynis Barber
Susannah	Sarah Maur-Thorp
Underwood	David Lodge
Johnny	Ben Cole
Newcomen	Ray Jewers
Maria	Lisa Davis
Flora	Jill Melford
Egglestone	Noel Coleman
Ann Underwood	Briony McRoberts
Lanyon	Mark Elliot
Coroner	Harry Landis
Mrs Egglestone	Jill Pearson
Mr Bollingham	Basil Hoskins

Margot..Ruth Burnett
Maggie..Carolyn Cortez
Cockney prostitute..............................Cathy Murphy
Liza..Claudia Udy

• SELECTED CREDITS

Directed by...............................Gérard Kikoïne
Produced by....Edward Simons/Harry Alan Towers
Screenplay by.......................J P Felix/Ron Raley
Associate Producers....James Swann/Maria Rohm
Music composed, orchestrated and conducted
by...Frederic Talgorn
Director of Photography...............Tony Spratling
Camera Operator.......................Gerard Loubeau
Production Designer.............Jean Charles Dedieu
Art Director.......................................Fred Carter
Editor...Malcolm Cooke
Sound Editor..............................Leslie Hodgson
Production Manager................Derek Whitehurst
1st Assistant Director.......................Do Combes
Make-up Supervisor........................Gordon Kaye
Hairdresser..................................Carol Bennett
Wardrobe Designer.........................Valerie Lanee
Continuity......................................Daphne Carr
Casting Director........................Maggie Sanguin
Executive Producer........................Peter A McRae
Allied Vision/Hungarofilm 90 [88] minutes
Eastmancolor

1992

Waxwork II: Lost in Time

• SELECTED CAST & CREDITS

Zach Galligan/Monika Schnarre/Martin Kemp/Bruce
Campbell/Michael Des Barres/Jim Metzler/Sophie Ward/
Marina Sirtis/Billy Kane/Joe Baker/Juliet Mills/John
Ireland/Patrick Macnee/David Carradine/Alexander
Godunov/Alex Butler (Jack the Ripper)
Director: Anthony Hickox/Producer: Nancy
Paloian/Written by Anthony Hickox/Original
Score: Steve Schiff/Director of Photography:
Gerry Lively/ Editor: Christopher Cibelli/
Executive Producer: Mario Sotela
Electric 108 minutes Colour

1993

Deadly Advice

• CAST

Jodie Greenwood................................Jane Horrocks
Iris Greenwood.................................Brenda Fricker
Beth Greenwood...........................Imelda Staunton
Dr Ted Philips...............................Jonathan Pryce
Major Herbert Armstrong..............Edward Woodward
Kate Webster....................................Billie Whitelaw

Dr Crippen..Hywel Bennett
George Joseph Smith..........................Jonathan Hyde
Jack the Ripper.....................................Sir John Mills
Bunny...Ian Abbey
Judge...Eleanor Bron
Gareth...Jo Stone-Fewings
Reverend Horace Cotton...........................Roger Frost
Mr Smethurst............................Gareth Gwyn-Jones
Constable Dickman...........................Richard Moore
Joyce Cream.....................................Alison Burrows
Veronica...Sarah Blackburn
Compère..Alan Fordham
Mary...Dillie Keane
Michael...Benedick Bates
Young Jodie....................................Elinor Blakeley
Jodie's dad.......................................Robert Hickson
Farmer..Andrew Watson
Waitress....................................Sue Jones-Davies
Young constable...............................Craig Edwards

• SELECTED CREDITS

Directed by...............................Mandie Fletcher
Produced by.........................Nigel Stafford-Clark
Screenplay...............................Glenn Chandler
Associate Producer....................Charles Salmon
Music...Richard Harvey
Director of Photography............Richard Greatrex
Camera Operator.............................Jim Alloway
Production Designer..............Christopher Hobbs
Art Director...........................Michael Buchanan
Editor...John Jarvis
Sound Editor...............................Rick Dunford
Production Coordinator.................Janine Lodge
Assistant Director........................Melanie Dicks
Second Assistant Director.............Robert Fabbri
Chief Make-up Artiste...................Aileen Seaton
Makeup Hair..............Robert McCann/Sian Grigg
Wardrobe Supervisor...............Cynthea Dowling
Casting...Sheila Trezise
SFX Chiefs...Dave Beavis/Arthur Beavis/Ken Lailey
Zenith 91 minutes Eastmancolor

1994

Ripper Man

• CAST

Mike Lazo...Mike Norris
Charles Walken/George Chapman [Jack the Ripper]........
....Timothy Bottoms
Frankel..Robert F Lyons
Harry...Charles Napier
Greg Onthi..Bruce Locke
Tony..Carey Scott
Gena..Sofia Shinas

Francie..Candi Milo
Laura..Patricia North
Kevin..Brock Pierce
Nancy..Valerie Norris
Addict/victim.....................................Deanne Carlin
Officer Bates.......................................Gailyn Addis
Sgt. Irvine...................................John Thomas Turk
Hecklers.............George 'Buck' Flower/Clarke Coleman/
....Myke Michaels
Coroner..John F Goff
Trance victim.....................................Dawn Gilbert
Lady Godiver (Volunteer)...................Tiffany Anderson
Exotic dancer.......................................Leanna Love
Male hypnotist volunteer....................Michael B Bayer
Watch commander.............................Tom Norwood
Twin comedy act....................Ed Johnson/Bob Johnson
Hospital thugs...............Thor Hammer/Raub McKim/
...................................Chris Person/Eric Leisher
Female thug..Maria Doest
Boy at hospital.............................Christian La Bella
Loomis..Joseph T Ferrero
Stunt players.................Greg Brazzel/Clarke Coleman/
...................................Pat Statham/Garrett Warren

• SELECTED CREDITS
Directed by...Phil Sears
Produced by.............Aaron Norris/Andy Howard
Screenplay by.......................................Phil Sears
Associate Producer.........................Valerie Norris
Music Composed by............................Jim Ervin
Director of Photography.................Blake T Evans
Production Designer/Art Director...Howard Smith
Editor.......................................Peter N Lonsdale
Recordist...Brian Smith
Unit Production Manager.......Donato Ricciardella
First Assistant Director.........................Rex Piano
Second Assistant Director..............Dan Leatham
Key Hair/Make-up.........................Myke Michaels
Costumes Designed by..................Dorothy Amos
Casting.....................Geno Havens/Iris Hampton
Special Effects..........Kam Cooney/Dick Anderson
Executive Producers...................Tom Steinmetz/
....Tony Mizrahi
Tanglewood/MAV 93 minutes Colour

1995

Babylon 5: Comes the Inquisitor
• CAST
Captain John Sheridan......................Bruce Boxleitner
Commander Susan Ivanova..............Claudia Christian
Security Chief Michael Garibaldi................Jerry Doyle
Delenn...Mira Furlan
Dr Stephen Franklin............................Richard Biggs

Talia Winters................................Andrea Thompson
Vir..Stephen Furst
Lennier...Bill Mumy
Lt. Warren Keffer..............................Robert Rusler
Na'Toth..................................Mary Kay Adams
G'Kar....................................Andreas Katsulas
Londo...Peter Jurasik
Sebastian [Jack the Ripper]...............Wayne Alexander
Mr Chase...Jack Kehler
Narn mother.......................................Diane Adair
Kosh.........................Ardwight Chamberlain
Centauri #1..Jim Chiros
Tech #1...Joshua Cox
Narn #1.................................Mark Hendrickson
Guard.........................Michael Francis Kelly
Narn #2...Kim Strauss
Human..Craig Thomas

• SELECTED CREDITS
Directed by...................................Michael Vejar
Produced by.................................John Copeland
Written by.........................J Michael Straczynski
Associate Producer.....................George Johnsen
Music...................................Christopher Franke
Director of Photography..............John C Flinn III
Camera Operator.....................Peter B Komalski
Production Designer.....................John Iacovelli
Art Director...........................Roland Rosenkran
Editor..Skip Robinson
Supervising Sound Editor...................Erin Hoien
Unit Production Manager............Kevin G Cremin
1st Assistant Director.................Pamela Eilerson
2nd Assistant Director...............Douglas Corring
Key Make-up Artist........................Cinzia Zanetti
Key Hairstylist..............................Traci Smithe
Costume Designer...........................Ann Bruice
Costume Supervisor........................Kim M Holly
Casting.............Mary Jo Slater/Steve Brooksbank
Executive Producers....................Douglas Netter/
...................................J. Michael Straczynski
Babylonian/Warners 45 minutes Colour

1997

Sliders: Murder Most Foul
• SELECTED CAST & CREDITS
Jerry O'Connell/Sabrina Lloyd/Cleavant Derricks/John
Rhys-Davies/Brian McNamara/Brigid Brannagh/David
Purdham/Adam Wylie/Lester Barrie/Suzanne Mara
Director: Jeff Woolnough/Producer: Richard
Compton/Mychelle Deschamps/Written by David
Peckinpah/Music: Stephen Graziano/ Executive
Producers: Tony Blake/ Paul Jackson
St. Clare/Universal 43 minutes Colour

The Ripper

• CAST

Inspector James Hansen........................Patrick Bergin
Florry Lewis.....................................Gabrielle Anwar
Prince Eddy [Jack the Ripper]..................Samuel West
Sgt Tommy Bell.................................Adam Couper
Evelyn Bookman.................................Essie Davis
Sir Charles Warren.............................Michael York
Lady Margaret.................................Olivia Hamnett
Mary Kelly....................................Karen Davitt
Officer Peters................................Damien Pree
Cullen.......................................Stewart Morritt
Sir William Fraiser............................Kevin Miles
Doctor William Gull...........................John Gregg
Doctor Pearce.................................Frank Whitten
Chalmers....................................Peter Collingwood
Lizzie......................................Josephine Keen
Thomas Delancey...............................Lisle Jones
Cartman.....................................Anthony Morton
Milkman.....................................Christopher Kemp
Policeman....................................Stephen Sheehan
Spectator....................................Caroline Huff
Doorman.....................................Denzil Howson
Cop #1.......................................Justin Parslow
Maid..Jessica Muschamp
Big man......................................David Clisby
Small man....................................Richie Akers
Old gent.....................................John Murphy
Bartender....................................Sally Anne Upton
Young cop....................................Curtis Barnott
Matron......................................Maureen Edwards
Prissy woman.................................Suzy Cato
Snobbish man.................................Peter Stratford
Handsome patrician............................Peter Hardy
Tenor.......................................Shaun Murphy
Baritone....................................Grant Smith
Old woman...................................Dawn Klingberg
Drunk.......................................Dean Barton-Ancliffe
Audience member..............................Hamish Hughes
Another audience member.......................Lawrence Price
Prince Eddy's valet............................Tim Wood
Guard with battle axe..........................John Turner
Major-Domo..................................Colin Duckworth
Captain.....................................Michael Fry
Theatrical troupe.....................Di Diddle/Anny Fodor/
.........................Ross Mathers/Santha Press
Pianist.....................................Stephen McIntyre
Old man.....................................Monty Maizels
Police photographer...........................Andrew Shortell
Prince Eddy's doubles.......Dean Caulfield/Jade Weitering
Hansen's double...............................Roy Edmunds
Florry's double...............................Szumai Anderson

Patrician's riding double.....................Lance Anderson
Prince Eddy's riding double.....................Clint Dodd
Coach drivers.......Cody Harris/Cheryl Batten/Terry Tulk/
.........................Fred Lewis/Dean Crighton

• SELECTED CREDITS

Directed by..................................Janet Meyers
Produced by.........................Allison Lyon Segan
Written by...................................Robert Rodat
Music......................................Mason Daring
Director of Photography...........Martin McGrath
Camera Operators..................Calum McFarlane/
.........................Murray Ware
Production Designer.........................Tim Ferrier
Art Director.........................Michelle McGahey
Editor..............................Elba Sánchez-Short
Sound Recordist.........................Gary Wilkins
Supervising Sound Editor..............Peter Austin
Unit Production Manager...............Barbie Taylor
1st Assistant Director....................Colin Fletcher
2nd Assistant Director....................Toni Raynes
Make-up.....................................Kirsten Veysey
Hairstylist................................Cheryl Williams
Costume Supervisor.........................Paula Ryan
Wardrobe Assistants...Michael Davies/John Power
Continuity.............................Chrissy O'Connell
Casting by............Mary Gail Artz/Barbara Cohen
Special Effects................Tim O'Brien/Jeff Little/
.........................Kevin Turner
Executive Producers....................Mark Gordon/
.........................Gary Levinsohn

Mutual/Universal 100 minutes Colour

Timecop: A Rip in Time

• CAST

Jack Logan..T W King

Timecop (1997)

Claire Hemmings.............................Cristi Conaway
Eugene Matuzek..Don Stark
Dr Dale Easter...Kurt Fuller
Inspector Wells..........................W Morgan Sheppard
Ian Pascoe...Tom O'Brien
Anne Thompson.................................Anna Galvin
Catherine Eddowes......................Belinda Waymouth
Ferrett...Ric Sarabia
Charles..John Maynard
Bride.....................................Saige Ophelia Spinney
Technician.....................................Michael Holden
Constable #1...Tim O'Hare
Constable #2..Simon Billig

• SELECTED CREDITS
Directed by......................................Allan Arkush
Produced by..............Philip J. Sgriccia/Chris Long
Teleplay by..................Alfred Gough/Miles Millar
from the Dark Horse comic by Mike Richardson/Mark
Verheiden
Music..Brad Fidel
Supervising Music Editor..............Allan K. Rosen
Director of Photography...............Ross Berryman
Production Designer.............................Jim Pohl
Set Decorator........................W. Joseph Kroesser
Editor......................................John F Showalter
Supervising Sound Editor..............Robb Navrides
Unit Production Manager...........Wayne A Farlow
First Assistant Director...............Joseph P Moore
Second Assistant Director............Sean Kavanagh
Key Make-up..................................Carla Fabrizi
Key Hairstylist.................................Linle White
Costume Designer.........................Darryl Levine
Casting by..............Robert J Ulrich/Eric Dawson/

Love Lies Bleeding (1998)

....Carol Kritzer
Executive Producers................Lawrence Gordon/
.......................Robert Singer/ Mike Richardson/
.............................Lloyd Levin/Art Monterastelli
Dark Horse/Universal 43 minutes Colour

1998

Love Lies Bleeding

• CAST
Dr Jonathan Stephens...............................Paul Rhys
Catherine Winwood........................Emily Raymond
Malcolm Mead...........................Malcolm McDowell
Inspector Abberline..............................Wayne Rogers
Josephine Butler...............................Faye Dunaway
Emmet Lloyd.......................................Noel Le Bon
Edward Winwood..............................Robert Russell
Mrs Winwood....................................Barbara Day
Constable Neal.....................................John Comer
Jack Pizer..Pavel Vokoun
Polly Nichols....................................Nancy Bishop
Mary Kelly................................Andrea Miltnerova
Drunken Sailor...Peter Alton
Fraser..David Nykl

• CREDITS
Directed by................................William Tannen
Produced by..Jan Bilek
Line Producer...............................Ricardo Freixa
Supervising Producer.....................Michael Lake
Screenplay by.....................................Tony Rush
Music....................................Michel Dvorak
Director of Photography.............Vladimir Smutny
Costume Designer................Simona Zapletalova
Art Director....................................Martin Maly
Editor...Peter Cohen
Sound Mixer...........................Tomas Cervenka
1st Asst Director...................Michaela Strnadova
Executive Production Manager..............Ales Tybl
Unit Manager......................................Petr Bilek
Stunt Coordinator.....................Ladislav Lahoda
Village Roadshow/Icon International 89 minutes
Colour

1999

The Outer Limits: Ripper

• CAST
Doctor John York [Jack the Ripper]..............Cary Elwes
Lady Ellen...Clare Sims
Sophie..Eliza Murbach
Sergeant...Robert Saunders
Madame...France Nuyen
Countess Julia....................................Frances Fisher
Inspector Harold Langford....................David Warner

Annie Chapman....................................Deni DeLory
Lizzie Stride..Marnie Alton
Worthington......................................Colin Skinner
Lord Reston...Scott Elam
Mary Jane Kelly..............................Mary Ann Skoll
Woman in cream dress......................Candice Connelly
Reporter..Brian Linds
Newsboy..Danielle Ayotte
Wickett..Jim Boardman
Young prostitute........................Marie-Sophie Girard
Blonde woman..............................Bonnie Catterson
Street prostitute #1.........................Carmen Casanova
Street prostitute #2................................Janet Flink
Street prostitute #3.............................Maya Changu

• SELECTED CREDITS
Directed by..............................Mario Azzopardi
Produced by.........................Brent Karl Clackson
Written by...............................Chris Ruppenthal
Associate Producer..........................Ben Brafman
Music....................................John Van Tongeren
Director of Photography................Rick Wincenty
Camera Operator.........................Paul Mitchnick
Production Designer.....................Steve Geaghan
Art Director...................................Susan Parker
Film Editor................................Daria Ellerman
Sound Supervisor...........................Adam Gejdos
Sound Editor.............................Brian Campbell
Production Manager..........................Lynn Barr
1st assistant Director....................Brian Giddens
2nd Assistant Director.................Ella Kutschera
Make-up Artist........................Fay Von Schroeder
Hairstylist...Susan Boyd
Costume Designer....................Stephanie Nolin
Casting by...................Mary Jo Slater/Paul Weber
Special Effects.............................Dave Allinson
Executive Producers...........................Sam Egan/
..................Richard Barton Lewis/Pen Densham/
....John Watson
Trilogy/Alliance Atlantis/M-G-M 44 minutes Colour

2000

Jill the Ripper
• SELECTED CAST & CREDITS
Dolph Lundgren/Danielle Brett/Sandi Ross/Charles
Sexias/Kristi Angus/Greg Ellwand/Susan Kottman/Victor
Pedtchenko/Kylie Bax/Richard Fitzpatrick
Director: Anthony Hickox/Producers: Tracee
Stanley, Noble Henry/Written by Gareth Wardell,
Kevin Bernhardt from the novel by Fredrick
Lindsay/ Music: Steve Gurevitch, Thomas
Barquee/Associate Producer: Helder
Golcalves/Director of Photography: David

Pelletier/Production Designer: Tim Boyd/Editor:
Brett Hedlund/Executive Producer: Damian Lee
Phoenician/Annex 98 minutes FotoKem colour

Jill the Ripper (2000)

The Others: Don't Dream It's Over
• CAST
Marian Kitt.................................Julianne Nicholson
Dr Mark Gabriel..............................Gabriel Macht
Ellen 'Satori' Polaski............................Melissa Crider
Elmer Greentree...Bill Cobbs
Prof Miles Ballard...........................John Billingsley
Warren Day..................................Kevin J O'Connor
Mary Jane Kelly................................Tushka Bergen
Jack the Ripper.....................................John Vickery
Jimmy..Aubrey Morris
Albert McGonagle..............................Jon Aylward
George Hutchinson...............................Clive Barker
Nurse..Jill C Klein
Cop...David Jean-Thomas
Paramedic.......................................Rachelle Leffer
Customer..James N Gale
Street person................................Floyd Van Bostick

• SELECTED CREDITS
Directed by......................................Mick Garris
Produced by...................................Sarah Caplan
Written by..Mick Garris
Associate Producer.....................Randy S Nelson
Music......................Shirley Walker/Klaus Badelt
Director of Photography..............Shelly Johnson
Production Designer......................Victoria Paul
Editors............................Chris G. Willingham/
..............................Patrick McMahon/Fred Toye
Supervising Sound Editor...........Mace Matiosian
Unit Production Manager..............Sharon Mann
First Assistant Director....................Seth Cirker/
....Noga Isackson

The Others (2000)

Second Assistant Director................J J Unsalata
Costume Designer.........................Karen Patch
Casting by........Janet Gilmore/Megan McConnell
Visual Effects Supervisor..................James Lima
Executive Producers....................John Brancato/
..........Michael Ferris/ James Wong/Glen Morgan
Delusional/Dreamworks/NBC 44 minutes Colour

2001
Bad Karma
• CAST

Maureen Hatcher/Agnes........................Patsy Kensit
Trey Campbell [Jack the Ripper]..........Patrick Muldoon
Carly Campbell....................................Amy Locane
Jenny Postelli.................................Amy Huberman
Detective Arboles...............................Patrick Byrnes
Teresa Campbell.............................Amy O'Sullivan
Mr. Miller...Damian Chapa
Arthur...Vinnie McCabe
Denise...Rachel O'Riordan
Richard...Sean Power
Edie...Merrina Mulsapp
Dod...Nick Hardin
Redhead......................................Denise McCarton
English prostitute.............................Fiona Reynard
Female security guard............................Maria Tecca
Policewoman...................................Jeanette Omos
Eskimo..Christopher Kelly
Paramedic...David Flynn
Detective...Gerry O'Grady
Police..................Sean Bermingham/Tony McKenna/
....Colm O'Conghaile
Stunts.............Dominic/Trina Griffin/Duncan Lacroix/
....................................Jeanette Omos/Gary Robinson

• SELECTED CREDITS
Directed by.......................................John Hough
Produced by..................................Brian R Etting
Written by.....................................Randall Frakes
from the novel by Douglas Clegg (as Andrew Harper)

Associate Producer..............Terese Linden-Kohn
Music by.................................Harry Manfredini
Director of Photography.............Jacques Haitkin
Production Designer........Anthony Rivero Stabley
Set Decorator.........................Catherine Dalton
Editor...Richard Trevor
Supervising Sound Editor..........Jeremy Hoenack
Unit Production Manager......Columba Heneghan
First Assistant Director.................Ivan McMahon
Second Assistant Director...........Laura Company
2nd Unit Directors......Paul Hough/Brian R Etting
Key Hair/Make-up...................Caroline McCurdy
Costume Designers...Susanna Puisto/Aisling Byrne
Casting By...............................Gillian Reynolds
Stunt Coordinator..........................Eamon Kelly
Executive Producer........................Mark L Lester
American World 94 minutes Fotokem colour

From Hell
• CAST

Inspector Frederick Abberline....................Johnny Depp
Mary Kelly.....................................Heather Graham
Sir William Gull [Jack the Ripper]................Ian Holm
Sir Charles Warren.............................Ian Richardson
Peter Godley.................................Robbie Coltrane
Dark Annie Chapman........................Katrin Cartlidge
Robert Best...Byron Fear
Liz Stride...Susan Lynch
Victoria Abberline................................Sophia Miles
Catherine 'Kate' Eddowes........................Lesley Sharp
Ben Kidney.....................................Terence Harvey
Ada...Estelle Skornik
Dr Ferral..Paul Rhys
Officer Bolt.............................Nicholas McGaughey
John Netley...................................Jason Flemyng
Polly..Annabelle Apsion
Annie Crook....................................Joanna Page
Albert Sickert/Prince Edward....................Mark Dexter
Constable Withers.........................Danny Midwinter
Martha Tabram.............................Samantha Spiro
McQueen......................................David Schofield
Lord Hallsham.....................................Peter Eyre
Mac, bartender.....................................Cliff Parisi
Gordie...Ralph Ineson
Gull's maid...Amy Huck
Doss landlord...............................Rupert Farley
Hospital director.............................Donald Douglas
Marylebone governor.............................John Owens
Opium den owner.................................Tony Tang
Queen Victoria...................................Liz Moscrop
Sidewalk preacher...............................Roger Frost
Robert Drudge.....................................Ian McNeice

Special Branch constable................Steve John Shepherd
Stonecutter.....................................Al Hunter Ashton
Alice Crook...Poppy Rogers
Ann Crook's father.............................Bruce Byron
Ann Crook's mother............................Melanie Hill
Carpenter...Andy Linden
Carpenter/letter writer.........................David Fisher
Constable #1..Gary Powell
Constable #2.......................................Steve Chaplin
George Lusk....................................Vincent Franklin
Bold hooker..Louise Atkins
John Merrick...................................Anthony Parker
Masonic governor................................James Greene
Constable #3................................Dominic Cooper
Police photographer............................Carey Thring
Rag & Bone man..........................Vladimir Kulhavy
Records clerk.......................................Graham Kent
Sailor..................................Rupert Holliday-Evans
Thomas Bond...................................Simon Harrison
Young doctor..Paul Moody
Young labourer.......................................Glen Barry
Labourer #2......................................Charlie Parish
Horse rider...John Dent
Funeral minister/letter writer................Gerry Grennell

• SELECTED CREDITS
Directed by..............Albert Hughes/Allen Hughes
Produced by.............Don Murphy/Jane Hamsher
Screenplay by............Terry Hayes/Rafael Yglesias
from the graphic novel by Alan Moore/Eddie Campbell
Original Music.......Trevor Jones/Marilyn Manson
Cinematography............................Peter Deming
Production Design.........................Martin Childs
Art Director...................................Mark Raggett
Film Editors.............George Bowers/Dan Lebenta
Sound Mixer..........................Steven D Williams
Assistant Sound Editors...Paul Apted/Steve F. Price
Production Manager........................Elena Zokas
Assistant Director..................John R Woodward
Second Assistant Director..........Sallie Anne Hard
Key Make-up artist............................Jiří Farkas
Makeup/Hair Designer...................Lisa Westcott
Costume Design.............................Kym Barrett
Casting.................Joyce Gallie/Christian Kaplan
Special Effects...............................George Gibbs
Executive Producers...........Thomas M Hammel/
....Amy Robinson
20th Century-Fox 121 minutes De Luxe colour

Sir Arthur Conan Doyle's The Lost World:
The Knife
• CAST
Professor George Challenger.................Peter McCauley

Marguerite Krux.................................Rachel Blakely
Veronica Layton.................................Jennifer O'Dell
Edward 'Ned' Malone............................David Orth
Lord John Roxton.....................................Will Snow
Inspector Robert Anderson........................John Noble
Dr William Gull..Nick Tate
with Chas Green/Jack Henry/John Coffey/Daniel Pitt
• SELECTED CREDITS
Directed by...................................Michael Offer
Produced by...................................Darryl Sheen
Written by..Guy Mullally
based on a novel by Sir Arthur Conan Doyle
Music by..........Garry McDonald/Lawrence Stone
Director of Photography.......................Ben Nott
Camera Operator...........................Butch Sawko
Art Director..................................J D Wingrove
Production Designer......................Eugene Intas
Editor..Anne Ker
Sound Recordist...............................Paul Clark
Production Manager....................Basia Plachecki
Assistant Director........................Darren Mallett
Second Assistant Director.............Rachel Bagley
Makeup and Hair supervisor........Veronique Keys
Costume Designer................Lucinda McGuigan
Casting Director........................Tom McSweeney
Effects Supervisor.........Brian Holmes McAlinden
Co-Producer...........................Marc van Buuren
Line Producer...............................Irene Dobson
Executive Creative Consultants...........Judith and
......................................Garfield Reeves-Stevens
Executive Producers.................Peter Bergmann/
.............Arnie Soloway/Jeffrey Hayes/Greg Coote/
....Guy Mullally
Coote-Hayes/New Line/AOL Time-Warner
45 minutes Colour

Ripper: Letter from Hell
• SELECTED CAST & CREDITS
A J Cook/Bruce Payne/Clare Keim/Ryan Northcott/
Derek Hamilton/ Courtenay J. Stevens/Emmanuelle
Vaugier/Daniella Evangellista/Kelly Brook/Jurgen
Prochnow
Director: John E Eyres/Producers: Evan Tylor,
John Curtis/Music: Peter Allen/Screenplay: Pat
Bermel/Story: John Curtis, Evan Tylor/Associate
Producer: Melanie Kilgour/Director of
Photography: Thomas M Harting/ Production
Designer: Mark Harris/Editor: Amanda I Kirpaul/
Executive Producers: John Curtis, Gary Howsam,
David W.G. Mackenzie, Petros Tsaparas
Prophecy/Studio Eight 116 minutes Colour

Bibliography

As was made plain in the text, Jack the Ripper has been the subject of innumerable books, pamphlets, magazine articles and now web sites – since the time of the Whitechapel Murders themselves. To list them all would serve no purpose as these same titles appear again and again in each new work about him. I have decided instead to confine myself to materials which were particularly instrumental in aiding me with the writing of this book. My thanks go to their authors and creators.

- Complete history of Jack the Ripper, The
  Philip Sugden/Robinson PublishingLtd/London/1994
- Diaries and Letters of Marie Belloc Lowndes: 1911-1947
  Susan Lowndes/Chatto and Windus/London/1971
- East End 1888
  W J Fishman/Duckworth/London/1988
- Encyclopedia of Serial Killers, The
  Brian Lane and Wilfred Gregg/Headline/London/1992
- Fantastic Television
  Gary Gerani with Paul H Schulman/Harmony/New York/1977
- From Hell: being a melodrama in sixteen parts
  Alan Moore and Eddie Campbell/Knockabout/London/1996
- Jack the Ripper: The Final Solution
  Stephen Knight/Grafton/HarperCollins/London/1997
- Jack the Ripper A to Z, The
  Paul Begg, Martin Fido and Keith Skinner/Headline/London/1991
- Jack the Ripper: His Life and Crimes in Popular Entertainment
  Gary Coville and Patrick Lucanio/McFarland/Jefferson NC/1999
- Limehouse Nights
  Thomas Burke/Horizon/New York/1973
- Lodger, The
  Marie Belloc Lowndes/Academy Chicago (Ripper centenary edition)/Chicago/1988
- London Monster: A Sanguinary Tale, The
  Jan Bondeson/Free Association/London/2000
- London: Portrait of a City
  Roger Hudson/Folio/London/1998
- Man Who Hunted Jack the Ripper: Edmund Reid and the Police Perspective, The
  Nicholas Connell and Stewart P Evans/Rupert/Cambridge/1999
- Merry Wives of Westminster, The
  Marie Belloc Lowndes/Macmillan/London/1946
- Mystery of Jack the Ripper, The
  Leonard Matters/Arrow/London/1964
- Penny Dreadfuls and Other Victorian Horrors
  Michael Anglo/Jupiter/London/1977
- Prince Jack: The True Story of Jack the Ripper
  Frank Spiering/Doubleday/New York/1978
- Tea-Shop in Limehouse, A
  Thomas Burke/Books for Libraries/Freeport, NY/1969
- Victorian Underworld, The
  Donald Thomas/John Murray/London/1998
- www.hollywoodrippermovies.com
  last but definitely not least, the invaluable
- www.casebook.org

Index

Page numbers suffixed with asterisks, as 89*, refer to illustrations
Index entries in italics refer to films etc